QUILTS IN COMMUNITY

OHIO'S TRADITIONS

QUILTS

WITH THE SUPPORT OF

American Association for State and Local History
Helping Hand Quilting Craft Foundation
Ohio Arts Council
Ohio Historical Society
The Stocker Foundation

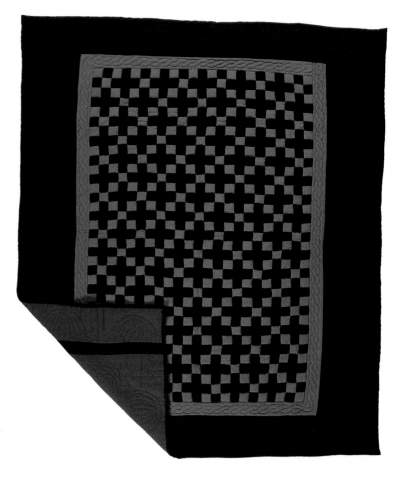

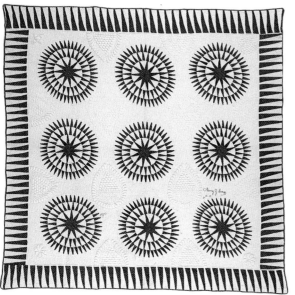

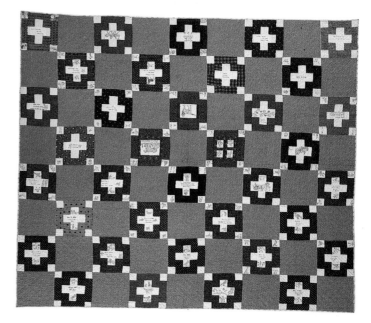

IN COMMUNITY
OHIO'S TRADITIONS

Ricky Clark, George W. Knepper, and Ellice Ronsheim
EDITED BY Ricky Clark

RUTLEDGE HILL PRESS
NASHVILLE, TENNESSEE

The *Quilts in Community: Ohio's Traditions*
exhibitions are co-sponsored by the Ohio Quilt Research Project,
the Dayton Art Institute,
and the Ohio Historical Society.

Published in Nashville, Tennessee, by Rutledge Hill Press,
513 Third Avenue South, Nashville, Tennessee 37210

Typography by Bailey Typography, Inc., Nashville, Tennessee
Design by Harriette Bateman

Library of Congress Cataloging-in-Publication Data
Clark, Ricky.
　　Quilts in community : Ohio's traditions / Ricky Clark, George W.
Knepper, and Ellice Ronsheim ; edited by Ricky Clark ; with the
support of American Association for State and Local History . . . [et
al.].
　　　　p.　cm.
　　Includes bibliographcal references and index.
　　ISBN 1-55853-101-7
　　1. Quilts—Ohio—History.　2. Quiltmakers—Ohio—Biography.
I. Knepper, George W., 1926–　　. II. Ronsheim, Ellice, 1951–
III. American Association for State and Local History.　IV. Title.
NK9112.C555　1991
746.9′7′09771—dc20　　　　　　　　　　　　　　　　　91-9132
　　　　　　　　　　　　　　　　　　　　　　　　　　　　　CIP

Printed in Singapore
1 2 3 4 5 6 7 8 9 — 96 95 94 93 92 91

PREFACE

Tim Lloyd started it. For several years he had been hearing the same refrain from women in different parts of Ohio: "We've been seeing [documenting, exhibiting] quilts in Gallia [Knox, Huron] County. We expected to see fifty [100, 150] and in fact saw 100 [200, 500]. We have learned so much about their history [their makers' history, Ohio's history]; let's expand this to a statewide project." As director of the Ohio Arts Council's Traditional and Ethnic Arts Program Tim convened a meeting of these quilt enthusiasts in June 1984. When the meeting ended, the Ohio Quilt Research Project began.

The project's goal was to document Ohio's nineteenth- and twentieth-century quilts, quiltmakers, and quiltmaking traditions. Our objective was to interpret our findings, present them to the public through a book and related museum exhibitions, and create a continuing, accessible archive.

We established our documentation procedure by studying similar projects in other states, as well as two recent regional studies within Ohio. We are indebted especially to the authors of several earlier projects that we consider outstanding models. They are the South Carolina Quilt History Project, organized by Laurel Horton, whose clear goals and methodology impressed us; Jeannette Lasansky's remarkable series of monographs on the material culture of central Pennsylvania; and the Kentucky Quilt Project, whose beautiful publication reports the first statewide attempt at quilt research.

Working through contacts in Ohio's strong networks of quilters and quilt guilds, county extension agents, and historical museums, we arranged public quilt documentation days throughout the state to which owners brought their quilts to be documented. Each quilt day was organized by local contact people who secured a date and location, found quilt day volunteers, and publicized the event. Members of the project trained these local volunteers and joined them to photograph and document the quilts and to interview makers and owners. Some interviews were tape recorded. We designed a series of forms on which we recorded information about each quilt's history, physical characteristics, and maker's history. Our photographers took at least two color and two black and white photographs of each quilt. Because of the large number of woven coverlets brought to quilt days (Ohio has a strong tradition of coverlet weaving) we also developed a documentation form for woven coverlets. Although we have not included coverlets in this book or our exhibitions, the records will remain in the Ohio Quilt Research Project archive for the use of future researchers. We no longer hold quilt documentation days; however, individuals and teams continue to document private and institutional collections for the archives. In five years of research we held fifty-three quilt days throughout Ohio and documented almost seven thousand quilts.

Because the publications of statewide quilt documentation projects appropriately differ according to the nature of each particular state, a word about our rationale is in order. First, the project's underlying premise is that quilts are not only beautiful textiles but, more importantly, historical documents. Like vernacular architecture, home furnishings, and gravestones, quilts reflect the lifestyles and world-views of their makers and users. Because we discovered both continuity and change in quilts and quiltmaking traditions from the earliest period to the present, we decided against a terminal date in our public presentations. We recognize that the wide availability of quilt magazines and nationally renowned designers and teachers has led to the proliferation of nationalized quilt styles. Since our focus is Ohio's quilts and quiltmaking traditions, we have therefore included among recent quilts only those that are distinctly Ohio-related, or continue a quiltmaking tradition established here earlier.

Second, quilts included in this book and the related exhibitions are only those made in Ohio and traditional in style. Where we believe Ohio quiltmakers work in traditions learned elsewhere, we have noted those influences. Most quilts brought to our attention, both historical and contemporary, were traditional. It must be noted, however, that Ohio's strong contemporary art quilt movement is directly related to the state's rich heritage of traditional quilts and involves many Ohio residents, both artists and interpreters. Quilt artist Nancy Crow of Baltimore (Fairfield County), who established Quilt National in Athens, America's prestigious biennial exhibition of contemporary art quilts, credits the traditional quilts she saw during her childhood with influencing her own quilt production. In her autobiography, *Quilts and Influences*, she includes several traditional quilts "with patterns that have intrigued me almost from the beginning of my own quiltmaking." Quilt researcher and art curator Penny McMorris of Bowling Green (Wood County), author of the definitive *Crazy Quilts*, has also written an outstanding book on quilts made by contemporary artists, *The Art Quilt*.

Finally, we selected *community* as the organizing concept for this book because that is where the quilts led us. Two years into our research period we reviewed our data, seeking a common thread that might suggest a theme for the book and exhibitions. We discovered that the quilts we had documented thus far reflected their communities of origin: geographic settlements, families, religious institutions, and reform societies. Our theme was obvious—*community*—and we chose as a title *Quilts in Community: Ohio's Traditions*.

Our research strategy, and especially our decision to have quilt documentation days organized at the grassroots level by local volunteers, rather than by Ohio Quilt Research Project administrators, was instructive. Not only did we learn a great deal about Ohio's quilts, we also learned much about our state and its people. We discovered these facts:

Ohio is a county-conscious state. When we asked where quiltmakers lived, many people named counties before they named towns.

Women are the primary tradition bearers. Far more women than men made quilts and attended quilt days, and most quilts are left to women in the family.

Rural women responded to our project in greater numbers than urban women, although urban women also own or make quilts. Quilt documentation days with the smallest attendance were those held in Toledo, Columbus, and Cleveland. The quilt day with the largest attendance was held in the reclaimed Black Swamp in rural Paulding County. In February.

Some Ohio women define their communities in religious terms. Those quilt documentation days organized by Quakers or Mennonites attracted primarily members of those sects. Quakers especially, historically a recording people, provided extraordinarily thorough family records.

Ohio's quiltmakers are nostalgic. In 1990 this is most clearly evident in their attitude toward the Amish, whose largest settlement is in Holmes County, Ohio. Quiltmakers from all over Ohio report purchasing quilting materials at fabric shops in Holmes County, although it may take them half a day to drive there. As historian Levi Miller wryly notes, "The Amish have moved from a tolerated minority to being viewed as a national treasure." James Mast, lifelong resident of Holmes County, agrees. In an interview with the Ohio Quilt Research Project he perceptively observed that visitors to Holmes County "go in the quilt shops—and that's no reflection on the nice quilts that are here—but I believe they enjoy driving up and down the road and looking at a lifestyle that maybe they've heard Grandma and Grandpa talk about, and . . . they realize that there's something here that they have lost, or has long since passed them by. . . ."

Ohio has been a significant region of quilt production from its earliest days. Although we documented an impressive number of Ohio-made quilts, the seven thousand in our archives are just the tip of the iceberg. We believe, however, that our sample is large enough and sufficiently comprehensive in terms of temporal and geographic scope that we can interpret it with some validity. We documented quilts in all areas of the state, although some population groups are underrepresented. For instance, there are many more black quiltmakers in Ohio than we met through our quilt days or through direct contact. Nor are all religious communities represented in our data. Although strong Jewish communities have existed throughout Ohio since the Civil War, we documented almost no quilts attributed to Jewish quiltmakers.

These are among the most obvious areas for further study; the many questions raised through regional quilt projects are exciting for researchers. We hope that documenting Ohio's quilts in the context of state and national history will contribute to an understanding of the influence of historic events, technology, and economics on Ohio's quiltmakers. Interpreting and presenting the results of our research publicly will lead to insight into regional and cultural preferences and the richly varied roles quilts play in the lives of their makers and owners. Our interpretation of Ohio's quilts, quiltmakers, and quiltmaking traditions will culminate in the fall of 1991, when this book is released to coincide with the opening of simultaneous exhibitions at the Dayton Art Institute and the Ohio Historical Center (Columbus). We anticipate that the publicity generated by these presentations will elicit information on more Ohio-made quilts, and we will add this to the existing archives. After the close of the exhibitions we will deposit the archives with the Library and Manuscript Division of the Ohio Historical Society for the use of researchers. We invite owners of Ohio-made quilts to contribute to this rich record of Ohio's quiltmaking heritage.

Ricky Clark, Editor

CONTENTS

[1] *Ohio Star in Garden Maze Setting*. Maybell E. Kerr, (1880–1929), Annapolis (Jefferson County), before 1929. 81" x 75" (205 cm x 190 cm). Pieced. Cotton. Collection of Flora Leonhart.

Quilts in Ohio's eastern counties are often constructed of tiny pieces. The Ohio Star blocks in Maybell Kerr's quilt measure only 3" by 3". Her effective Garden Maze sash is comparatively rare in Ohio quilts.

Maybell E. Kerr, daughter of Ezekiel Kerr and Flora Mills Kerr, lived all her life in Annapolis. She was of Scots-Irish descent.

[2] Maybell E. Kerr

EARLY MIGRANTS TO OHIO

GEORGE W. KNEPPER

ermanent settlement was well underway in the trans-Appalachian West before that part which is now the state of Ohio received its share of the westward migration. During the American Revolution, a few Moravian missionaries, Indian traders, and land scouts settled temporarily beyond the Ohio River, but they had no lasting impact on the land. Years after western Pennsylvania, western Virginia, Kentucky, and Tennessee boasted small wilderness settlements, Ohio remained Indian country. In the 1780s, Congress addressed the problem of how to manage western lands newly acquired by treaty with Great Britain and by the cession of state land claims. It first attempted to clear Indian titles from a portion of this new public domain and accomplished this to its satisfaction (but not to the Indians') in the Treaty of Fort McIntosh (1785) and later treaties. Congress proclaimed that this ceded land—principally what is now eastern and southern Ohio—was to remain closed to settlers until land survey and sale procedures were established. Procedures or blueprints for organizing the land northwest of the Ohio River were outlined in the Land Ordinance of 1785 (see illustration 3), and those for governing it in the Northwest Ordinance of 1787.

Migration to Ohio was but part of a much larger transmontane movement which populated portions of the West with amazing rapidity after the War of Independence, but Ohio received perhaps the most cosmopolitan mixture of domestic migrants and foreign immigrants that one can find during the early national period. Migrants (those from within the nation) came in substantial numbers from New England, the Middle Atlantic states, the Upland South, and, to a lesser extent, from the Tidewater South. Limited numbers of free blacks and escaped slaves found homes in Ohio. Small Indian bands continued to live in the state until the 1840s.

THERE SHALL BE neither slavery nor involuntary servitude in the said territory . . . .
    Article VI, The Northwest Ordinance
    1787

Foreign immigrants came early to Ohio from every important overseas source. Prominent among them were Germans, Irish, English, Scots, Welsh, French, and Swiss. In some cases immigrants stayed for a time in the East before making their way into Ohio. Some established separate communities, as did certain groups of domestic migrants; some were quickly interspersed among persons of other traditions.

Each group coming to Ohio, foreign or domestic, brought along its traditional way of doing things, its "cultural baggage." Many of these groups were large enough, and persistent enough, to retain their distinct cultural practices, yet no single migrant or immigrant group was strong enough to impose its traditions upon the entire state. What historian John D. Barnhart said of the entire Ohio Valley is equally true of Ohio: "The nature of the population movements created sectional settlements; but they tended to counteract each other, and the established customs of any one section were not able to dominate the entire territory."

From its first days, Ohio was an amalgam of peoples. It was not a melting pot, nor would it be until the urban-industrial sector eclipsed the rural-agricultural sector in the twentieth century. Early Ohio was a "salad bowl." One could identify each ingredient: Scots-Irish uplander, Yankee, Pennsylvania German, southern Quaker. Even when living in close proximity to one another they remained distinct. Eventually a common cultural "salad dressing" influenced all and tended to conceal underlying cultural differences. In extreme cases—the Old Order Amish, for instance—cultural separateness persists to the present day. More commonly, what were once distinct cultural traditions—the New England tradition of the Western Reserve, for instance—faded over time.

Among the first people entering Ohio were Scots-Irish settlers from western Virginia, western Pennsylvania, and Kentucky, some of whom arrived before the country was legally opened to settlement. The United States Army tried unsuccessfully to keep these squatters out in conformance with the congressional proclamation banning premature settlement beyond the Ohio.

The Scots-Irish squatter typically was a hunter-farmer who cleared a small patch of land on which he

planted corn and perhaps tobacco. He turned his hogs loose in the woods and supplemented the family diet with fish and wild game. Conservative easterners considered squatters "too idle, too talkative, too passionate, too prodigal, and too shiftless to acquire either property or character." Doubtless some fit this description, but many squatters regarded themselves as upright citizens taking what was properly theirs in a free society. Some westerners saw them as the embodiment of the American spirit: proud and independent individualists, the cutting edge of civilization in the wilderness.

Of course not all squatters were Scots-Irish, and certainly not all Scots-Irish were squatters. Scots-Irish frontiersmen have been characterized by historian Edgar Hassler as bold, determined, industrious. They were "sharp at bargains, fond of religious and political controversy," and unusually touchy about their rights. Their cabins contained "a Bible, a rifle, and a whiskey jug." They harbored an intense hatred for Indians. After legal settlement commenced, many Scots-Irish, who were persons of economic and social substance, migrated to Ohio seeking new land and new economic opportunity.

In the territorial period and the first decades of statehood, Scots-Irish influence was greatest in a band of varying width paralleling the Ohio River all along the Ohio border (see illustrations 1, 4, and 6). The Scots-Irish were especially prominent in what were called the "eastern counties" (for instance, Jefferson, Belmont, Monroe), but they became so widely dispersed that many areas of the state had a good representation. Their cultural traditions were perhaps best observed in the eastern counties where their Presbyterian faith was strong (see illustrations 8 and 9), but true to their nature, Scots-Irish Presbyterians fragmented into competing, particularistic sects: Old Seceders, New Seceders, Reformed Presbyterian, and so on.

New Englanders were the next migrants to arrive in force. The Ohio Company of Associates, which founded Marietta, Ohio's first legally constituted settlement, sent its advance party to the mouth of the Muskingum in April 1788. Others followed regularly, making the 600-mile-trip by way of the Pennsylvania (Forbes) Road and then by boat to their Ohio destinations. It was a difficult journey of more than forty days' duration. Land attracted them, and limited opportunity at home pushed them toward Ohio. Given Marietta's essentially "pure" New England character, it was relatively easy for the settlement's talented leadership to put familiar practices in place. Marietta was laid out in the manner of a New England village with in-lots and out-lots (farms) set out in orderly fashion. The in-lots fronted on wide streets. A concession to the wilderness required erection of a strong fortification to which these classically educated leaders gave the name *Campus Martius* ("armed camp"). By the 1790s, new settlements developed outside Marietta in what is now Washington County.

A much larger New England community was formed in the Connecticut Reserve or Western Reserve in what is now the northeastern section of Ohio (see illustration 10). Stretching 120 miles westward from Pennsylvania between the forty-first parallel and the Lake Erie shore, the Reserve embraced over three million acres. The Reserve's first few settlers arrived in 1796, but nothing resembling a community was established until about 1799. Settlement was slow and the region remained isolated until canals opened it to the outside world. As with their kindred in the Ohio Company settlements, these migrants were lured by the pull of good land at affordable prices. Most came from rural and small town Connecticut, Massachusetts, and Vermont.

The Western Reserve continued to be dominated by its New England traditions for many decades (see illustrations 11 and 12). Once the Ohio-Erie Canal (built 1825–32) ended its isolation, newcomers of varying sorts, including Irish and German canal laborers, started to make an impact. Yet large portions of the Reserve remained relatively isolated well into the twentieth century; in its small towns, the New England character remained surprisingly intact until the automotive and mass media age achieved its full impact (see illustrations 14 and 15).

Ohio's New England influence was not confined to the Marietta region and the Western Reserve. Yankees established towns elsewhere in the state. Putnam was pure New England before becoming absorbed into its larger neighbor, Zanesville. Granville was settled in 1805 by a congregation from Granville, Massachusetts. The founder of Worthington was a New England Episcopal priest, James Kilbourne, who brought his fellow Connecticut Yankees to establish the town. But Yankees did not always emigrate in groups. Thousands of individuals were spread around the state. Cincinnati, for instance, had a substantial New England element in its cosmopolitan population.

In 1788, almost coincident with the founding of Marietta, a group of New Jersey people and migrants

[4] *Children of Israel*. Saraptia Fidora Swank Patterson (1853–1944), Olive Green (Noble County), 1880–1900. 80″ x 80″ (203 cm x 203 cm). Pieced. Cotton. From a private collection.

Like Maybell Kerr, Saraptia Patterson preferred to work with very small fabric pieces. Each pieced block in her quilt measures 17″ by 17″ and contains more than 100 small blue and white squares, in addition to the larger geometric units. This preference for tiny pieces may be a regional variant of the postage stamp quilts popular throughout Ohio beginning in the 1870s. The borders surrounding the center area are also characteristic of quilts in this region.

Saraptia Patterson was of Scots-Irish descent and lived all her life in Noble County. Her husband, Samuel Patterson, was a carpenter and farmer.

[5] Saraptia Fidora Swank Patterson

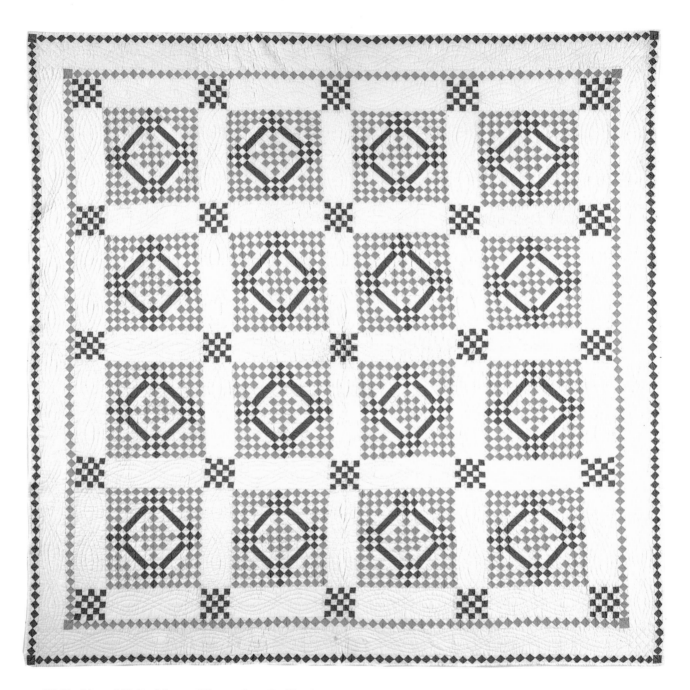

[6] *Double and Twisted Laws o'Massey.* Irma L. Henderson
Smith (b. 1912), Hammondsville (Harrison County), 1927. 77"
x 77" (194 cm x 194 cm). Pieced. Cotton. From a private
collection.

Irma Smith's quilt, with its unique pattern name, is strikingly
similar to Saraptia Patterson's (see illustration 4). The
quiltmakers lived only a few miles apart. Irma Smith also
preferred working with small units. She surrounded her quilt
with a triple border: a wide border flanked by narrow, pieced
borders. This border treatment was favored by many
quiltmakers in the eastern counties.
   Irma made this quilt when she was in the seventh grade. She
and her younger sister, Hazel, who made an identical quilt in
blue and gold, walked four miles to their grandmother's house
in Harrisville to get the pattern. Of the many quilts Irma Smith
has made, this is her favorite.

[7] Irma L. Henderson
Smith

from Kentucky began to settle between the Miami rivers in the Symmes (Miami) Purchase. These Jerseyites and Kentuckians established Columbia, Losantiville (Cincinnati), and North Bend. Cincinnati was to become the dominant settlement, its centrality assured in 1789 with the erection of Fort Washington.

As its rich hinterland began sending grain, pork, and other products to Cincinnati for processing and shipping, that city became ever more cosmopolitan. Settlers from the Middle Atlantic states and Kentucky were soon joined by Virginians and New Englanders. The latter moved into the commercial, financial, and professional life of the community. Blacks concentrated in Cincinnati because jobs were available for unskilled workers. By 1825 Irish canal workers were arriving as was the large German influx which did so much to condition Cincinnati historically. It is little wonder that Dr. Daniel Drake, Cincinnati's distinguished citizen, could find no "points of coincidence" in the population of his town.

East of the Symmes Purchase, between the Little Miami and the Scioto, lay the Virginia Military District. Virginia reserved this tract when surrendering various western land claims to Congress in 1784. After 1790 Congress allowed Virginia to commence settlement therein. The first settlers were nearly all Virginians or former Virginians who had lived for some years in Kentucky. Most were Scots-Irish Presbyterians, Methodists, or Baptists. The Military District operated under Virginia custom. A small but impressive leadership clique quickly emerged around Chillicothe (established 1796), the District's unofficial capital. The clique dominated the territorial assembly and led the successful move to statehood.

In the early statehood period, rich new Ohio lands in a slave-free environment, which was guaranteed first by the Northwest Ordinance and later (1802) by Ohio's constitution, attracted groups that had maintained cultural cohesion in the settled East and South. One such group, the so-called Pennsylvania Dutch, were German-Americans whose ancestors had lived in eastern Pennsylvania. Most were pietistic Protestant: Mennonites, Amish, Dunkards (German Baptist Brethren). They maintained distinctive dress, farming styles, food, housing, commerce, worship, and social customs (see illustrations 16 and 17). They settled in force in the so-called "backbone" counties including Columbiana, Stark, Richland, Crawford, Wayne, Knox, and Holmes. Mennonites and Amish also settled in Butler County in southwestern Ohio. One small group of anti-slavery Baptist Germans came to Lancaster (Fairfield County) in 1801 from Rockingham County, Virginia. By 1809 their church at Pleasant Run exceeded seventy members. Others located in Highland County.

■ **NO PERSON, demeaning himself in a peaceable and orderly manner, shall ever be molested on account of his mode of worship or religious sentiments, in the said territory.**
  Article I, The Northwest Ordinance
  1787
■

[8] *Sunburst.* Nancy Jane Gregg (b. 1856), Noble County, c. 1880. 69″ x 69″ (175 cm x 175 cm). Pieced, stuffed. Cotton. Collection of Nancy Rudge.

This Sunburst, with forty-five points in its outer ring, is another pattern favored by Noble County quiltmakers from the 1880s through the 1930s.

[9] *Laurel Leaf.* Mrs. Webb and Nancy McIlravy Major (1831–1890), Harrison County, completed 1854. 87″ x 87″ (221 cm x 221 cm). Appliquéd, pieced. Cotton. Collection of Willis and Faith Godden.

Although this quilt is primarily appliquéd, the center area is surrounded by a triple border similar to the one used by Irma Smith, also of Harrison County (see illustration 6).

The quilt, an intergenerational family project, was documented in 1931 by Dora Major, who recorded its history on a note she attached to the quilt back: "This Quilt is called the 'Laurel Wreath' [*sic*] and the quilting design is called the 'True Lover's Knot.' My great grandmother Webb pieced it and my Grandmother Major gave it to Father and Mother when they were married, Nov 4 1854 and my mother quilted it soon after. She had it in the frames three months with the help of her friends."

[10] The Western Reserve in 1826. Collection of the Western Reserve Historical Society.

[11] *Morning Patch*. Keziah Pope (1773–1850), Strongsville (Cuyahoga County), before 1850. 88″ x 82″ (224 cm x 209 cm). Pieced. Cotton. Collection of Stella Mallory Dickerman.

Keziah Pope's quilt is in a style popular in the Western Reserve throughout the nineteenth century. The region's settlers brought it with them from New England, where it was also the prevailing style at the time. These quilts are pieced of structurally identical blocks, sometimes alternating with plain blocks. Unlike the bordered quilts found in Ohio's eastern counties and illustrated above, the blocks in Western Reserve quilts extend to the edges of the quilt.

Keziah Pope, pioneer settler of Strongsville, came from Massachusetts with her family in 1819. In addition to making quilts for her family, she quilted with the Ladies' Benevolent Sewing Society (see illustration 130 on page 114).

While pietistic Germans settled in homogeneous rural communities, other Germans located in nearly every Ohio county during the early decades of statehood. Some came directly from the old country, but most were from Pennsylvania, Maryland, and Virginia. In the larger towns they mingled with persons of other traditions, but when they settled in German-speaking communities, they tended to maintain their cultural identity for generations. German language newspapers could be found in Lisbon (Columbiana County) by 1808 and Lancaster in 1809. In 1817 the Ohio General Assembly authorized printing of the constitution and the laws of Ohio in the German language. Considerable numbers resided in the Great Miami Valley, and the great German influx to Cincinnati occurred in the 1830s and thereafter.

Before the Civil War nearly every sizable Ohio community had German elements within it. Persons of German descent belonged to many different religious persuasions. Lutherans and Roman Catholics were perhaps most numerous. They did not mingle. Later in the nineteenth century, north-central and western Ohio boasted rural villages which were exclusively German Catholic or German Lutheran (see illustration 22 on page 22). In such enclaves German custom prevailed. Sermons were in German, and schools taught the German language and tradition. Other Germans belonged to the Reformed, the Brethren, and the Methodist churches. In time small numbers of German Jews settled in Ohio, primarily in Cincinnati where they made a conspicuous contribution to the city's life.

The Welsh were yet another group that settled early Ohio. They banded together, partly out of preference and partly because their traditional occupations, especially mining, dictated that they locate where such jobs were concentrated. Jackson and Gallia counties attracted Welsh miners. Welsh settlements could be found in Portage County, at Radnor in Delaware County, Paddy's Run

A NEW AMERICAN women's gathering is coming into use around here now. Six, seven, or eight neighbors visit, all at one house, in the afternoon and make quilts of matched patches sewed together. We sit on chairs and benches around a wooden form, talking, complaining, trading advice, troubles, and homesickness. The quilts are bright and useful. It is good medicine for all the visitors.

　　Liwwät Böke
　　St. John (Mercer County)
　　c. 1850

in Butler County, Gomer in Allen County, and the Welsh Hills of Licking County. Many Welsh settlers came from Cambria County, Pennsylvania, about eighty miles east of Pittsburgh. The Welsh language, songs, and the Congregational and Methodist religions flourished in these regions for several generations after their founding.

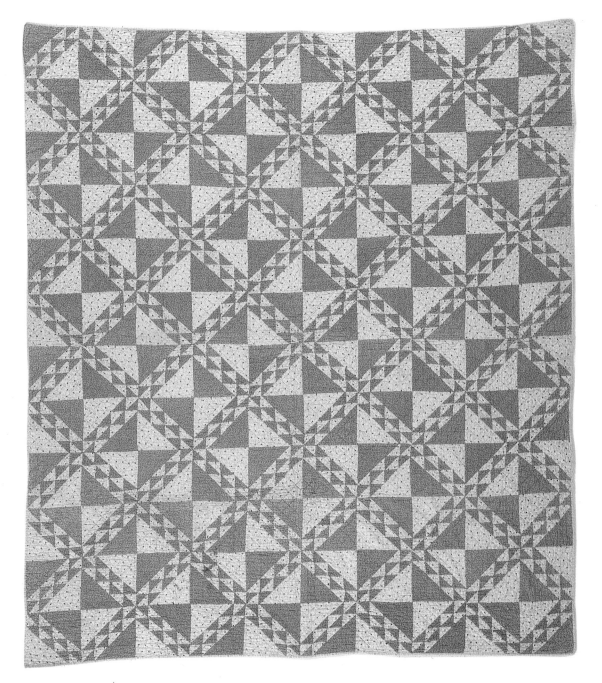

[12] *Northwind.* Sarah Wharram Goble (1837–1899) and E[ffie] Josephine Goble (1864–1962), Oxford Township (Erie County), 1890. 76″ x 66″ (193 cm x 168 cm). Pieced. Cotton. Collection of Dr. Gordon R. Meeker.

Sarah Goble pieced this quilt, and her daughter Josephine quilted it forty years after Keziah Pope made hers (see illustration 11). It is in the same Western Reserve style, however: an all-over pattern of identical pieced blocks carried to the edges of the quilt.

The Gobles came to Erie County in 1861 from Lehman, Pennsylvania, bringing "with them a new set of Josiah Wedgewood china dishes," as Josephine recorded in her diary. Sarah taught her four daughters to sew, and they "were always trying out something . . . like making wax flowers, knitting, crocheting, ornamenting picture frames with braided leather, leaves and roses, crystalizing dried wild grass with pretty seedpods."

[13] Sarah Wharram Goble and Chauncy Fuller Goble with their daughters *(left to right)* Effie Josephine, Emma, Esther, and Ella.

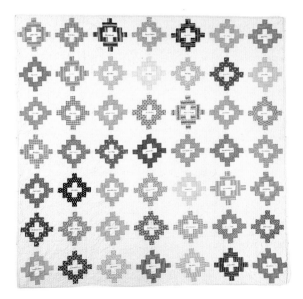

[14] *Christian Cross.* Church Society, Rome (Ashtabula County), 1850. 90″ x 90″ (229 cm x 229 cm). Pieced. Cotton. Collection of the Western Reserve Historical Society.

Within the Western Reserve style, the Christian Cross was a favorite pattern, particularly for signature quilts like this. Most of the women whose names are signed on this quilt were original settlers of Rome and relatives, as well as fellow church members. They arranged their signed blocks in family groups, with blocks signed by mothers, daughters, and sisters in the same rows. Signature quilts were sometimes made for a woman leaving her home during the period of westward expansion.

Two inscriptions identify New London, Connecticut, as the home of the signers, underscoring the bonds between New England and the Western Reserve.

[15] *Christian Cross.* Charlotte Eliza Wilcox Wilbor, Black River (Lorain County), c.1875. 82″ x 81″ (208 cm x 206 cm). Pieced. Cotton. Collection of Mr. and Mrs. James Abbott III.

This Christian Cross signature quilt was made twenty-five years after the one in illustration 14 and almost one hundred miles farther west. The Western Reserve style and Christian Cross pattern were still favorites, however, and the makers arranged their signatures in family groups. For another Western Reserve quilt in this style and pattern, see illustration 77 on page 63.

The Irish (Roman Catholics from southern Ireland), like the Germans, formed distinct communities in some instances, but in others became individually dispersed throughout the general population (see illustration 18). Among the former were those settling in Perry County where Ohio's first Roman Catholic church was established in 1818. The Perry County Irish were miners. Irish communities sprang up all along Ohio's canals. The Irish were especially drawn to urban life and concentrated in manufacturing and mining centers where they supported the Catholic church, found employment in city services, and soon demonstrated a proclivity for urban politics.

Before statehood, Quakers started to migrate to Ohio. They came from New Jersey, Pennsylvania, Maryland, Virginia, and the Carolinas (see illustration 19). Those migrating from free states were attracted by cheap land and the chance to make a new start in a promising region. Those from the South had an additional motive; they were escaping from slavery. As early as 1797, groups from the Carolinas and Virginia had settled in Ross County on the east bank of the Scioto River. In 1800 North Carolina Quakers moved into Ohio's eastern counties eventually establishing the well-known Mount Pleasant Meeting in Jefferson County. Quakers from South Carolina led the way into Warren County and were soon followed by others from North Carolina and Virginia. Quakers from Salem, New Jersey, established Salem, Ohio, in Columbiana County.

The Quakers, of course, were "plain" people who shunned ostentation. However, they entered fully into the life of the community and supported social reform movements. Like the German pietists, they were pacifists.

It is clear that well before the War of 1812 (which was to some degree a watershed in migration patterns) Ohio had attracted people from many regions who brought with them their particular customs and traditions. This list is by no means complete. Small numbers of people came into the territory or state from other sources. For example, the unfortunate French émigrés who settled on Ohio Company lands in 1790 stayed at Gallipolis (Gallia County) and at the French Grant farther down the Ohio, but they were too few to leave a distinct material inheritance (although they left a romantic one) on the region.

Blacks were another small but visible population cohort (see illustration 20). The largest number lived in the southern third of the state: from 1830 until after the Civil War, Cincinnati contained about one-tenth of Ohio's blacks. Blacks were systematically excluded from Ohio's social institutions; thus, their impact on the state's early development was minimal.

The 1850 federal census showed the place of origin of Ohio's people. Immigrant groups could now be readily identified. English immigrants were heavily concentrated in the Western Reserve, in pottery and clay products centers such as East Liverpool and Zanesville, and in commercial centers. They were also found along railroad

corridors after 1850. French and Swiss settlers often located near one another because many of the French were Alsacians, similar in ethnic background to the Swiss. Small concentrations of French were found in Stark, Wayne, and Muskingum counties and in southwestern and northwestern Ohio. Swiss farmers and dairymen settled Wayne, Tuscarawas, and Monroe counties. In 1837, a group of Swiss Mennonites settled Bluffton in Allen County. Scots were not numerous; they appear to have concentrated in Cuyahoga, Ashland, Columbiana, Mahoning, and Washington counties. Finally, Canadians migrated to the Western Reserve, the Refugee Tract east of Columbus, and northwestern Ohio.

[16] *Rainbow Blend*. Fannie Kuhns Hostetler (1892–1946), Madison County, 1938–1940. 85″ x 85″ (216 cm x 216 cm). Pieced. Cotton. From a private collection.

This pattern, sometimes called Broken Star, has been a favorite of Amish and Mennonite quiltmakers from 1880 to the present. Like most quilts made by Ohio's Germanic sectarians, it is surrounded by multiple borders and a contrasting binding. The borders in this quilt are unusual in their Nine-Patch corner blocks. As is true of all Amish quilts in Ohio, the fabrics are in solid-colored, rather than patterned, fabrics.

Fannie Kuhns, an Old Order Amish woman, was born in Indiana in 1892 and in 1918 married Mose M. Hostetler. After their marriage they lived in an Amish community in Madison County, Ohio. Fannie died in 1946. For another quilt by Fannie Kuhns Hostetler, see illustration 59 on page 43.

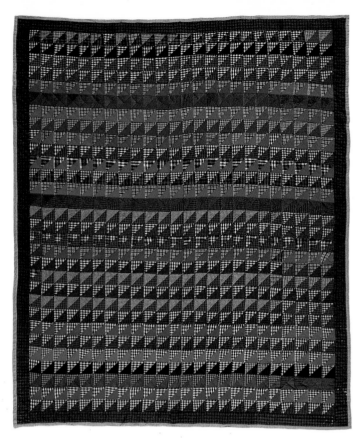

[17] *Thousands of Triangles*. Wilhelmina Dischinger Kappel (1866–1947), Zoar (Tuscarawas County), before 1947. 83″ x 69″ (211 cm x 175 cm). Pieced. Wool, cotton binding. From a private collection.

One of the most interesting of Ohio's Germanic sectarian groups was the Society of Separatists of Zoar, who settled there in 1817. To ensure their economic and communal survival, the Zoarites became a self-supporting, communitarian society within two years of their arrival. Among their most noted and successful industries was a woolen mill managed by Gottfried Kappel. His son, William C. Kappel, married quiltmaker Wilhelmina (Minnie) Dischinger, also a native Zoarite.

Minnie made a number of quilts during her lifetime, both from woolens woven at Zoar and from cottons purchased by society members. The top of this quilt is made entirely from Zoar woolens and provides a sample of the solid and checked fabrics the society produced. The checked backing and binding were made from purchased cottons. For another quilt by Minnie Kappel, see illustration 47 on page 36.

Social ferment is an important American characteristic. The nation's diverse cultural and social traditions persist for a time depending upon the strength of the tradition and its degree of isolation from contaminating factors. Given the number and strength of Ohio's various traditions, it was many generations before the stronger ones faded.

Today cultural remnants of the early migrant and immigrant groups persist in Ohio. In certain small Western Reserve villages one is reminded of New England. Sometimes, as in Hudson with its village green, its classic homes and public structures, and its academy, much of the village is a reminder. In Tallmadge, on the other hand, only a white frame Congregational church and the old town hall sitting on the village green convey the New England flavor. Extensive Ohio lands are worked today by the Old Order Amish in their time-honored way, differing little from the tradition first brought to the Buckeye State 180 years ago. In Chillicothe one can still see buildings and vistas with the feel of the South about them. Adena, the country estate of Thomas Worthington, could have been lifted bodily from old Virginia and transplanted in the hills above Chillicothe.

Ohio has never been one state in sentiment and outlook. Its diverse traditions and its strong, competing groups keep it from speaking with one heart and one voice. Perhaps in its diversity, early Ohio came closer than any other part of the United States to being a microcosm of America. To this day, no single political appeal, no one economic direction, no unique social program claims the allegiance of a continuous, dominant majority of the state's people.

[18] *Princess Feather*. Mary Rebecca Morrow (1863–1913), Bartlett (Washington County), 1889. 85″ x 83″ (216 cm x 210 cm). Appliquéd. Cotton. From a private collection.

Mary Morrow was one of six children born to John and Mary Hamill Morrow, both Irish immigrants. Her Princess Feather quilt is an apparently original variation of the appliquéd quilts in similar patterns that were popular throughout Ohio during the second half of the nineteenth century and were usually worked in red and green (see "Germanic Aesthetics, Germanic Communities"). Mary's quilt indicates that Irish women in Ohio were quilters. However, we found no distinctive style associated either with Irish quiltmakers or with Washington County quilts.

[19] *Sawtooth*. Emma Harlan Redfern (1854–1932), Clarksville (Clinton County), 1875–1900. 95″ x 74″ (241 cm x 188 cm). Pieced. Cotton. Collection of Dorotha Flint.

Emma Harlan Redfern, daughter of John and Elizabeth Harlan, was a member of the Quaker community of Clarksville in Clinton County. Unlike the elegant silk Quaker quilts found in and around Philadelphia, Emma's quilt, a traditional pieced quilt in subdued colors, cannot be associated with a particular Quaker quilting tradition. This is not surprising. Clinton County's Friends migrated from South Carolina, not from Pennsylvania; and they brought with them cultural traditions associated with South Carolina.

Except for a disproportionate number of signature quilts, those quilts made in Ohio's Quaker communities show considerable acculturation. Their distinctive Quaker characteristics are reflected not in their style, but in the thorough and accurate historical records their owners provided.

[20] *Pine Burr*. Mary Bell Johnson (b. 1893), Massillon (Stark County), 1975. 80″ x 75″ (203 cm x 191 cm). Pieced. Cottons and blends. Collection of Robbie M. Moore.

Mary Johnson's Pine Burr quilt is in a lively pattern more often seen in the South than in Ohio. Since she was forty-two when she moved to Massillon, Mary brought with her the quilting traditions she had learned in her native state of Alabama.

Born in Ramer, Alabama, in 1893, Mary Johnson was one of many blacks who migrated to Ohio from the South between the first and second world wars. She was a prolific quilter, working with quilters at the Shiloh Baptist Church in Massillon, as well as in her own home. In an interview in 1989, when she was ninety-four, she said she had made "too many quilts to count."

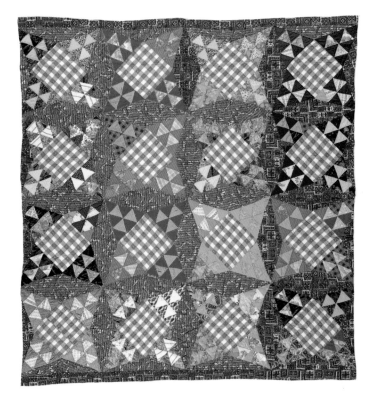

[21] Mary Bell Johnson

[22] *Pride of Iowa*. Nuns of Our Lady of the Visitation Order, Minster (Auglaize County), 1861–1865. 86″ x 84″ (217 cm x 212 cm). Appliquéd. Cotton. From a private collection.

Elegant appliquéd quilts like this were extremely popular in Ohio in the mid nineteenth century, particularly among church Germans. They incorporate floral motifs worked predominantly in red and green on a white ground, with details in a third color, often gold as in this case.

Mary Catherine Steinemann Decker (1843–1884) commissioned the nuns of Our Lady of the Visitation convent to make this quilt to be used by Archbishop John Purcell on his visits to Minster, a German Catholic community in western

Ohio. Minster remained predominantly German throughout the nineteenth century; as late as 1900, both German and English were taught to children in the first six grades.

GERMANIC AESTHETICS, GERMANIC COMMUNITIES

RICKY CLARK

The Pride of Iowa quilt, made by nuns in Our Lady of the Visitation Convent in Auglaize County during the 1860s, is highly decorative and technically elaborate (see illustration 22). Appliquéd in red, green, and gold on a white background, it portrays four large urns of flowers, leaves, and stuffed berries surrounded by a related appliquéd border.

Elizabeth Hegy Mast's Sawtooth Star quilt, made in Holmes County in 1881, is far simpler, while equally dramatic (see illustration 23). Elizabeth's quilt, in the same color scheme, is pieced primarily of red and gold repeated blocks with a dark green background, surrounded by wide outer and narrow inner plain borders. Both quilts are edged in narrow bindings of bright, contrasting colors.

The quilts were made twenty years and 130 miles apart. The nuns' quilt is appliquéd and representational, Elizabeth's pieced and stylized. The floral designs in the nuns' quilt lie on a white ground, those in Elizabeth's, on a dark ground. The nuns chose a quilt style popular throughout Ohio during the mid nineteenth century. Elizabeth worked in a style also found in many parts of Ohio, but which was particularly prevalent in Ohio's Amish, Mennonite, and Brethren communities from the 1880s to the present. The makers of both quilts were Germanic and lived in exclusively Germanic communities. The makers of the appliquéd quilt were Roman Catholic and the maker of the pieced quilt, Amish Mennonite.

Unlike the quilts illustrating "Early Migrants to Ohio," which are associated with discrete geographic regions, these two styles were more widely dispersed. Both were especially popular with Germanic women. Further, the two styles were favored by Germanic women of different religious backgrounds: the floral appliqué style by Roman Catholics and church Protestants; the simpler, pieced style by Germanic sectarians.

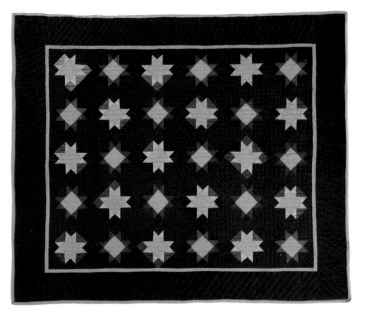

[23] *Sawtooth Star.* Elizabeth Hege Mast (1820–1902), Martin's Creek (Holmes County), 1881. 81″ x 69″ (206 cm x 175 cm). Pieced. Cotton. Collection of James Mast.

Elizabeth Mast's quilt is in a style favored by Germanic sectarians (Amish, Mennonites, Brethren) from the late 1870s to the present. It is made of pieced blocks alternating with plain blocks and set on point, surrounded by a wide outer and narrow inner border and bound in a contrasting color.

Elizabeth Hege was born in Bavaria. Her family emigrated to Pennsylvania in 1826 and in 1831 moved to Holmes County. Friederich Hege, Elizabeth's father, was one of the first bishops of the Martin's Creek Amish church. Elizabeth married Samuel Mast, a minister of the same church. In the early 1860s the Martin's Creek Amish church, along with other Amish churches in Holmes county, divided over various issues; and the Masts withdrew to organize the more liberal Martin's Creek Amish Mennonite church. Samuel Mast was their first minister.

In 1881 Elizabeth made this quilt for her grandson, Samuel Ephraim Mast, who was born that year. The quilt, still with descendents, has been passed down through men in the family.

THE FLORAL APPLIQUÉ QUILT STYLE

Floral appliqué quilts are among Ohio's most decorative and admired bedcoverings. They are bold and colorful and, rather than blending quietly into a restful decor, demand to be seen. Their makers understood a basic canon of artists and advertisers: complementary colors in adjacent areas intensify each other. This is why we often use complementary (opposite) colors to attract attention, such as red and green for Christmas decorations, yellow and lavender for Easter eggs, and turquoise and orange for Howard Johnson's. Further, the color scheme in these quilts is simple and direct. Their makers chose only one pair of complementary colors and effectively placed them on a plain white background. (Some Pennsylvania quiltmakers, working in the same style, chose a yellow background.) Colors are predominantly red and green, with occasional details in a third color, such as orange, yellow, or pink. In some cases, quiltmakers substituted blue for green. Bindings are narrow and brightly colored, usually red or green.

Bright and exuberant when seen from a distance, floral appliqué quilts also invite close scrutiny. Many are enhanced with skillful needlework techniques: elaborate stuffed work, delicate embroidery, and fine quilting. The contrasts between fine needlework in the white areas, where they are most effective, and bold colors in the appliquéd areas, contrasts between delicacy and drama, make these quilts appealing to almost all quilt enthusiasts.

BESIDES THE ARTICLES for which the committee awarded premiums, there were many of great excellence and beauty; the display of quilts, especially, exceeded anything of the kind we ever saw. The flowers upon many of them were so true to nature, that they seemed to have grown there; and the quilting was also exceedingly neat and regular.
First Fair of Stark County Agricultural Society 1850

Although some floral quilts were pieced, most were appliquéd. The design usually consists of a center field of repeated floral motifs, arranged either in repeated blocks or quadrants and framed by a related, appliquéd border. While each design is unique, variations of the Pride of Iowa and three other patterns identified by Carrie Hall and Rose Kretsinger as Princess Feather, Rose of Sharon, and various floral wreaths were repeated by many quiltmakers (see illustrations 24, 25, 26, and 28).

Like the Pride of Iowa quilt, those found today are often in fine or unused condition, suggesting that some were made for special occasions, rather than entirely for utility. The histories that accompany them support this:

[24] *Urn.* Ann P. Webster, Barnesville (Belmont County), c. 1840. 83″ x 80″ (211 cm x 202 cm). Cotton. Appliquéd and stuffed. Collection of Ruth Naylor.

Less elaborate than the Pride of Iowa in illustration 22, Ann Webster's quilt is nonetheless a variation of the flower-filled urn pattern. Rather than decorate her border with colored appliqué, Ann quilted and stuffed a serpentine vine. The large areas of white background in the center are also enhanced by spectacular stuffed wreaths and floral motifs, as are her quilted and stuffed signatures at the centers of the side borders.

One-third of the c. 1850 examples were made for dowries or weddings, others as gifts for various occasions. Some are marked, usually in embroidery, with names, initials, and/or dates (see illustration 161 on page 130). Again, the largest number of signed quilts dates from the earliest period.

Floral appliqué quilts did not originate in Ohio; similar ones were made in eastern states during the same period. In Ohio the style reached its peak around 1850–1860, declining gradually until the turn of the century, with a revival in the 1920s. Quilts in this elaborate style reflect an affluent society of women with leisure to create highly decorative quilts made with time-consuming techniques. They are Ohio quiltmakers' interpretation of an exuberant decorating style popular during the mid nineteenth century, which favored red and green color combinations and large, floral motifs. Baltimore album

[25] *Princess Feather.* Rachel Stickle Thome (1830–1895), Nashville (Holmes County), c. 1870. 83″ x 83″ (210 cm x 210 cm). Appliquéd. Cotton. Collection of Lavern Pennell.

One of the most frequently repeated patterns in this style was Princess Feather, here arranged in four large blocks.

Rachel Stickle lived in Holmes County all her life. In 1860 she married Thomas Thome, a farmer. She was a prolific quiltmaker and worked in a variety of styles.

[26] *Rose of Sharon.* Clara Jane Carl Shreve (1857–1888), Shreve (Wayne County), 1879. 77″ x 77″ (196 cm x 196 cm). Appliquéd. Cotton. From a private collection.

The Rose of Sharon was another popular pattern with many quiltmakers. Clara Jane Carl arranged her motifs in a quadrant; more often, the roses were smaller and arranged in repeated blocks. In some quilts blue substitutes for more commonly used green.

Clara Jane Carl, born in 1857, was one of eleven children of George Carl and Christina Wezel, German Lutheran immigrants who met and married in Big Prairie, north of Wooster (Wayne County). In 1879 she married Ezra Shreve, a civil engineer whose grandfather had founded the town named for him. Clara made this quilt for her wedding. The Shreves had four children before they moved to Mexico; only two survived. Clara died in 1888, after only nine years of marriage; and her daughters, then only five and seven, were sent back to Ezra's parents where they were raised by Ezra's unmarried sister.

[27] Clara Jane Carl Shreve

[28] *President's Wreath*. Margery Be[a]ham Sunnafrank (1810–1896), Cambridge (Guernsey County), 1830–1850. 97" x 97" (246 cm x 246 cm). Appliquéd. Cotton. From a private collection.

This and other wreath patterns were extremely popular with makers of floral quilts. As in this case, the wreaths were usually arranged in repeated blocks. The triple rows of diagonal quilting are a hallmark of early Ohio quilts.

Margery Be[a]ham, born in Adams Township (Guernsey County), was the daughter of a pioneer settler. In 1831 she married John Sunnafrank, whose parents also came early to Guernsey County. John kept taverns near two of Ohio's most important early "highways," Zane's Trace and the National Pike. The Sunnafranks and their children were charter members of the Methodist Church in Cambridge, which Margery attended until her death in 1896.

quilts made during the same period reflect another region's interpretation of the same decorating preference.

A sample of 140 floral appliqué quilts made in Ohio between 1834 and 1900 indicates that forty-two (30 percent) of the makers were ethnic Germans. (We define *ethnic* as immigrants and first-generation Americans.) This sample includes 74 quilts for which we know the ethnic background of the maker. Of those, forty-two (57 percent) were made by Germanic women, seventeen (23 percent) by women of English background, and fifteen (20 percent) by quiltmakers from all other ethnic backgrounds combined (see illustration 29). In either case, the number of Germanic quiltmakers is distinctly high in proportion to the Germanic residents of Ohio. According to the 1850 population census, only 6 percent of Ohio's residents were born in Germany and 10 percent in Pennsylvania, the largest source of Germanic migrants to Ohio. Thus, while fewer than 16 percent of Ohio's 1850 residents were Germanic, among those working in this style, 30 percent of the total or 57 percent of the ethnically documented quiltmakers were Germanic.

Although the makers of the Pride of Iowa quilt were Roman Catholic, most makers of floral appliqué quilts were church Protestants (members of mainstream Protestant churches, such as Lutheran, Reformed, Methodist, or Baptist). Of fifty-seven documented quiltmakers with known religious preferences, forty-eight (84 percent) were church Protestants, six (11 percent) were Roman Catholic, and only three (5 percent) were Germanic sectarians, a group discussed below (see illustration 30).

The Pride of Iowa quilt was made for Archbishop John Baptist Purcell, a popular and dedicated cleric. A Cincinnati resident, he first visited the Roman Catholic parish in Minster, Ohio (Auglaize, then Mercer, County), in 1835 and, beginning in 1854, came every two years. In the early 1860s Mary Catherine Steinemann Decker, a loyal member of the Minster parish, decided to honor the dignitary with something special. She commissioned the nuns of Our Lady of the Visitation convent in Minster to make this quilt. Each time Archbishop Purcell was expected in this German Catholic community, a messenger collected the quilt from Mary Catherine to put on the archbishop's bed. When he left, the quilt was returned to Mary Catherine, who stored it until his next visit. No one except Archbishop Purcell has ever slept under the quilt.

Although Germanic women comprised the largest group of quiltmakers making floral appliqué quilts, other women made quilts in this style as well. Some were non-Germanic women living in strongly Germanic counties. A fine example is the Pineapple quilt made by Julia Hayden Marshall and her daughter, Frances Marshall McClung of Greer (Knox County), during the Civil War (see illustration 31). See also the quilt by Serena Tucker, illustration 161 on page 130.

The Marshalls were thoroughly involved in textiles; textile manufacturing was their reason for living in Ohio. Born in 1815 in Otsego, New York, Julia Hayden was the daughter of Hezekiah and Hannah Hayden.

Hezekiah Hayden owned a textile mill in Otsego and was one of the city's first commercial manufacturers of cloth. Julia's husband, Edward W. Marshall, who descended both from a Connecticut governor and a signer of the Declaration of Independence, was a coverlet weaver from Windsor, Connecticut. Edward and Julia Marshall moved to Ohio in the late 1830s and lived in a number of eastern Ohio communities with woolen mills: first Steubenville (Jefferson County), then three townships in Knox County. Eastern Ohio had a high concentration of coverlet weavers during the mid nineteenth century. Unlike Edward Marshall, most were German immigrants or Germanic migrants from Pennsylvania. Like Edward Marshall, many moved frequently. Weavers of Jacquard coverlets can sometimes be traced through the signature blocks on their coverlets.

The design of the Marshall quilt is probably influenced both by the Germanic population of Knox and Holmes counties (Greer is in Knox County at the Holmes County border) and by the coverlets Edward Marshall wove, which would have been primarily for Germanic customers. The symmetrical, four-unit design of the appliquéd motif is similar to many coverlet patterns found in the area. The grapes and high-footed urn of flowers in the border are taken directly from Edward Marshall's coverlet designs (see illustration 99 on page 81) and were universally popular images in textiles, wallpaper, and china. These motifs, as well as the whirling swastika in the center of the appliquéd motifs, appear on other quilts, as well as on chests and woven coverlets made by Germanic residents in adjacent Holmes County. The pineapple, an unusual subject for quilts, was used by a Holmes County quiltmaker whose quilt and accompanying pineapple template have been preserved. Items of Ohio Germanic material culture decorated with these motifs are regularly displayed by the German Culture Museum in Walnut Creek (Holmes County) and illustrated in their publications (*Germanic Folk Culture in Eastern Ohio, Moravians in Ohio*, and *Amish in Eastern Ohio*).

[31] *Pineapple.* Julia Hayden Marshall (1815–1885) and Frances Marshall McClung. Greer (Knox County), c. 1860. 88″ x 88″ (224 cm x 224 cm). Appliqué. Cotton. Collection of the Ohio Historical Society.

The design of this quilt, made by the wife of a coverlet weaver and their daughter, recalls patterns seen on Jacquard coverlets made in this section of Ohio at exactly the same time (see illustration 99 on page 81). Field patterns on coverlets were usually repeated blocks of symmetrical "quaternity crosses," and the Pot of Flowers and grapevines were popular border designs. The whirling swastika is an age-old Germanic design; Edward Marshall would have woven his coverlets primarily for Germanic customers at this time, as the family lived in a strongly Germanic region.

Julia and her husband, Edward Marshall, both came from families involved in textile production. Julia's parents owned a textile mill in Otsego, New York; and Edward had been a coverlet weaver in Connecticut.

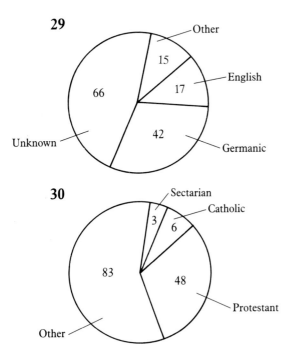

[29] Ethnic backgrounds of Germanic quiltmakers (1834–1900)

[30] Religious backgrounds of Germanic quiltmakers (1834–1900)

Floral appliqué quilts were at the height of popularity in the mid nineteenth century. One of the earliest quilts in this style documented by the Ohio Quilt Research Project was Mary Ann Whetzel's Water Lily (see illustration 32). It is made from red and green fabrics in two alternating lily motifs, one pieced and the other appliquéd. Although the central area is framed, the border is plain white cotton and consequently appears simpler than later examples. The quilt is bound in a rust-colored cotton.

Mary Ann Whetzel was born on Christmas Day in 1820, in Groveport (Franklin County). Her Pennsylvania-German parents, Henry Whetzel and Elizabeth Saylor, had migrated to Ohio shortly before her birth. In 1838, when Mary Ann was eighteen, she pieced her quilt, then set it aside for eight years. Just before her September 1846 wedding to Vermont native Sylvester Hinckley Grennell, she enlisted the aid of her sister Nancy and their mother in completing the quilt.

In 1899 Mary Ann gave the quilt to her daughter Ella, who documented it before passing it on to her own daughter. A note stitched to the back of the quilt reads:

This quilt was pieced by Mary Ann Whetsel [sic] in 1838 and quilted in the summer of 1846 by herself and sister Nancy and her mother who quilted the little diamonds all around the edge of the quilt. This was just before Mary was married to S. H. Grennell she gave this quilt to me in June 1899, and I told Ethel she could have it bye and by.
Ella F. (Grennell) Whiting

In spite of the limited palette and subject matter, as well as the popularity of the oft-repeated Princess Feather, Rose of Sharon, and floral wreaths, the diversity of design within the red and green appliqué style is astonishing. There is no apparent correlation between design preference and ethnicity, region, or time period. Germanic quiltmakers, for instance, created both light designs (see illustration 32) and heavy ones (see illustration 37). So did non-Germanic women (see illustrations 34 and 28). Patterns were arranged in repeated blocks or quadrants in about equal numbers (see illustrations 39 and 40).

During the colonial revival period of the early twentieth century, when Americans nostalgically recreated their perceived material past, women produced or reproduced a number of floral appliqué quilts. One of the loveliest was made by Maude Laurenna Lieurance Cluxton, a Quaker woman from Martinsville (Clinton County), c. 1900 (see illustration 42). The center field of Maude's quilt was pieced, rather than appliquéd, although she used an appliquéd undulating vine for her border. Her colors, design organization, and Feathered Star pattern all recall earlier Ohio quilts, as does the inset of piping inside her border.

Maude was born in Martinsville in 1883, studied music at Wilmington College, and sang in choral groups. She loved sewing and was known for her ability as a seamstress. She participated in Ladies' Aid quilting groups at the Newberry Friends Meeting, working with her friends on quilts that were sold as fundraisers. Often the women quilted all day.

Maude's parents considered their only child too frail to work or marry. However, she eventually worked as housekeeper to the Cluxton family and married Clayton Cluxton in 1933 after the death of his first wife. They lived on a farm outside Martinsville until 1945, when she and her husband moved to Florida. Maude died in 1968 and is buried in the Martinsville cemetery.

[32] *Water Lily.* Mary Ann Whetzel Grennell (1820–1910) and family, Groveport (Franklin County), 1838–1846. 104″ x 82″ (263 cm x 207 cm). Pieced, appliquéd. Cotton. Collection of Mr. and Mrs. Wayne Cooper.

This is the earliest floral appliqué quilt we saw with firm documentation. Because the surrounding border is plain white, rather than appliquéd, the quilt appears simpler and the design lighter than later examples. Its almost equal amounts of piecing and appliqué are another unusual feature.

Mary Ann Whetzel was born December 25, 1820, in Groveport, the daughter of Pennsylvania German parents. In 1846 she married Sylvester Hinckley Grennell, a farmer who had come to Ohio from Vermont. With the help of her sister and mother, she finished her quilt in time for her wedding. In 1854 the Grennells moved with their three children to Waupun, Wisconsin, where three more daughters were born. Mary died in Wisconsin in 1910.

[33] Mary Ann Whetzel Grennell and husband, Sylvester Hinckley Grennell

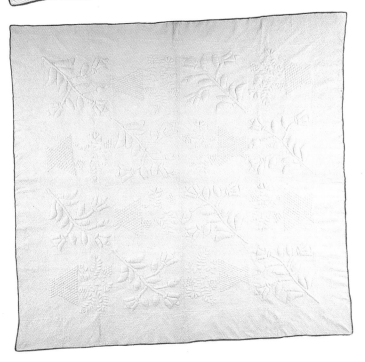

[35] Hester Stephenson

[34] *Tulip.* Hester Stephenson (1842–1928), Bellefontaine (Logan County), 1858. 79″ x 77″ (200 cm x 196 cm). Appliquéd. Cotton. Collection of Kris Sorgenfrei.

Hester Stephenson's Tulip quilt, made when she was sixteen, appears light and airy because she has placed plain white blocks between the appliquéd sprays of tulips and has used a simple vine of delicate green leaves as a border design. The quilt is lively, nevertheless, because the tulip sprays are directional and lead the viewer's eye diagonally across the quilt. The appliquéd tulips are stuffed, as are the masterfully quilted baskets in the plain blocks.

The contrast between the colorful tulips and the restful white alternate blocks is pleasing when we view the quilt from the front. When seen from the back, the quilt presents a contrast between strong, outlined tulip sprays and delicate, detailed flower baskets.

[36] Back of quilt in illustration 34

[37] *Sunflower.* Ellen Walton Rigdon (1862–1938), Wapakoneta (Auglaize County), c. 1880. 82″ x 80″ (208 cm x 203 cm). Appliquéd with reverse appliqué. Cotton. From a private collection.

Ellen Rigdon thoroughly filled the space in her Sunflower quilt. The repeated blocks are elaborate enough to establish secondary patterns where they come together. The curvilinear border seems to grow out of the center area, rather than framing it, as is the case in some other floral quilts.

Ellen grew up in Auglaize County, the daughter of Pennsylvania German parents. She was a seamstress, which probably accounts for the variety of needlework techniques she employed, such as reverse appliqué and decorative buttonhole stitch. Ellen died in Columbus in 1938.

[39] *Rose Wreath*. Rachel Tomlinson Daniel (1836–1877), Hillsboro (Highland County), 1856–1876. 83″ x 83″ (211 cm x 211 cm). Appliquéd. Cotton. From a private collection.

Rachel Daniel's Rose Wreath invites close scrutiny. She achieved an effect of great delicacy with narrow stems and soft colors, as well as by layering the petals of her roses and gathering their centers. An identical gathering technique was used in the yo-yo quilts popular during the 1930s (see Virginia Gunn, "Yo-Yo or Bed-of-Roses Quilts: Nineteenth Century Origins," *Uncoverings* 8 [1987]).

Rachel Tomlinson was born in the "Old Tomlinson Place," a two-story log cabin in Hillsboro. The Tomlinsons were Quakers, members of Fall Creek Friends Meeting near their home. In December 1858, Rachel married Joseph Smith Daniel, also of Highland County. They had four sons. Rachel died in 1877.

[38] Ellen Walton Rigdon

[40] *Plume*. Catharine Custer Spacht (1798–1892), New Stark (Hancock County), c. 1850. 73″ x 72″ (185 cm x 182 cm). Appliquéd. Cotton. Collection of Mrs. Lois Rodabaugh.

Catharine Spacht's quilt seems massive when compared with other quilts illustrated here. She has used color and shape effectively to achieve this. Complementary colors of equal value placed side by side, like the strong red and green she selected, reinforce each other, making each color seem more intense. The simple shapes with their smooth, unbroken edges and large areas of solid color also contribute to this effect. The multiple, plain borders on her quilt are characteristic of the Germanic sectarian style and may reflect the influence of the Swiss Mennonite and Brethren communities in New Stark.

Catharine Custer was born in 1798, probably in Lancaster County, Pennsylvania. She lived most of her life in Hancock County where she and her husband, John Spacht, raised five children. Catharine died in 1892.

[41] Catharine Custer Spacht

[42] *Feathered Star.* Maude Laurenna Lieurance Cluxton (1883–1968). Martinsville (Clinton County), c. 1900. 93″ x 89″ (237 cm x 225 cm). Pieced, appliquéd. Cotton. Collection of Rebecca Cluxton.

This Feathered Star is pieced with an appliquéd border, but is otherwise in the same style as those discussed above. Its insets of piping recall quilts made from 1850 to 1875. If the owner's estimated date is correct, Maude Cluxton may have been reviving an earlier pattern.

Maude Lieurance Cluxton was a Quaker woman of English and Scots-Irish ancestry. She lived in Martinsville until 1945, when she and her husband moved to Florida. She was interested in sewing all her life and was active in the Ladies' Aid quilting group at Newberry Friends Meeting.

[43] Maude Laurenna Lieurance Cluxton

THE GERMANIC SECTARIAN QUILT STYLE

Almost thirty years after the height of the floral appliqué quilt style, another group of Germanic quiltmakers in Ohio adopted a different design tradition (see illustration 23). These women were sectarians, religiously distinct from the church Protestants and Roman Catholics associated with the floral appliqué style. Members of Germanic sects who came to Ohio early and whose cultures still persist include Amish, Mennonites, Brethren, and Moravians. The communitarian Society of Separatists of Zoar settled in Tuscarawas County in 1817 and disbanded in 1898.

A sect is a religious group that withdraws from an established denomination to revitalize some aspect of faith the sectarians believe the parent church is neglecting. Most of Ohio's Germanic sects originated in Germany and Switzerland during the sixteenth-century Reformation when the governments of these countries sanctioned only one official church. Sectarians, believing those state churches had lost the purity and simplicity of the early Christian church, sought to revive it. They believed that the true church was a visible community of devout believers, rather than an entire nation of individuals who varied widely in their personal religious commitments. Consequently, they withdrew from the state church to live in complete obedience to biblical precepts as they understood them. Further objecting to the state church's strong ties to government, sectarians refused to take oaths, serve in public office, or participate in military service.

Primarily because of their doctrines of nonviolence and church-state separation—radical concepts that threatened the structure of European society—Germanic sectarians were bitterly persecuted in their homelands. In the late seventeenth and early eighteenth centuries, they came to America to escape the effects of this persecution and adverse economic conditions. Settling first in Pennsylvania and Virginia, they began migrating to Ohio before it became a state in 1803. Moravian missionaries were among the first white people in the region that would become Ohio, arriving in 1772. The first Brethren came in 1795, Mennonites in 1801, Amish in 1808, and Zoarites in 1817. Several groups of Bernese Swiss Mennonites immigrated directly to Ohio in the early nineteenth century and established Swiss-speaking congregations in Ohio unaffiliated with those Mennonite congregations established earlier. These later Mennonite settlers are known as Swiss Mennonites.

Beliefs and practices among the various sectarian groups differ and have ranged, for example, from the practice of infant baptism (Moravians) to sanctioning only believers' baptism (Amish, Mennonites, Brethren) to outright rejection of baptism and all other traditional sacraments (Zoarites). Today each extant sect incorporates divergent views that have led to the formation of subgroups within the sect, although their basic historical beliefs in humility, separatism, nonconformity, and nonresistance are still held in common. Ohio is home to the world's largest community of Old Order Amish, as well as to smaller groups such as the ultraconservative Swartzentruber Amish and the comparatively liberal Beachy Amish. Although they disagree on some issues, all Amish and the most conservative Mennonites and Brethren still dress in traditional "plain" garb.

Probably because of the persecution they suffered for their faith and a resultant tradition of mutual aid, Germanic sectarians developed a strong sense of community, which they define in religious terms. They settled in Ohio not as individualistic adventurers or Revolutionary War veterans, as many other pioneers did, but as religiously based communities. The Amish use the word *gemeinde* (or *G'ma*) to express their communal identity, a word that means both "congregation" and "community"; to the Amish the concepts are identical. The term *Brethren* indicates the significance of community both to the Brethren and to the Moravians, whose historical name, *Unitas Fratrum*, means "Unity of the Brethren." For each of these sectarian groups, community takes precedence over the individuals within it.

Many of the beliefs of these groups apply as well to another important group of Ohio quiltmakers, the Religious Society of Friends (Quakers). Together these groups are often called the "peace churches," based on their common doctrine of nonresistance. However, the Quakers are not a Germanic sect, and the stylistic characteristics we found in Germanic sectarian quilts are not present in those made by Ohio's Friends, whose quilts

[44] *Cross Roads to Jericho.* Elizabeth Miller Schrock (d. 1904), Walnut Creek (Holmes County), before 1904. 80″ x 66″ (203 cm x 168 cm). Pieced. Cotton. Collection of the German Culture Museum.

The design in Elizabeth Schrock's quilt is characteristic of quilts in the Germanic sectarian style: it is pieced; the pieced blocks alternate with plain blocks and are set on point; the central area is surrounded by a wide outer and narrow inner border; and the quilt is bound in a contrasting color. In this and similar quilts, the binding repeats a color used in the center field.

Elizabeth Miller Schrock was an Old Order Amish woman. As in this example, most Amish quiltmakers use only solid-colored fabrics in the quilts they make for family use.

are rarely different from those made by other Ohio quiltmakers.

The quilt style widely favored by Germanic sectarians is determined by its organization of design elements. A characteristic quilt consists of a center field of pieced blocks alternating with plain blocks and "set on point" (arranged diagonally across the surface) to create a dynamic design. This central area is framed by a narrow inner and wide outer border and, finally, by a narrow binding in a contrasting color. Although there are minor variations such as multiple plain borders, an occasional sawtooth inner border, or allover central patterns, this style is essentially as it appears in the Amish quilt in illustration 44.

When made by Amish women, such quilts can be distinguished by their use of saturated, solid colors, in contrast to those of other sectarians that incorporate patterned fabrics as well (see illustrations 45, 46, and 47). Block designs, while almost always pieced, are as diverse as in quilts made by non-Germanic quiltmakers. Regardless of the pattern variations in the pieced area of these sectarian quilts, there is a strong preference for multiple borders. The combination of wide outer and narrow inner borders on pieced quilts is otherwise rare in Ohio, except in the eastern counties.

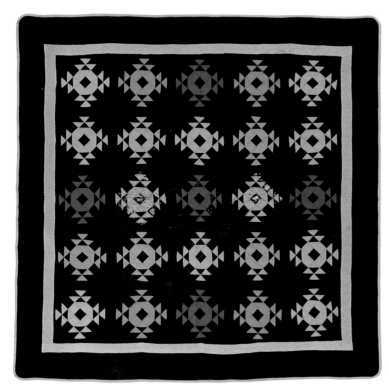

[45] *Crown of Thorns*. Mattie Raber Hershberger, Charm (Holmes County), 1946. 77" x 75" (196 cm x 191 cm). Pieced. Cotton. Collection of Stanley A. Kaufman.

This Crown of Thorns was made as a gift from the maker to her future son-in-law, David C. Wengerd, on his twenty-first birthday. It is inscribed in quilting "May 9/1946/DCW/Age 21." Although heavily worn, it exhibits the saturated colors of so many Ohio Amish quilts, dramatized by the black background that is also a hallmark of Amish quilts in Ohio.

[46] *Double Irish Chain*. Rebecca Smiley Ramseyer (1856–1932), Smithville (Wayne County), 1920–1930. 85" x 73" (215 cm x 185 cm). Pieced. Cotton. Collection of Marie Beechy.

This quilt is in the same style as those in illustrations 44 and 45. However, this quilt is made from patterned fabrics. Rebecca Smiley Ramseyer was a Mennonite and, unlike Amish quiltmakers, was free to use both plain and patterned materials. The top of this quilt appears to be much older than its backing and binding; it may have been quilted recently.

Rebecca Smiley was born in the Mennonite community of Goshen, Indiana, in 1856. After her 1877 marriage to Daniel Ramseyer, the couple moved to a farm in Smithville where they joined the Oak Grove Mennonite Church. Rebecca died in 1932.

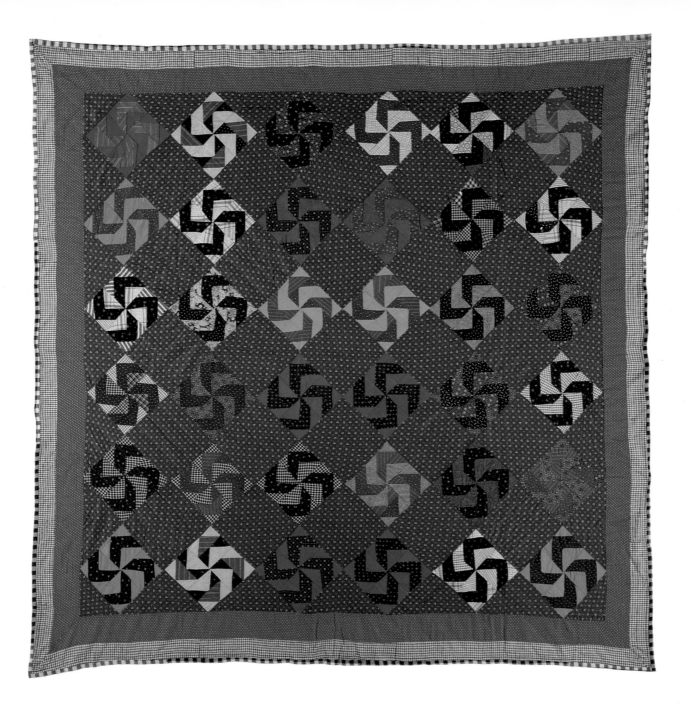

[47] *Dutchman's Puzzle*. Wilhelmina Dischinger Kappel (1866–1947), Zoar (Tuscarawas County), before 1947. 79″ x 79″ (199 cm x 199 cm). Pieced. Cotton. From a private collection.

Wilhelmina (Minnie) Dischinger and her husband, William C. Kappel, were both members of the Society of Separatists of Zoar, a communal society that existed from 1817 until 1898. William's father was the society's weaver, and Zoar was noted for the woolens woven there (for a quilt made by Minnie from Zoar woolens, see illustration 17 on page 20). Zoarites purchased their cotton fabrics, however, and this quilt is made from a variety of them. Minnie's fondness for checks is evident in the fabrics she chose for her outer border and unusually wide binding; many of the Zoar woolens were checks.

[48] Ohio counties with high concentrations of Germanic sectarian congregations, 1980.

▲ Amish
■ Brethren
● Mennonite
★ Moravian

The Germanic sectarian style is especially prevalent in Wayne, Holmes, Stark, and Tuscarawas counties, an area with a high concentration of Germanic sectarian communities (see illustration 48). We consider this an ethnic, rather than a regional, style, however, because examples in other areas of Ohio were made predominantly by Amish, Mennonite, or Brethren women (see illustration 49). There is only one Moravian congregation outside this four-county area.

Sarah Troyer of Holmes County and Mary Ann Kauffman Beachy of Madison County, for instance, were members of Amish congregations one hundred miles apart (see illustrations 50 and 51). The Lehman family of Wayne County and Barbara Welty of Putnam County were Swiss Mennonites living in widely separated communities (see illustrations 52 and 53). The same is true of Brethren quiltmakers Amanda Workman Fulmer of Ashland County and Laura Ruff Culler of Stark County (see illustrations 55 and 56).

It should be noted, however, that the two quilt styles preferred by Germanic quiltmakers are not the only ones in which they work (see illustration 58). Throughout the state's history, most Ohio quiltmakers have worked in a variety of techniques. The large collections of quilts that families bring to quilt documentation days frequently include pieced, appliquéd, crazy, and embroidered quilts made by a single quiltmaker over several decades. This is true of Germanic sectarians as well.

It is less true for the Amish, who are the most separatist and conservative of the Germanic sectarians. Their preferred technique is piecing, although not all Amish quilts are in the repeated block style. A particularly favored pattern is Broken Star, a radial design (see illustration 16 on page 19). Even with this focal change, however, Amish quiltmakers frame the center area with borders and contrasting binding, as they do in the sectarian style. And although Amish women currently make appliquéd quilts in patterned fabrics to sell to the "English," as the Amish call those outside their church, they still make only pieced quilts for their families. Some of these are in two styles apparently unique to the Amish.

The first is a long, narrow quilt of unusual proportions, when compared with bed quilts (see illustration 59). Many are designed in the Germanic sectarian style; their distinction lies in their unusual proportions. Quilts like this are made to cover the lounges or day beds commonly used in many Amish living rooms. Their shape is determined by their function, as they are made to cover the tops of a particular piece of furniture. All the lounge quilts we saw were made after 1900, although such quilts were in use earlier; Eve Wheatcroft Granick reports finding a lounge quilt listed in an 1892 Holmes County estate inventory (*The Amish Quilt*). Pieced lounge quilts have been illustrated in recent publications on Amish quilts. Most lounge quilts that we saw, however, were also plain quilts (see illustration 60).

The plain quilt is the second style we associate with Amish quiltmakers from the 1880s to the present. As its name suggests, it is simply a wholecloth quilt with one or more inner borders in a second color. Like the example in

[Text continued on page 42]

[49] This 1902 photo by Sam Amstutz shows a group of women in the Bluffton-Pandora Swiss Mennonite community making a quilt in the Germanic sectarian style. As is true in other photos by Sam Amstutz, the subjects display valued objects, in this case photographic portraits, a photo album, and a potted plant precariously balanced on the quilting frame. The quilters are (*left to right*) Rose Miller, Emma Diller Bitel, Sarah Diller Reichenbach, and Ida Amstutz. Noah C. Amstutz and Mary Amstutz stand behind them. *Photo courtesy the Swiss Community Historical Society.*

[50] *Gem Block*. Family of Sarah P. Troyer, Berlin Township (Holmes County), c. 1925. 90″ x 78″ (227 cm x 198 cm). Pieced. Cotton sateen. Collection of Stanley A. Kaufman.

Some Amish quilts, like this example, are made in only two colors. In Ohio, especially after 1920, black was frequently the primary color used by Amish quiltmakers, particularly in eastern Ohio.

[51] *Basket with Flowers*. Mary Ann Kauffman Beachy (b. 1899), Plain City (Madison County), 1944. 88″ x 78″ (224 cm x 197 cm). Pieced. Cotton. From a private collection.

Made in western Ohio in 1944, Mary Ann Beachy's quilt has all the hallmarks of the Germanic sectarian style. Although the baskets are aligned vertically, the blocks that include them are arranged diagonally; in basket patterns, the baskets emerge from a corner of the block. The quilt is filled with a flannel sheet.

Mary Ann Kauffman Beachy quilted for her family and also attended church quiltings. She made this quilt for her daughter.

[52] *Evening Star.* Catherine Zimmerly (1861–1952) or Leah Zuercher (1896–1988, Wayne County, 1900–1925. 77" x 71" (196 cm x 180 cm). Pieced. Wool. Collection of the Lehman family.

This Evening Star comes from Sonnenberg, a Swiss Mennonite community established east of Wooster (Wayne County) in the early nineteenth century. It is in the Germanic sectarian style, with a pieced, rather than plain, inner border. The backing fabric is a printed floral stripe, which is almost a hallmark of Sonnenberg quilts. The quilt glows with intense color because it is made from solid-colored wool.

The quiltmaker was either Catherine Zimmerly of East Union Township or her daughter, Leah Zuercher of Sugar Creek Township. The Sonnenberg community spanned both townships.

[53] *Ocean Waves.* Barbara Amstutz Welty (1868–1958), Pandora (Putnam County), c. 1920. 77″ x 71″ (196 cm x 180 cm). Pieced. Cotton. From a private collection.

The center of Barbara Welty's quilt is composed of pieced blocks joined in horizontal rows (a "straight set"), rather than on point, as is more often true in this style. Despite this, the center area is surrounded by multiple borders and a contrasting binding. Regardless of the pattern variations in the center field, most Germanic sectarian quiltmakers surrounded them with multiple borders. Barbara used dressmaking scraps for this quilt. Mennonite women do not avoid patterned fabric in their garments, as Amish women do; therefore, their dressmaking scraps include many with printed patterns.

    Barbara Amstutz Welty lived all her life in the Bluffton-Pandora Swiss Mennonite community. Born in 1868, she married Solomon Welty in 1890. They raised eight children. Barbara quilted regularly with the women of her church and in later years quilted professionally as well. She died in 1958.

[54] Barbara Amstutz Welty

[55] *Double Sawtooth*. Amanda Workman Fulmer (1857–1919), Loudonville (Ashland County), before 1919. 71″ x 69″ (180 cm x 175 cm). Pieced. Cotton. Collection of Doris Strang.

Amanda Fulmer's Double Sawtooth blocks are filled with crazy patches. Her blocks are surrounded with multiple borders and a contrasting binding. This quilt is by a Brethren woman working in the Germanic sectarian style.

Amanda Workman lived in Loudonville throughout her life. She and her husband, William Fulmer, whom she married in 1877, had three children. *Photo by Jean Alexander, courtesy Bobo • Alexander.*

[56] *Nine-Patch* or *Single Irish Chain*. Laura Ruff Culler (1865–1945), Freeburg (Stark County), c. 1910. 76″ x 69″ (192 cm x 175 cm). Pieced. Cotton. From a private collection.

Laura Ruff Culler was also a Brethren woman working in the Germanic sectarian style. Her quilt is composed of Nine-Patch blocks on point and alternating with plain blocks. When arranged this way, the resulting pattern appears to be a rectilinear grid. Laura used a marvelous variety of blue printed fabrics. This quilt illustrates the effectiveness of a very simple pattern, when the blocks are set on point.

Laura Ruff was born in 1865. In 1888 she married Henry Culler, and they had seven children. Laura began teaching her daughter to quilt "as soon as [she] could climb up on a chair." She died in 1945.

[57] Laura Ruff Culler

[58] Quilting at Center Church of the Brethren, Louisville (Stark County), 1901. Center Church women met once a month to make a quilt "to be sent to the needy in Europe." They also wove the rug in the foreground. The signed and initialed Fan quilt in this photograph indicates that Germanic sectarian women worked in a variety of styles; this pattern was universally popular at the time. The white ribbons worn by many of the individuals suggest this occasion was a special event in the life of Center Church. *Photo courtesy Kathryn Lavy.*

[59] *Nine-Patch.* Fannie Kuhns Hostetler (1892–1946), Plain City (Madison County), c. 1930. 83″ x 53″ (210 cm x 135 cm). Pieced. Cotton. From a private collection.

This long, narrow, pieced quilt was made to cover a lounge in an Amish home. Lounge quilts are designed the same as bed quilts; only their proportions differ. It is unusual to find white fabric in Amish quilts, as it is not a costume color. Some Amish women were forbidden to use white in their quilts.

Fannie Kuhns, an Old Order Amish quiltmaker, was born in 1892 in Nappanee, Indiana. After her 1918 marriage to Mose M. Hostetler, the couple moved to Plain City, where they had four children. Fannie made quilts as bedcovers and as gifts to her children. Her patterns came from friends and relatives, as well as from newspapers and quilt batting wrappers. She died in 1946.

[60] *Plain Lounge Quilt.* Amish quiltmaker, Holmes County, 1900–1940. 71″ x 39″ (179 cm x 98 cm). Pieced, reversible. Cotton sateen. From a private collection.

Most lounge quilts we saw were plain, as this is. The reverse is also purple, with two inner green borders. Plain quilts are a wonderful canvas for expert quilting designs.

illustration 61, many plain quilts are reversible. One made by Esther Beachy Yoder of Plain City (Madison County) in 1949 shows the influence of non-Amish quilts in its unusual binding of prairie points, a device popular at that time among the "English" (see illustration 62).

Like quiltmakers everywhere, most Amish quilt-makers report ordering patterns from newspapers and magazines or using those inherited from their mothers or traded with friends. Some sketched favorite patterns in notebooks. Others recorded them by making a quilt block in each pattern that appealed to them (see illustration 63). This fabric record of quilt patterns, now owned by the maker's daughter, comprises an impressive block collection.

As noted, Amish quilts made in the Germanic sectarian style can be distinguished from similar quilts made by other Germanic sectarians primarily by their incorporation of solid-colored fabrics in intense colors. Colors in Amish quilts usually reflect those used in Amish clothing, which are established in the *ordnungen*, or "rules for living," that govern behavior within Amish communities. These rules change slightly over time and from one congregation to another. They are usually transmitted orally, although a few written examples exist. *Ordnungen* are detailed and specific concerning appropriate colors and fabrics and therefore dictate the fabric scraps Amish quiltmakers use in their quilts. *Ordnungsbriefe* (written *ordnungen*) established in three of Ohio's Old Order Amish communities in 1865, 1950, and 1955 are detailed by Gertrude Enders Huntington ("Dove at the Window: A Study of an Old Order Amish Community in Ohio"). They all prohibit the use of patterned fabric in clothing and curtains. The 1950 *ordnung* from Pike County prohibits bright red, orange, yellow, and pink fabrics in clothing, and requires black for window curtains. The 1955 *ordnung* from an east central Ohio Amish congregation, probably in Tuscarawas County, forbids married women (church members) to dress in yellow or bright red, but permits blues, greens, lavenders, greys, blacks, and browns. It encourages white or blue cotton for curtains, and discourages lavender and yellow. This *ordnung* addresses materials as well, encouraging the use of cotton, linen, or wool, permitting acetate, and discouraging "miracle fabric."

Honoring these restrictions is sometimes difficult, as Amish women are at the mercy of the textile industry;

[61] *Plain Quilt.* Family of Bishop Ammon Troyer, Sugar Creek (Tuscarawas County), 1918. 76″ x 67″ (193 cm x 170 cm). Pieced, reversible. Cotton. Collection of the German Culture Museum.

Plain quilts were also made as bed quilts. This one, dated "1918" in red embroidery, is one of several reversible quilts we documented in Amish communities. Their makers tell us the quilts have a definite front and back, but sometimes they were used with the back up to save wear on the front. The light color in the borders and binding is a faded lavender.

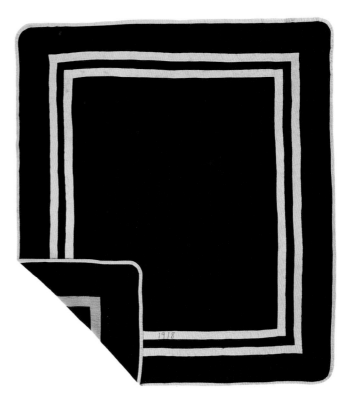

[62] *Plain Quilt.* Esther Beachy Yoder (b. 1900), Plain City (Madison County), 1949. 84″ x 74″ (212 cm x 188 cm). Pieced, reversible. Cotton. Collection of Fannie Troyer.

Esther Yoder's traditional Amish plain quilt reflects the influence of the "English" on Amish material culture. Yellow is an unusual color to find in an Amish quilt or clothing, although solid-colored dresses in "copen blue" and "maize" were popular outside Amish communities during the 1940s. Many non-Amish quiltmakers edged their quilts with prairie points (folded triangles); however, this is the only Amish quilt we saw with this edging.

Esther Beachy was born in 1900 in Arthur, Illinois. She married Henry B. Yoder in 1920 and has lived in Plain City since then. They have raised ten children. According to her daughter, Esther was a fine quilter, although she sometimes had her quilting done by older ladies in her community.

[63] *Collection of quilt blocks.* Amish quiltmaker, Baltic (Coshocton County), before 1962. Pieced. Cotton. From a private collection.

Whenever this quiltmaker saw a quilt pattern she liked, she made a representative block and kept it as a sampler. She wrote pattern names and comments about colors or design either on the blocks themselves (see the Pinetree block) or on paper labels, which she then pinned to the blocks. Sometimes she pinned pieces of selected fabrics to the sample blocks.

This collection is an extraordinary record of a quiltmaker's aesthetic preferences, of a variety of patterns popular among Amish quiltmakers in Ohio, and of Amish costume colors.

available fabrics and colors are those on the market. One Amish quiltmaker still loves the bright green and purple that were plentiful in the 1950s but were hard to find in her area (Ashtabula County) in the 1980s. Another purchases some of her fabrics by mail from Gohn's, a fabric business in Indiana that serves Amish communities, to get colors unavailable locally (Trumbull County). A Holmes County Amish quiltmaker, attempting in 1988 to replicate an old quilt from her family's collection, discovered that the color she wanted was available only in double knit fabric and encountered enormous problems in trying to piece small triangles of the stretchy material.

Double knits are the newest fabric to appear in Amish costume and quilts. Avoiding ostentation, most Amish quiltmakers used cotton until the 1970s and avoided the silks and velvets popular among the "English" during the earlier crazy quilt era (1880–1900). Many Amish quilts made between 1920 and 1950 incorporate cotton sateen, a lustrous fabric often used for linings.

Perhaps the most unusual fabric used in an Amish quilt is wool challis. In 1987 an Amish quiltmaker in Madison County made a Nine-Patch quilt from this fabric, using scraps from her 1942 black baptismal dress and her 1946 royal blue wedding dress, both of which had been partially destroyed by moths (see illustration 64). She purchased red wool, which she combined with recycled black wool to make the back of her reversible quilt. This woman's wedding dress was blue; however, favored colors vary from one Amish congregation to another. One of her neighbors reported that red was the traditional color for wedding dresses in the Indiana Amish community in which she grew up.

Because their everyday costume is so distinctive in color, we asked our Amish informants about unexpected colors we saw in Amish quilts. They always had a logical explanation. A quiltmaker in Windsor (Ashtabula County) told us that most Amish quiltmakers in her area buy their fabrics at Spector's in Middlefield (Geauga County), a chain of fabric stores situated in Amish communities. She explained that quiltmakers often purchase prepackaged bundles of cloth that sometimes include yellow and white. Although neither color is acceptable in clothing, there are no restrictions in her congregation concerning colors in quilts. On the other hand, an Amish quiltmaker in Geauga County reported that during the 1940s her congregation forbade the use of white in quilts.

A Double Wedding Ring made by an Old Order Amish quiltmaker in 1975 incorporates a variety of fabric scraps, in addition to the purchased background fabric in her favorite green (see illustration 65). The bright red in her wedding rings stands out among the other fabrics, which reflect contemporary Amish costume colors. The maker reported that every spring her father purchased several yards of bright red cotton, which he tore into strips and tied to the horses' bridles. He believed the flies that usually tormented the horses throughout the summer were repelled by the bright color.

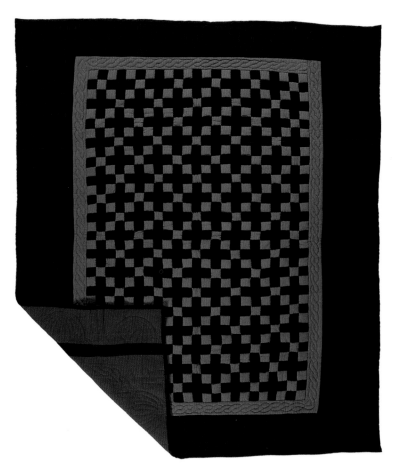

[64] *Nine-Patch*. Amish quiltmaker, Madison County, 1987. 88" x 73" (224 cm x 185 cm). Pieced, reversible. Wool challis. From a private collection.

This quilt was made recently of scraps cut from the owner's wedding dress (blue) and baptismal dress (black), which had been damaged by moths since her baptism in 1940 and wedding in 1944. She purchased new red fabric, which she combined with black scraps, for the back. Black is a traditional color for Amish baptismal dresses in her community because it symbolizes the death of Jesus. Blue was not required for wedding dresses, but in 1944 "everybody wanted it." The quilting pattern in the border was one the maker inherited from her mother.

GERMANIC AESTHETICS

Ohio's Germanic quiltmakers historically have favored two quilt styles: one being the red and green floral appliqué and the other, pieced blocks set on point and framed with multiple plain borders. The floral appliqué style was particularly popular during the mid nineteenth century among Roman Catholics and church Protestants, the pieced style from the late nineteenth century to the present among sectarians. Probably neither style originated with Germanic quiltmakers. Most of the appliquéd quilts we documented were made during the mid nineteenth century, and most of the pieced quilts during the last quarter of the same century. It is likely that Germanic women adopted these already existing techniques and styles in much the same way that Plains Indians in the 1970s adopted Star quilts, recognizing the similarity between the quilt designs and significant motifs from their own culture.

The temporal and stylistic differences, as well as the religious ones, raise intriguing questions. Why did the sectarians apparently begin quilting in earnest so much later than their Catholic or church Protestant compatriots? Perhaps the sectarians—separatist, traditional, and still German-speaking in most cases—were slower to adopt American customs. The nature of bedding found in the strongly Germanic east-central counties supports this. Straw-filled chaff bags used as mattresses and feather beds, the traditional German bedcovering, were still used by some sectarians in Holmes and Wayne counties as recently as 1935. Further, sectarians may have preferred blankets made from their own wool to "American" quilts. Plain blankets and overshot coverlets woven at several mills in this area are found in many sectarian homes. The sectarians' emphases on humility and community—"in, but not of, the world"—probably account for their preference for plain blankets and pieced quilts.

By contrast, highly decorative Jacquard coverlets available from many of the same mills at the same time are more frequently found in the homes of Lutheran or German Reformed families, the same families that made or used floral appliqué quilts.

Do these two groups of Germanic quilts have anything in common? Despite working in apparently diverse styles, their makers share a love of color; and their preferred quilt designs recall other Germanic decorative arts. Amish flower gardens are noted throughout Ohio for their strong and exuberant colors. *Fraktur* (decorated manuscripts), furniture, and enameled glassware decorated with realistic floral motifs like those on floral appliqué quilts grace many Germanic homes. The on point arrangement of quilt blocks in the sectarian style recalls the diamond motif still visible in Ohio's nineteenth-century Germanic furniture, metal work, and architecture (most notably at Zoar), as well as on the covers of much earlier Bibles and *ausbunden* (hymnals).

Most significantly, both groups favor wide borders framing the center field and colorful, contrasting bindings. Although borders are not exclusive to Germanic quilts, they are the single design element common to quilts in both styles. The preference for borders has been so strong among Germanic women that, as their quilt patterns have been increasingly influenced by popular fads (crazy, outline, and postage stamp quilts, for instance), the center areas are still framed by wide, multiple borders.

Floral appliquéd quilts are treasured masterpieces from Ohio's past. Dramatically beautiful quilts in the sectarian style are still being made. Both styles make a significant contribution to Ohio's quiltmaking traditions.

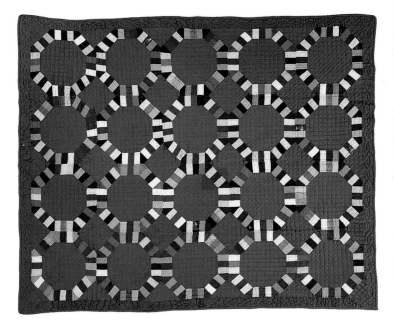

[65] *Double Wedding Ring*. Amish quiltmaker, Baltic (Coshocton County), 1975. 92" x 76" (234 cm x 192 cm). Pieced. Cotton sateen. From a private collection.

The maker of this Double Wedding Ring quilt used fabric scraps for the rings and purchased material in her favorite green for the background. Except for the fire-engine red, most of the scraps reflect the colors of Amish costume over several decades. The bright red scraps date to her childhood fifty years ago, when her father bought several yards of red cotton each year. He tore it into strips which he tied to the horses' bridles, believing the flies that normally bothered the animals during the summer were repelled by the bright color.

[66] *Sawtooth Strips*. Elizabeth Shafer Keller (1800–1887), Seneca Township (Guernsey, now Noble County), c. 1840. 83" x 74" (211 cm x 188 cm). Pieced. Wool. Collection of Glendola Pryor.

Born in Loudoun County, Virginia, Elizabeth Keller and her husband, Levi, were living in Guernsey County by 1830. She was the mother of twelve children. According to her great-granddaughter, the wool fabric for this quilt was produced on the Keller farm and the maker dyed at least some of the wool with native vegetable dyes. The varying shades of red are an indication of unstable dye.

The quilt has both a wool backing and batting. The blue and red plaid backing is typical of hand woven wool fabric of early-nineteenth-century Ohio. The quilt has been patched and the edges rebound.

[67] Elizabeth and Levi Keller

FROM BOLT TO BED:
QUILTS IN CONTEXT

ELLICE RONSHEIM

All objects formed by man are affected by the circumstances in which they are made. In documenting innumerable quilts over the years, we began to see them not as isolated objects of the past but as part of a flowing continuum, each a product of its time and environment. In this chapter we examine some of the factors that influenced the quilts made in Ohio. These include developments in the textile industry, the relationship of dress goods and fashion to quilt styles, the effect of the popular press, and Ohio's transformation from a frontier to settled rural and urban communities.

In addition to the quilt research project findings, our research was based on readings of nineteenth-century publications available to Ohioans and an examination of other Ohio textiles, costumes, and bedding. The quilt data are limited to the approximately seven thousand quilts people chose to bring into one of the fifty-three Quilt Discovery Days. We relied upon oral family history because so few quilts were signed and dated. Later we checked fabrics, styles, and written sources to see if they substantiated the oral history. Anonymous quilts, no matter how wonderful, were not assumed to be made in Ohio and therefore were not incorporated in the project's conclusions.

Response to the documentation varied across the state, and some types of quilts may be under- or over-represented. People save special items, not the ordinary; attics are filled with christening and wedding dresses, Grandmother's best china, and a great-aunt's prettiest quilt. The everyday dishes are broken, the house dress or play clothes given away or outgrown, and the simple utilitarian quilt worn out. Consequently, there is a disproportionate amount of special occasion quilts in family and museum collections. Another consideration favors the quilts made more recently, for their survival chances are better. Also, because the population of Ohio was considerably smaller during the early part of the nineteenth century (938,000 in 1830 and 3,199,000 in 1880), there were fewer people to make quilts, and fewer quilts were produced.

Compiling statistical breakdowns on almost seven thousand quilts will be greatly enhanced when all the project's data are computerized. For most of these articles, thousands of pieces of paper were hand tabulated; hence, the rounding off of the numbers. Our research has answered some questions but has raised others. We hope further research will continue to provide a greater understanding of Ohio quilts.

We never documented a quilt where we were provided with too much information. To help preserve the history of quilts in Ohio, we ask readers to take the time to find out about the quilts in their own families and to pass the information on to future generations. Quilt histories should be written on a piece of muslin and should include the maker of the quilt, when and where it was made, and anything else that might seem significant. The piece of muslin should then be hand sewn to the quilt backing. Thus, the quilt will be documented for future historians and for descendants.

UTILITARIAN QUILTS AND COMFORTS

Quilts were made to be used, to provide warmth. They also display different levels of workmanship and complexities of style. Elaborate appliqué or pieced quilts constructed with minute stitches differ greatly from thick, coarsely made quilts and comforts, both visually and in the expenditure in time and money incurred for their construction.

A quilt's visual appeal is subjective. While working at the Quilt Discovery Days, project volunteers frequently debated the merits of needlework, design, and overall impact. The intricate quilting patterns or multitudes of tiny pieces in some quilts were compared with the seemingly spontaneous color combinations in the simply quilted or tied woolen comforts.

Examining differences in the time consumed and expense of making the two types of quilts was more objective. The elaborate quilts, which may have primarily functioned as decorative bed coverings rather than as warm bedding, had smaller pieces and more intricate quilting. Hence, they required more time to complete. Since many of the floral appliqué quilts and the earlier framed medallion quilts used large amounts of the same fabric, cloth may have been specially purchased for these quilts (see pages 24–32 and 83–86 for additional discussion of floral appliqué quilts).

■

THERE ARE many who have not the time to piece quilts, but if they wish to use the scraps that accumulate so rapidly, they can make covers for comforts from them. Cut all the pieces the same width and so long as you can out of the material. Sew them together, using the light and dark alternately, until you have a strip long enough for the comfort. Sew the other strips in the same way and join them all together, or put strips of plain calico between. All the work may be easily and quickly done on the sewing machine, then tack or quilt the comfort.

The Ohio Farmer
September 20, 1894

■

The opposite of the labor-intensive decorative quilt is the quickly made utilitarian quilt or comfort. The terms *quilt* and *comfort* were used interchangeably in mid-to-late-nineteenth-century household guides. Here we call thick, coarsely quilted bedding a quilt and pieced quilts that are tied comforts or comforters. These utilitarian beddings share common characteristics. Their batting is thicker than that in their decorative counterparts; and to hold the bulky filler in place, the top filler and backing must be attached either with stitches or by tying the layers together. Tying is the process in which

thread or yarn is drawn through the layers at regular intervals and knotted to hold the batting in place. In Ohio the quilt patterns are simple geometric designs utilizing large pieces with alternating plain squares; they are often finished without borders. Dark colored wools or cottons were favored for the face of the quilt.

The project did not find any significant numbers of utilitarian cotton quilts or comforts. The earliest (pre-1850) Ohio utilitarian quilts consisted of hand woven wool with a wool batt as the filler (see illustrations 68 and 69). Backings varied from wool to a linen and cotton mixture. Most of these quilts descended in the maker's family and were reported to have been spun, woven, and quilted by the maker. The later nineteenth-century quilts used heavier suiting-weight wool and corduroy filled with cotton batting. Their backings were usually a plaid or striped cotton flannel. All the utilitarian quilts, both early and late, were quilted using simple patterns, grids, or diamonds; and the stitches were large and widely spaced.

■

A COMFORTABLE FOR a large or double bed ought to be three yards long and three yards wide. You may make it of glazed coloured muslin, (in which case it cannot be washed,) or of furniture chintz, or cheap calico. It is best to have both the lining and the outside of the same material. Having run the breadths together, place it in a quilting-frame, and lay on the cotton bats [*sic*] thickly and evenly, each one a very little over the edge of the other. A comfortable of the above size will require three pounds of carded cotton bats. It should be quilted in very large diamonds, laid out with chalk and a long ruler, or with a cord line dipped in raw starch, wetted to a thin paste with cold water. In quilting a comfortable, you need not attempt to take close, short stitches.

Miss Leslie's Lady's House-Book
1853

■

Directions for tying comforts did not appear until the early 1840s, and then the most frequent references were to knotting silk parlor throws (see log cabin quilts, pages 93–96 for additional information). Perhaps because of the popularity of the log cabin quilts in the 1870s, tying became a widespread method of joining front to back. It was practical as it facilitated the awkward task of cleaning the heavy, thick quilts. The ties could be clipped and removed and the layers separated, washed, and reassembled. Removing the batt eliminated the difficulty of maneuvering a waterlogged quilt during cleaning. If the batt was wool, the chore could be lessened by taking the separated batting to a mill to be replenished and recarded. The Rastetter Woolen Mill near Millersburg (Holmes County) still provides this service.

WE HAVE for a long time made our comforts by tacking them in quilting frames, and after adding as much cotton as we wish—which is generally four to six pounds—we draw our top straight and tightly over it. . . . We take [tie] ours about four inches apart each way. Some like them tied a little further apart, and some nearer. . . . We make all our comforts this way. Run the outer edges lightly together, and when they become soiled clip the thread that holds the rosette, rip the edges apart, wash the calico, then put the same rosettes back on them.

We like comforts made in this way better than quilted, because we can avoid the necessity of washing the cotton batting that is in them. Every person who has tried it knows how unsatisfactory a comfort is that has been washed with the cotton in it. . . .

The National Stockman and Farmer
June 3, 1886

Other hints to facilitate cleaning appeared in household columns of newspapers and magazines. One recommended facing the neck edge with cotton, tacked or pinned into place, to save the quilt from soiling and prevented the wool from irritating the sleeper's neck.

DURABLE BEDDING—A woman who has raised a large family recommends housekeepers to take a good quality of unbleached cotton, run up the breadths for top and lining of quilt, and then color it with any cheap domestic dye, such as japonica, annatto, white oak bark, or any such thing. Quilt them coursely [sic], and put more cotton batting in than would be needed for ordinary bed quilts. They will wear years longer than ordinary new calico, and are especially to be desired in large families of boys. If desired, outside spreads may be made of more fanciful materials.

The Ohio Farmer
December 4, 1875

These utilitarian comforts and quilts were practical for inexpensive, warm bedding that could be quickly made by a person with a minimum of skill. Most nineteenth-century periodicals dealing with household concerns recommended this type of bedding highly, but few utilitarian quilts or comforts, especially any made before the Civil War, were brought to quilt days. If they were made in Ohio in the quantities suggested by the household guides, they may have been heavily used, worn out, and discarded. It is also thought that owners considered them too ordinary or too worn to be of interest.

Ohio probate records and estate sales are of little help in trying to determine the use of quilts or comforts. The scanty descriptions there rarely distinguish between *old* and *worn* and are therefore of little value in identifying inexpensive utilitarian bedding.

Pre-Civil War quilts may be especially scarce because during the war women helped supply the Union soldiers with bedding. Over 30,000 pieces were sent by Ohio Soldiers' Aid societies, including blankets, comforts, sheets, and quilts. Thus it is possible that a signifi-

Ozias Burr's Estate

BLANKETS

3	checked	$1 each
1	checked	$1.23
1	checked	.12 cents
1	flannel	$1.50
1	flannel	.37½ cents
2	linsey	.75 each

Quilts

1	woolen	.73 cents
1	cotton	$3.33

Comfortable [comfort]

1	1.50
1	.23 cents
1	1.00

Franklin County Probate Records
1846

---

cant proportion of early-nineteenth-century pieced cotton quilts and utilitarian quilts and comforts were destroyed during the war.

Virginia Gunn's article, "Quilts for Union Soldiers in the Civil War" (*Uncoverings* [1985]), relates directions distributed by the Soldier's Aid Society for making "comfortables, 8 feet long, 4 feet wide of cheap dark print, wadded with cotton." Many women may have produced these quickly made "comfortables" and sent them with their older, worn quilts. If this is the case, a higher proportion of treasured family quilts probably are still in existence.

Another possible reason for the scarcity of early nineteenth-century utilitarian quilting is related to cost and time factors. A family raising its own sheep and weaving the resulting wool could produce blankets as easily as yardage for woolen quilts. Even when made of recycled cloth, quilts need the addition of a batt and backing to complete, and printed fabric for cotton quilts would have had to be purchased. Therefore, a domestically produced woolen blanket may have been a cheaper alternative to quilts.

By midcentury, the reverse was true. Most families were purchasing wool cloth rather than producing it. The price of cotton prints had been reduced by the success of the cotton textile industry. Thus, later in the century it was cheaper to make a tied comfort than to buy a high quality blanket.

Comforts could also be purchased. These ready-made comforts, often called "comfortables," were made from continuous lengths of fabric thickly filled and either quilted or tied. Household guides suggested having them match the decor of the rest of the room. Frequently made in various grades of large-scale floral furnishing prints, they were sold throughout the late nineteenth and early twentieth centuries. The fluffy cotton sateen or rayon comforters popular in the 1920s and 1930s were successors to these earlier comfortables.

[68] *Sixteen Patch*. Member of the Forward family, Jackson Township (Champaign County), c. 1812. 96″ x 79″ (244 cm x 201 cm). Pieced. Wool, cotton, and linen. Collection of the Ohio Historical Society.

According to the family history, the wool for this quilt was handspun and woven. The batting is wool, and it is quilted in a simple diamond pattern. The backing appears to be a twill weave cotton and linen combination. The first Forward family was among the settlers in Jackson Township, moving there in 1802, three years before the county was formed. Early accounts relate the problems of wolves attacking the sheep. In order to protect their source of wool, pens with high walls were built near the houses and the sheep kept in the pen at night.

[69] The blue and brown fabric in the large block is not pieced. The weaver changed the color of the weft.

PATCHWORK QUILTS, unless in silk, are rarely seen in cities, the glory of our grandmothers having passed away. Comforters, that is to say, two widths of furniture—chintz, with a layer of cotton batting between, and tacked together, or blankets, are used for winter covers. Comforters may be had at any upholsterer's from $1.50 to $3.00, according to the fineness of the chintz, which is about as cheap as they can be made at home, unless time is plenty; they are lighter and warmer than quilts.

Blankets range from three to thirty dollars a pair, the best French blankets costing that extravagant amount: A good pair of fine wide English blankets ranges from six to ten dollars, according to the width; they are the warmest and most comfortable of all bed-covers, and, if well taken care of, will last two generations.

Godey's Lady's Book
October 1855

[71] Gracie Pearl Sheets Graham with her husband, Elbert Graham

No comfortables were brought to any of the Quilt Discovery Days, possibly because the owners did not consider this type of bedding to be a quilt.

Most of the post-1900 comforts the project documented came from the rural southeastern counties of Ohio, the same area that has retained the traditions of quiltmaking throughout the twentieth century (see illustration 70). Many post-World War II cotton pieced quilts were also documented in the area, but very few pre-1880 quilts. Quilts in this section of Ohio seem to have been made for utilitarian purposes, used, and replaced as part of the ongoing quiltmaking tradition.

[70] *Shoo Fly.* Gracie Pearl Sheets Graham (1893–1975), Guyan Township (Gallia County), 1920–1935. 77" x 72" (194 cm x 183 cm). Pieced, tied. Wool and cotton. Collection of Jackie Graham.

Warm quilts were a necessity on the Graham farm; family members recall going to bed with "4 comforts and a hot brick" in cold weather. Mrs. Graham was raised in a quiltmaking family and married into one as well. The project documented over twenty quilts from various family members, the majority of which were tied comforts made in the second quarter of the twentieth century.

Fabric scraps were traded among family members and many of the quilts utilize wool suitings and pants fabrics. For one quilt, Gracie Pearl Graham dyed pink the fabric from an old pair of her husband's pants, to give the quilt some color. Many of the quilts utilized simple pieced shapes and were tied with carpet warp of a contrasting color. Outing flannel was purchased in Gallipolis for ten cents a yard and used as backing fabric.

THE IMPACT OF TECHNOLOGY ON THE AVAILABILITY OF DRESS GOODS IN OHIO

Since the history of quilts is affected by the availability of fabric, an examination of the fabrics available to Ohio quiltmakers in the nineteenth century is essential to understanding the quilts made there. In the early decades of the century, quilts reflected the scarcity of textiles. Most of the surviving pre-1840 quilts can be divided into two categories: simple woolen quilts, whose primary function was warmth; and more elaborate cotton pieced quilts made from imported printed chintz and calico (see illustrations 72, 73, and 74). The majority of Ohio quilts we documented were made after 1840 from printed cotton dress goods. This increase in quiltmaking directly correlates with the dramatic improvements in textile production during the first part of the nineteenth century. Also interrelated are the effects of transportation improvements, economic influences, the impact of the sewing machine, women's fashions, and the garment industry. It is important to keep in mind that these changes were not immediate, nor did they all happen concurrently everywhere in Ohio.

All textiles—bedding, clothing, and household linens—were essential parts of early Ohio households. Just how important they were can be seen by studying probate inventories and estate sale records. These records are not without error, varying widely in the description and completeness of inventory as well as accuracy of values. However, they do provide clues to the relative worth, amounts, and types of textiles found in pre-Civil War Ohio households. After the war, descriptions of individual items became rare. Quilts, blankets, and sheets are grouped under the single term *bedding*, making comparisons between early and late nineteenth-century bedding difficult.

By today's standards, a house interior described in early Ohio estate records would seem sparsely furnished and devoid of the softness textiles provide. Few curtains adorned the windows, and little or no carpeting covered the floor. Upholstered furniture was scarce as it did not become common until midcentury. Items such as sheets, towels, curtains, and garments are enumerated in these records, which emphasize that textiles were expensive and difficult to obtain in early-nineteenth-century Ohio. Often the most valuable household items listed would be bedding, including the layers of textiles on the bed as well as the wooden bedstead. Typical bedding consisted of a coarse linen ticking filled with straw or corn husks used as a mattress, possibly topped with another tick filled with feathers. Pillows, linen sheets, various blankets, coverlets, comforters, and/or quilts would complete the bedding, depending on the taste and economics of the household.

An examination of the 1824 estate inventory of Rufus Putnam reveals a wealth of information on early Ohio textiles. Putnam, one of the founders of Marietta, had a higher standard of living than did the average Ohioan. Nevertheless, the wide variety of textiles listed is an indication of

relative worth and availability throughout Ohio. Bedding, including the beds, ranged in value from $14.00 to $30.00, blankets from 50¢ to $4.00, quilts from $2.50 to $4.00. In comparison, chairs were 25¢ to $1.25 each. Most early probate records list the clothing items of the deceased. If the listings are accurate, a few changes are all most people owned. When David Loomes, a shoemaker, died in 1812 in Portage County, his clothing consisted of seven shirts, four vests, and two pairs of pants, along with a hat and footwear totaling $15.50, 28 percent of his estate. Another indication of small wardrobes was the lack of closets in nineteenth-century homes. A chest of drawers or wardrobe would suffice for storage for most families.

Southwest Chamber

SIX GREEN CHAIRS @ $1.25	$7.50
One Stand Table and Cover	$1.70
One Clothes Press	$8.00
One Case Drawers	$5.00
One Bedstead Bed Bolsters under bed and Pillows	$14.00
Three Cambrick window Curtains	$1.00
One Trunk	$3.00
One Suit curtains say 20 yrds @ 30	$6.00
Five pr. Blankets @ $2.50	$12.50
Two pr Rose Blankets @	$5.00
Two old Gridley Blankets	$5.00
One Domestic Blanket	$2.30
One old domestic Blanket	.60
One quilted blue coverlid	$2.00
One Stamped Counterpane	$2.00
One Callico Quilt	$3.00
One Callico Quilt	$4.00
One Callico Quilt	$2.50
One Woolen Quilt	$2.50
One Woolen Quilt	$4.00
Five pr. fine linen sheets @ $2.50	$12.50
Eight pr. Coarse Sheets @ $1.75	$14.00
Five Pr. Coarser Sheets @ $0.20	$2.00
One Damask Diaper Table Cloth	$6.00
One Damask Table Cloth	$2.00
One plane [sic] linen fringed Cloth	.62½
One Diaper linen fringed Cloth	$1.50
One New Cotton Table Cloth	$2.00
2 Towels @ .25	.50
Nine Towels @ .30	$2.70
Carpet say 14 yards	$9.00
One looking Glass	$1.25

Southeast Chamber

One Stand table and cover	$1.00
Three chairs @ .75	$2.25
One bedstead bed bolsters and pillows	$8.00
One Bed bolster and pillows on floor	$6.00
One looking glass	$1.25
One colonel chest	.50
One old chest "in the passage"	.25

Rufus Putnam estate inventory
Washington County, 1824

[72] *Framed Medallion*. Betsy Crocker, Dayton (Montgomery County), 1825. 105″ x 105″ (267 cm x 267 cm). Pieced, appliquéd. Glazed chintz and cotton dress prints. Collection of Margaret R. Loughry.

Susan Foster received this quilt from "Aunt" Betsy Crocker in 1825 with the instructions to give it to the child who would take the best care of it. It has continued to be handed down under the same conditions.

Only a few quilts made in this elaborate style were documented as being made in Ohio. More common in the South and mid-Atlantic states, the use of imported glazed chintz is typical of the framed medallion style. Cut-out chintz appliqués alternate with pieced stars in one of the seven borders surrounding the central square. Decorative quilts such as this were used as bed coverings and not solely for warmth. The shiny appearance of the chintz would be diminished through repeated washings.

[73] Detail of illustration 72

These relatively scarce and valuable textiles could be purchased, or they could be made in the home. The two sources were not mutually exclusive. Many households were involved in some facet of production of woolen and linen fabrics, while purchasing other fabric such as silk and printed cottons. For other needs it was possible to hire a professional weaver to make fancy weave articles, such as woolen and cotton coverlets or linen tablecloths.

Home manufacture of any textile—linen, wool, or cotton—is a tedious process, with linen production being the most time consuming. From sowing the flax seed to weaving the thread takes fourteen or more months, entailing up to twelve steps. While statistics for the amount of flax grown in Ohio are sketchy, the number of surviving flax spinning wheels, hand woven linens, and personal accounts attests to the significant amount of linen produced in Ohio during the first few decades of the nineteenth century.

Besides being used in the home, linen yardage was taken as trade or payment in general stores and resold as "country linen," usually at a lower price than imported linen. Isaac Evans, advertising in the *Chillicothe Supporter* on August 18, 1809, noted that he would consider "salt, shirting linen and sugar taken in exchange for merchandize." Because linen production is so labor intensive, the invention of the cotton gin in the late eighteenth century and the advent of machine spun cotton thread in the early nineteenth century led to the decline of home linen production.

The other important home-produced textile was wool, and early Ohioans kept sheep for the same reason they raised flax: to have raw materials for textiles. Sheep raising was one of the first agricultural endeavors in Ohio, and by the Civil War it was one of the major wool-producing states. Problems with wolves and poor quality wool lessened as the area became more settled and the

---

EVERY FAMILY was a manufacturing establishment to a certain extent. We raised flax and made thread, carded, spun, wove, colored, cut and made our own garments. Oak bark and the shucks of walnuts and butternuts served as coloring materials. We purchased needles and pins of occasional peddlers. My first needle was a birthday present from an aunt, and for years I carefully preserved it—my only needle. The deficiency in pins was supplied by a certain kind of thorn which were plentiful.

"Pioneer Incidents in the Life of Susan A. (Kellogg) Wilbor (1804–1875), of Milan [Huron County]," *Firelands Pioneer.* September 1876

[74] *Le Moyne Star.* Mary Jolliffe Higgins and/or Lydia Bruce Higgins, Higginsport (Brown County), 1800–1825. 109″ x 103″ (277 cm x 263 cm). Pieced, appliquéd. Cotton. Collection of Ohio Historical Society.

According to family records, Mary Jolliffe Higgins brought the fabric for this quilt to Ohio from Virginia shortly after her marriage to Colonel Robert Higgins in 1797. The Higgins family were founders of Higginsport, and their daughter Lydia was born there in 1801. Mary Jolliffe may have started the quilt before she died in 1806. Lydia Higgins could have completed it with additional fabrics at a later date.

The quilt combines pieced blocks of small-patterned dress goods and large-scale furnishing chintz, which form the central block and wide borders. Motifs were cut out of another furnishing chintz and appliquéd to the yellow blocks.

breeding stock improved. Spanish Merino sheep, known for their fine quality fleece, were imported at great cost. Gov. Thomas Worthington paid $250 in 1810 for a full-blooded Merino ram. If not owning sheep themselves, most settlers had access to the raw wool products of neighbors' animals. Wool-picking bees were a community effort in many areas. Then, after spinning, the wool could be woven into blankets and yardage.

To weave with skill takes years of practice, and most women did not have the time to achieve these skills and not every household owned a loom. Spinning wheels outnumber looms on estate inventories, seven to one. Before factory-spun thread was available, a single weaver could keep several spinners busy. Often a relatively small number of weavers produced cloth from the yarn spun in the surrounding households. These weavers might have been women who earned extra money by weaving for others or professional weavers who arrived with the early settlers and wove yard goods using customers' yarn.

An advertisement in *The Supporter* of Chillicothe on November 22, 1813, indicates the type of goods professionally produced. The advertisers, Crumpton and Smith, offered coverlets (both double and single weave), diapers, table linens, bed ticking, carpeting, and woolen and plain cloth. Records of home-produced linen and wool fabric include sheeting, bed ticking, table linens, toweling, carpeting, and blankets. Woolen and linen yardage were used for shirtings, undergarments, men's suits, and outerwear.

Ohio-produced fabrics were not the only sources for clothing or quilts. This is substantiated by examining the dresses and quilts that survive from the beginning of the nineteenth century. Two late-eighteenth- or early-nineteenth-century linen quilts were recorded by the Ohio Quilt Research Project, but they could not be documented as having been made in Ohio. The vast majority of existing examples are printed cotton or silk, neither of which was produced in Ohio. These fabrics had to be imported from the East Coast or from Europe (see illustration 75).

An advertisement placed in *The Centinel of the Northwest Territory* (Cincinnati) on February 15, 1794, states that David Zeigler had returned from Philadelphia with an assortment of dry goods, a general term used for textiles, notions, and articles made of textiles. Fifteen years later, in 1809, John Waddle of Chillicothe advertised an extensive list of yard goods imported from London and Liverpool "containing the latest London fashions and patterns." The list included wools of all weights and colors, calicos, ginghams, silks, velvets, and linens, as well as shawls, handkerchiefs, parasols, laces, ribbons, and hosiery. Waddle stated in his advertisement that the merchandise was available to his customers and to the public, which may indicate that his was a wholesale business and that his goods were distributed to a larger market outside the immediate area.

John T. Barr & Co.

The Supporter
Chillicothe (Ross County)
December 16, 1809

[75] *Lone Star.* Janet McCracken McCoy (c. 1790–1841),
Chillicothe (Ross County), 1835–1840. 89″ x 87″ (226 cm x 221
cm). Pieced, appliquéd. Cotton. Collection of Ross County
Historical Society.

Janet McCracken moved from Shippensburg, Pennsylvania, to
Ross County around 1800. She married John McCoy, another
Pennsylvania native and successful Chillicothe merchant, in
1808. Fabrics for her quilt were probably purchased in
Chillicothe, which had thirty-eight retail and two wholesale dry
goods stores by 1835.
  Stars, including the Lone, Ohio, and Blazing stars, were one
of the three recurring pattern types found in pre-1840 Ohio
pieced quilts. The other two were triangular patterns, such as
Birds in the Air, Flying Geese, and Double Sawtooth, and
designs based on squares, like Nine-Patch.

COMPARISON of wages and cost of goods in nineteenth-century Ohio.

Shirting	50 cents per yard
Calico	46 cents per yard
Gingham	56¼ cents per yard
Sheeting	62½ cents per yard
Apples	$6.80 per 2¾ bushels
Potatoes	2.25 per barrel

Prices may be slightly higher in this area than more settled parts of Ohio.

J. C. Ford, store ledger
Madison (Lake County)
1818–1822

■

Calico	28 cents per yard
Flannel	87½ cents per yard
Silk	90 cents per yard

Julia Galloway Worthington, account book
Chillicothe (Ross County)
1829
Ohio Historical Society

■

Monthly wages:

Laborers	$10–$27
Teacher (male)	$22
Blacksmith	$30
Owners and Managers	$62.50

Prices at Company Store

Food Stuff:

Coffee	12½ cents/lb.
Tea	$1/lb.
Beef	3 cents/lb.
Sugar	10 cents/lb.
Potatoes	56 cents/bushel
Rice	10 cents/lb.
Cheese	10 cents/lb.
Apples	25 cents/bushel

Dry Goods:

Blankets	$2.25 pair
Wool Shirt	$1.12½ each
Satinette	$1/yard

Alpacca	40 cents/yard
Shirting	16½ cents/yard
Thread	13 cents/spool
Muslin	10 cents/yard
Calico	15 cents/yard
Flannel	70½ cents/yard

Sundries and Incidentals:

Needles	6 cents/dozen
Paper Pins	10 cents each
Indigo	13 cents/ounce
Cooking Stove and trimmings	$22.50
House rent	$2 a month [possibly subsidized by company]

■

Glidden Company ledger
Scioto County
1846–1847

Average monthly wages:

Skilled Labor including Blacksmiths, Carpenters, Shoemakers	$71.50
Farm Laborers	$32.00
Common Labor	$37.25

Provisions and Groceries

Beef	12½ cents/lb.
Cheese	22¾ cents/lb.
Potatos [sic]	51 cents/bushel
Rice	13½ cents/bushel
Tea	$1.52/lb.
Coffee Roasted	33⅓ cents/lb.
Sugar, Coffee B	18 cents lb.
Fuel, wood, hand	4.74 per cord

Dry Goods

Cotton-flannel, med. quality	29 cents per yard
Tickings, good quality	37½ cents per yard
Prints, Merrimac	14 cents per yard
Mousseline de laines	22 cents per yard
Satinets, medium quality	84 cents per yard

House Rent

Four-room tenements	12.42 per month

"Labor in America"
United States Bureau of Statistics
circa 1875

■

An indication of the widespread availability of imported dress goods can be found in the journal kept by Englishman Timothy Flint while traveling in the northeastern portion of Ohio in 1818. He noted, "I have often seen among the inhabitants of the log houses of America, females with dresses composed of the muslins of Britain, the silks of India, and the crepes of China."

The Cincinnati Directory of 1831 listed 128 dry goods merchants whose inventories totaled $2.5 million the previous year. This accounts for half of all the imports into the port city. Many of these merchants, like John Waddle, may have been wholesale businessmen who distributed their goods throughout the surrounding states.

The increasing amount of fabric being imported into Ohio during the first several decades of the nineteenth century was conveyed to Ohio and distributed statewide by the improving transportation systems. The National Road stretched from Cumberland, Maryland, to Wheeling by 1817 and had reached Springfield (Clark County) by the late 1830s. Private turnpike companies linked towns together, and after 1825 canal systems opened up previously isolated areas. On the rivers and Lake Erie steamboats rapidly moved goods from one port to another. These improvements in transportation lowered the freight costs, reducing the prices of goods.

Another factor that had an immense impact on the
availability of printed cotton fabrics, as well as on all
other textiles, was improvement in the textile manufacturing process. In the last quarter of the eighteenth century, the textile industry in England and on the East
Coast began a remarkable trend toward mechanization.
At first, this represented assistance to the home and professional hand weaver by eliminating the hand process of
carding the unspun wool and by supplying factory-spun
cotton yarn. Eventually, it made hand weaving totally obsolete and impractical. The first American cotton spinning mill was established in Rhode Island in 1793. In
1809 there were eighty-seven cotton mills in operation in
the United States, concentrated in the New England
states. However, the products of these mills were still
woven into fabric by hand. Cotton warp was used in
mixed woolen goods, as well as in "domestics": coarse
plaids, stripes, checks, and gingham cotton fabric. By
1815 the power loom was in operation in this country. A
year later the first fully powered cotton factory was established in Massachusetts. The products were plain white
sheeting, as well as striped and checked domestics.
Mechanization of the textile industries made available a
larger variety of goods at cheaper prices than the hand
processes could produce.
    Shortly after 1800, textile mechanization moved into
Ohio. Of the fifty-seven Ohio counties listed in the 1820
Index of Manufacturers, forty-four reported having some
facilities for cloth production, primarily wool carding
and fulling mills. Fulling is a part of the finishing process
for wool cloth whereby the fabric is washed, shrunk, and
felted. After fulling, the nap is raised by brushing and

sheared to achieve a smooth surface. The most commonly manufactured textile in Ohio was woolen yard
goods.
    In 1820 Franklin County production of broadcloth,
cassimeres, satinet (a woolen and cotton mixture), flan-
nels, and yarn employed sixteen people and was valued at
$12,000. Three carding machines, three spinning ma-
chines, eight looms, one warping mill, one press, one
shearing machine, and two folding mills were utilized in
the production. Fabrics woven were suitable for men's
clothing and outerwear.
    Cotton yarn was often used in combination with the
wool, but little cotton yardage was produced in Ohio.
The 1820 *Index of Manufacturers* lists one cotton mill in
Jefferson County that produced "yarn, shirting plaids
and checks" valued at $4,523, but the proprietors were
"discouraged by the introduction of foreign fabrics."
    Ohio quiltmakers do not seem to have used this type
of plaid or checked cotton in their quilts. Of the relatively few pre-1840 Ohio quilts documented, none is
known to have been made from Ohio factory-produced
cotton or wool. Plain white factory cotton may have been
used for quilt backings, but there is no reliable method
for determining the visible difference between "home
spun" and factory-made cloth. We documented a few
early woolen quilts that were woven by the quiltmaker
(see illustration 66 on page 48), and the rest appear to
have been made from imported cotton prints that were
produced outside Ohio.

    The technological process having the greatest influ-
ence on quiltmaking was the development of cylinder
printing. This use of engraved metal rollers permitted
continuous printing of the decorative pattern, unlike the
previous block or plate printing methods; and manufacturers were able to increase dramatically the volume of
production. New England cotton mills began to implement the new printing process in the 1820s, and by the
mid 1830s the mills were manufacturing about 120 million yards of printed cottons annually. According to the

[76] *Double Sawtooth*. Anna Young, Wayne County, 1843. 87″ x 72″ (221 cm x 183 cm). Pieced. Cotton. From a private collection.

Anna Young used early-nineteenth-century sewing techniques in her 1843 pieced quilt. It is one of the earliest dated pieced quilts documented in Ohio. Her name and the date are cross-stitched on the back in the same type of embroidery used to mark household linens and undergarments.

The tiny white piping embellishing the border is a dressmaking technique popular from the mid 1820s until the 1870s. Flowered stripes and larger-scale floral prints in warm browns and soft tans were common in dress fabrics in the 1830s and early 1840s. Anna Young utilized sixteen different brown and tan prints in this quilt.

1850 *Statistics of Manufacturers*, there were forty-two calico printers in the New England and mid-Atlantic states producing cotton fabric valued at over $13,680,000.

It was this printing method that had the most impact on quiltmaking in Ohio. With the abundance of colorful printed cottons being manufactured, prices fell within the economic reach of many women for the first time. The author of *Eighty Years of Progress in the United States* (1867) described the drop in textile prices in these terms: "The price of a good calico is now 12 yards to a bushel of wheat. Forty years ago it was one yard for a bushel of wheat. The quality of goods at the same time has improved in a greater ration. The handsome prints that now replaced the 'factory checks' of that day, shows [*sic*] as great a change as does the price."

Not all cotton dress goods were produced in the United States. One-third of all imports from England between 1820 and 1860 were textiles. Victor Clark, in *History of Manufacturers of the United States*, said that

between 1827 and 1830 the average amount of cotton fabric imported from England was 3.5 yards per capita and was worth 21¢ a yard. Thirty years later, after textiles were fully factory produced, the price had dropped to 8.3¢ per yard. However, the per capita ratio had risen to 6.5 yards. Benefitting from lower prices and greater availability, Ohio quilters responded in the 1840s by producing an increasing number of quilts using roller printed cottons (see illustration 76).

As a result of improvements in the textile industry during the first half of the nineteenth century, the clothing worn by Ohioans changed. With fabric less expensive, most Ohioans could afford to own more clothing and to replace older, shabby garments before completely wearing them out. However, the cost savings may have been illusionary as mid-nineteenth-century fashions required an increased amount of fabric. For instance, the expanding skirts of the period necessitated additional yardage.

Quiltmaking profited in three ways from these changes in clothing. First, the construction of additional clothing produced more sewing scraps for quiltmaking. Second, replacing garments before they were completely worn out enabled quiltmakers to recycle less worn portions for quilts. Third, style changes affected quiltmaking because clothing was shaped to the body, becoming more form fitting. Previous styles tended to be looser fitting and were based on simple squares and rectangles, straight edges being the most efficient use of material. The new tight bodices and rounded sleeve shapes employed curved pattern pieces, resulting in greater waste. Thus, more scraps for quilts were produced (see illustration 77).

1874
Preble County
The Ohio Historical Society

Peterson's Magazine
June 1866

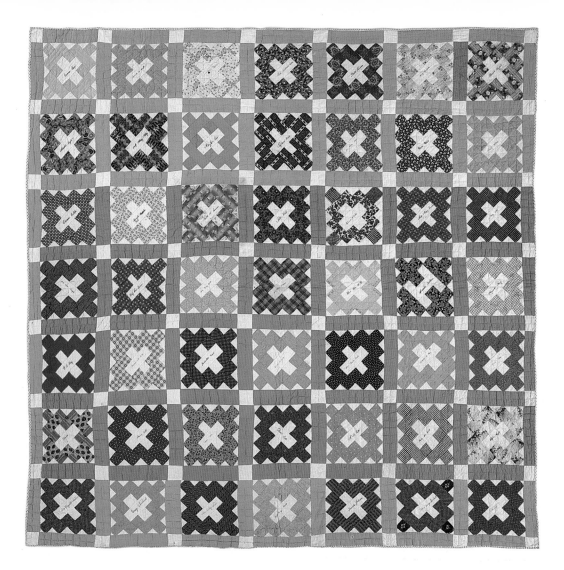

[77] *Christian Cross*. Rosina Butts, Auburn Corners (Geauga County), 1867—1880. 77" x 76" (196 cm x 193 cm). Pieced. Cotton. Collection of the Ohio Historical Society.

Rosina Butts made this quilt after her grandson, Daniel Bray, was born in August 1867. His name, that of his brother Gilbert, and the maker are written in the centers of the blocks. Names of other members of the community are recorded on this unusually bright album block quilt. This style of quilt contains a wealth of information for the researcher. Location, date, and names are customarily inscribed in ink; and the large pieces composing the blocks enable the fabric pattern to be clearly seen. These are some of the easiest quilts to place in context. They are a careful record of what a known group of people had available to them, in terms of printed cottons, during a particular time span, at a given location.

■

AUGUST 9, 1888
Ripped up 2 dresses, my wedding dress & an old brown dress that was Hollys, to make quilt of.
    Lucinda Cornell
    Westerville (Franklin County)
    August 9, 1888

■

The new styles also required more sewing time. By the late 1860s, spreading skirts were frequently topped by an additional decorative overskirt. Gradually these second skirts were bunched and gathered into increasing back fullness, terminating in the bustle of the 1870s and 1880s. However, the time-consuming trimming, pleat-ing, and ruffling on these dresses coincided with the development and increased availability of the sewing machine.

The sewing machine was not the work of a single inventor but the culmination of efforts by many individuals over a period of time. Although the first American patent was issued in 1846, it took approximately ten years and many modifications to provide a machine that was practical for the domestic market. According to U.S. census statistics, 111,000 were produced in 1860, a fact that becomes more significant when the retail cost of the machines is taken into account. Sewing machines ranged in price from $45 to $115, while the normal annual income for a skilled worker was $600. By the end of the century, the cost had dropped to $20 for a machine and cabinet.

The Ohio Farmer
January 7, 1860

Ladies' Dressing Gowns.

No. 53. Ladies' Calico Wrappers; we carry a large
stock in various patterns, - prices, 85c., $1.00, $1.25

No. 55. Best American Indigo Blue Calico Wrappers,
prices, - - - - - $1.40 and $1.50

Alms and Doepke catalog
Cincinnati (Hamilton County)
Fall/Winter, 1884–1885
Ohio Historical Society

In 1861 Wheeler and Wilson, a sewing machine manufacturer, published a time comparison between sewing a garment by hand and sewing the same garment by machine. It showed that a calico dress, which took six hours, thirty-seven minutes by hand took fifty-seven minutes by machine; a man's shirt took fourteen hours, twenty-six minutes by hand and one hour, sixteen minutes by machine. Machine sewing an apron would reduce the time involved from one hour, twenty-six minutes to nine minutes.

Both men and women endorsed this labor saving device. On August 1, 1857, the editor of the *Ohio Cultivator* urged farmers to relieve their wives who had been "tortured over vests, pants, coats, frocks, shirts, pinafores, [and] sacks." He added, "She will gain time to travel, time to think, time to be pleasant, cheerful [and] light-hearted." The owner of a sewing machine, it might be speculated, also gained time for quiltmaking. This theory can be substantiated by the fact that in Ohio the greatest number of quilts documented were made after the price of sewing machines had dropped to within the economic reach of the general population. However, other factors must be considered before embracing this theory wholeheartedly. These include the growing numbers of quiltmakers as the population increased and the likelihood that quilts made in the recent past are more likely than older ones to have survived.

Another time-saving development that may have contributed to the increase in quiltmaking in the second half of the nineteenth century was the increasing availability and acceptance of ready-to-wear clothing. Men's coats, vests, pants, and shirts had been available in Ohio during the first part of the century, with Cincinnati second only to New York in the production of ready-to-wear

clothing. Census records for 1850 and 1860 value the garments made at $4,427,500 and $6,381,190 respectively. Clothing establishments quickly embraced the sewing machine, expanding their production and markets. Machine sewing reduced the cost of construction, lowering the price for consumers. By the 1870s women's undergarments, cloaks, and loose-fitting wrappers could be purchased in stores and by mail order. Some of the prices for ready-to-wear men's and women's garments were so low it made home sewing seem a waste of time for women from middle- and higher-income families. These women may have preferred (as do many of their twentieth-century counterparts) to purchase some of the family's

ELLEN C. THOMPSON, a little girl between six and seven years old, had a Quilt of piece-work on exhibition at the late Fair. Her little fingers have been turned to some account at a very early age. We don't think that many little girls in this county can say as much.
Painesville Telegraph (Lake County)
October 28, 1858

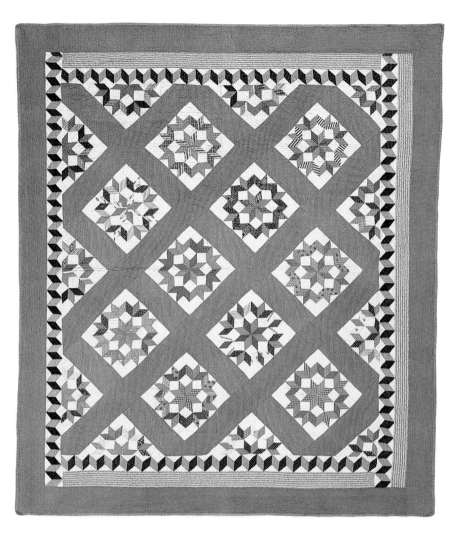

clothing and spend the time saved creating quilts (see illustration 78).

With both the sewing machine and the increased offerings of the garment industries, there was a decreasing need for time-consuming hand sewing used in clothing construction. The ability to sew fine seams, back stitches, or buttonholes was becoming a lost art by the early 1870s. Writers in farm magazines and household books noted the passing of skilled, plain sewing and often reminisced about how they learned to sew at a "tender age" by piecing their first quilt. These articles urged mothers to continue the tradition of teaching their little girls the useful skill of plain hand sewing. Nevertheless, we documented very few quilts known to have been made by girls under the age of fifteen. The passing of fine hand sewing skills is perceptible in the quilts documented. While the majority continued to be pieced and quilted by hand, intricate quilting patterns and elaborate stuffed work are rare on quilts produced during the last quarter of the nineteenth century. Quilting designs became simpler, and stitches increased in size. Appliqué work, with its characteristic precise stitching, gradually faded from popularity.

As the emphasis on skilled plain hand sewing diminished in the late 1860s and early 1870s, decorative surface

[78] *Carpenter's Wheel.* Wilhelmina Trost (1822–1897), Canal Winchester (Franklin County), c. 1875. 80″ x 69″ (203 cm x 175 cm). Pieced. Cotton. From a private collection.

Born in Germany, Wilhemina Trost immigrated in 1853 to the United States with her husband, John. They settled in Canal Winchester, where John Trost worked as a tailor. They raised a family of three sons and a daughter.

The quilt made by Wilhemina Trost exhibits many of the characteristics of quilts made by Germanic people in Ohio: blocks set on point, a pieced inner border, and wider outer border. Unusual characteristics are the treatment of the corners of the pieced inner border and the heavy sashing used between the blocks. Also evident in this quilt is the popularity of striped and double pink (pink on pink, or two shades of pink on white) dress fabric in the late 1860s to the mid 1870s.

embroidery emerged as the preferred needlework technique. It is best exemplified in the crazy quilts of the 1880s. Crazy quilts differed from previous quilt styles in three respects: the abundance of surface decoration they contained; the use of silk, rather than cotton, as material; and the availability for the first time of commercially produced patterns and fabric scraps (see illustration 79).

Employing a technique used first in log cabin quilts, the quiltmaker stitched irregularly shaped scraps of silk to a foundation block, then covered the seams with silk

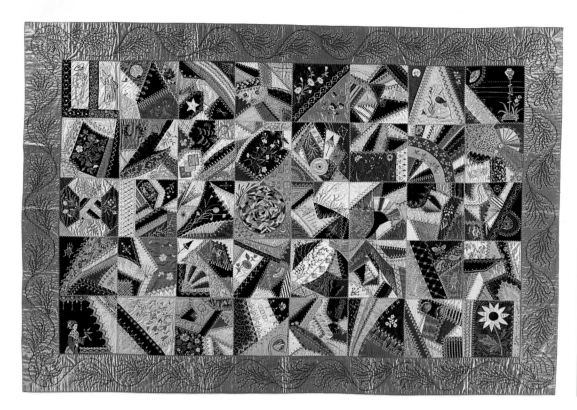

[79] *Crazy Quilt.* Maria Wilson Beardsley (1858–1946), Hamilton (Montgomery County), c. 1883. 80" x 55" (203 cm x 140 cm). Pieced, appliquéd, embroidered, hand painted. Silks, including velvets, taffetas, grosgrains, and brocades. Collection of the Ohio Historical Society.

Maria Beardsley created this quilt at the age of twenty-five. According to family tradition, she and her husband, a Hamilton business man, grouped the pieces on the floor, trying various combinations to achieve the most advantageous arrangement. The silk fabrics for the quilt were contributed by family

members and friends. After the patches were completed, the gold satin border and backing fabric were purchased.

The finished quilt was used for special occasions, "being thrown over the back of a sofa or chair when ladies came for teas or dinner parties."

At least one other elaborate crazy quilt was made in the neighborhood, and there appeared to be a gentle rivalry among quiltmakers. Maria's daughter remembers that her mother "would come home from a gathering and say she'd seen so-and-so's quilt, and maybe hers was better?"

embroidery. The silk fabric pieces were embellished with a variety of embroidery techniques, as well as by painting, ribbon work, and appliqué. Because of the delicate nature of the fabric and the small size of the quilts, they were more appropriate as decorative bedcoverings or parlor throws than as warm, easily soiled bedding.

A veritable kaleidoscope of colors and ornamentation, crazy quilts were well suited to Victorian taste. During this period, great emphasis was placed on home decoration, and handmade embellishments were considered a sign of a nurturing, creative household. Rooms were typically crowded from floor to ceiling with objects both useful and ornamental. Wallpaper, upholstery, carpeting, and drapery featured a wide array of floral designs, often used together within a single room. Furniture was adorned with carving, turning, and veneer. Crazy quilts were very much at home in such a setting.

They also had much in common with the costume of the time. Like crazy quilts, women's high fashion silk dresses of the late 1870s and 1880s combined colors and textures. Skirts and bodices were draped and swagged with contrasting satins and velvet brocades and lavishly

embellished with bows, laces, fringes, and ruffles (see illustration 81).

A major contributing factor to both Victorian dress and crazy quilts was the widening availability of silk after the Civil War. Had this fabric not been within the economic reach of the majority of women, the silk crazy quilt fad would never have gained such broad acceptance. In the antebellum period, silk had been a luxury item reserved for wedding and Sunday dresses, whose life span was often increased by redyeing or "making over." Fashionable magazines like *Godey's* urged their readers to use silk in their patchwork; but this practice was apparently not followed by Ohioans, for few pre-1870 silk quilts were brought to quilt documentation days. Not until the East Coast silk industry increased production of affordable silk was this fabric used lavishly in dresses and quilts.

Advances in the silk industry were stimulated by several factors, including the increased export of raw silk from the Orient and completion of the transcontinental railroad, which improved coast-to-coast shipping. The high cost of cotton after the Civil War and a high protec-

[81] Afternoon Dress. American, possibly Ohio. 1879–1881. *Courtesy of the Cincinnati Art Museum.*

Silk and Satins

WE CARRY pre-eminently the leading stock of Silks in Cincinnati, having received for this season's trade an unusually large and elegant line of the most famous and reliable makers of Silks in the world, we urge our friends to take advantage early of our success, while the assortment is full and the choice unlimited.

Colored silks—Gros Grain Dress Silks all widths 85 cents—2—a yd . . .

Velvets will be worn more than ever this season, both in combination with silks and other fabrics, and in full costume. . . .

We have imported especially for this season, a large and elegant line of the latest and most beautiful styles in Brocaded and Embossed novelties.

Colored brocades, the newest french styles 18"–23" $2.75, 3.25, 6.50, 7.50, 8.00, and $10.00

Colored Dress velvet—$6.50 26"

Brown, green, bronze, garnet, blue, prune, mulberry.

Alms and Doepke catalog
Cincinnati (Hamilton County)
Fall/Winter, 1884–1885
Ohio Historical Society

tive tariff on silk goods also aided America's silk industry. By 1874, silk worth $21 million was produced in the United States. This included braids, ribbons, and silk embroidery thread (an important component of crazy quilts), as well as yard goods.

The earliest crazy quilt we documented was started in 1882, the year that directions for making crazy quilts

THE MOST ECONOMICAL way to use silk pieces in patch-work, is crazy or Japanese work. It is made of pieces all shapes and sizes, as you happen to have. They have to be basted on a lining first. I use old muslin or sheeting, as that is easy to sew through. Cut this in squares eight inches large; now baste on the pieces of silk, taking care to turn in the edges nicely; have one or two quite good sized pieces in each block. Work around each piece with some contrasting color of silk, in feather, coral, briar, button-hole, or any fancy stitch. Then on any plain piece you can work some little pattern, a star, a flower, an animal, or anything your fancy suggests, the object being to get as much variety as possible; make no two blocks alike. Any one who has not seen work of this kind, has no idea how handsome it is, nor how fascinating to do.
I found many "cute" designs to embroider in outline on the blocks, in little children's books—Kate Greenaway figures for instance. The friend who first told me about this kind of work said, "You have no idea how your mind will develop to the subject after you once begin."—Alice

The Farm and Fireside
November 11, 1882

first appeared in various magazines. Very quickly there was a proliferation of design aids for these quilts. Whether these published embroidery patterns can be attributed to the influence of decorative arts schools and societies established to promote good design or to an opportune business venture is unknown. Nevertheless, crazy quilts were the first quilt style for which commercial patterns and design aids were widely available. Among the

The Farm and Fireside
October 1, 1885.

[82] Detail of Maria Wilson Beardsley's crazy quilt, illustration 79. This close-up reveals the maker's skilled hand embroidery. The multicolored bird in the lower left-hand block is an example of the appliquéd decorations commercially produced for use on crazy quilts.

The Farm and Fireside
October 1, 1885

published designs were flowers, insects, animals, children, and elaborately decorated letters, as well as a wide variety of embroidery stitches. Prompted by the public's fascination with the Japanese exhibit at the Philadelphia Centennial Exposition in 1876, commercial firms also published oriental motifs, such as fans, lanterns, butterflies, and kimono-clad figures. These designs were offered as paper patterns to trace, transfer patterns, stamping kits, or pre-embroidered appliqués (see illustration 82). Bundles of silk scraps could also be purchased from silk producers.

[83] *Crazy Quilt*. Minnie Peterman (1860–1933), York (Jefferson County), 1890–1900. 85″ x 85″ (216 cm x 216 cm). Pieced, wool embroidered. Wool. Collection of John and Judee Parkinson.

Minnie Peterman, whose sense of color and design is evident in this quilt, supported herself as a dressmaker in the Georgetown-York area of Harrison and Jefferson counties. Before the widespread availability (and respectability) of ready-made clothing for women and children, dressmakers like Minnie Peterman would be hired to help produce the next season's wardrobe. The arrival of the dressmaker was an annual event for many families, and she would live with them for several weeks, producing dresses, skirts, jackets, and coats before moving on to the next family.

Minnie Peterman was an exacting seamstress, as recalled by a former patron, who remembers trying on wool dresses when she was a small girl. She stood for what seemed like hours on a hot summer day while Minnie pinned and adjusted the fit. One day the weather was so hot and the fitting so long, the little girl fainted.

Minnie Peterman's occupation yielded an impressive variety of scraps. Her crazy quilt is a wealth of late nineteenth-century woolens. Crepes, twills, gabardines, and plaids were united with colorful woolen embroidery and edged with a one-inch ruffle, pieced from several different wool fabrics.

[84] Minnie Peterman *(left)*, with her sister, Asenath Peterman Parkinson

Bursting on the scene in the early 1880s, crazy quilts were a true fad. At first endorsed by the popular press, by the late 1880s they were falling from popularity. As early as 1887, magazine editors were declaring crazy quilts passé. Ohio women seemed to be in agreement. Although we saw a few from the early twentieth century, the majority of silk crazy quilts documented in Ohio were made between 1882 and the early 1890s. By the mid-to-late 1890s, some Ohio women who were still making crazy quilts had switched from silk to woolen fabric and embroidery yarn. Embroidery stitches covering the

SCRAPS OF FLANNEL or other woolen goods may be pieced by a pattern or put together crazy fashion, outlining the seams with silk zephyr or crewel in bright colors.
The Ohio Farmer
September 20, 1894

seams and the embroidered designs were simplified because of the thickness of the wool. Woolen crazy quilts are sometimes referred to as "country crazies," and we did find more of them in rural areas, with more of the elaborate silk ones in good-sized towns like Chillicothe (Ross County) and Hamilton (Butler County). Nevertheless, Ohio farm magazines published directions for silk crazy quilts and advertisements for corresponding patterns (see illustration 83).

As the crazy quilt fad receded, it was replaced by a related style, the embroidered outline quilt. Usually worked in the color-fast red embroidery thread recommended by magazines, these quilts were most popular at

WE REGRETTED much the time and energy spent on the most childish, and unsatisfactory of all work done with the needle, "crazy" patch-work. . . .
Godey's Lady's Book
December 1887

the turn of the century. Kits for stamping the designs on white backgrounds were available, or the quiltmaker could purchase prestamped quilt blocks, which some of our informants called "penny squares." Many of the outline designs from the earlier crazy quilts were transferred to this new style of quilt and embroidered in red, or occasionally blue, cotton embroidery thread (see illustration 85). A variation of this style was particularly popular as church fundraisers (see "Sisters, Saints, and Sewing Societies: Quiltmakers' Communities," pages 115–158).

Not everyone was enamored with the decorative crazy and outline embroidery quilts. Many Ohio quiltmakers continued to produce pieced quilts in a multitude of cotton prints utilizing the diversity of dress prints from the cotton factories (see illustration 86).

One reason for the increasing variety of cotton prints was the expanded range of dyes available to the textile manufacturer. This expansion was made possible because of progress made in the synthetic dye industry. The discovery of aniline, a coal tar derivative, in 1856 gradually increased the color palette. Synthetic dyes produced more consistent results using a less expensive and simpler process. They were not without their drawbacks, however. Many of these new dyes were not entirely color-fast, rapidly fading to colors unrelated to the original hue.

[85] *Red Embroidered Quilt.* Elizabeth Jarvis Ellis (1842–1924), Youngstown (Mahoning County), 1898. 82″ x 77″ (208 cm x 196 cm). Embroidered. Cotton. Collection of Mrs. Charles H. Maltbie.

Elizabeth Jarvis Ellis was born in County Clywd, North Wales, and immigrated to eastern Pennsylvania with her husband, Benjamin Ellis, in 1875. After Benjamin was killed in a coal mining accident, Elizabeth Ellis moved to Youngstown with her two newly married daughters and their husbands.

She made the quilt after moving, personalizing it with her name, date, and several quotations: "Native of North Wales," "America," and "We're from the Owl Country." The owls are larger versions of ones embroidered on crazy quilts, and the floral wreaths are quite similar to those designed for pillow shams.

[86] Printed Cotton Dress Fabrics, 1875–1890. Courtesy of Arnold Savage.

Tan, chocolate brown, and coppery red backgrounds with large, widely spaced floral sprigs or geometric shapes were popular prints for mid-1870s and early-1880s fabrics. By the late 1880s, there was a greater variety in the color palette with the addition of wines, purples, more indigo, and blacks. Some of the prints became realistic, depicting acorns, feathers, horseshoes, and horseheads. Other prints were more abstract or geometric. With literally thousands of cotton prints produced for clothing and furnishings during the last quarter of the nineteenth century, it becomes very difficult to date swatches of fabric exactly.

[87] *Sawtooth*. Alice Mary Glynn Coulson (1868–1940), Russia Township (Lorain County), 1885–1895. 80″ x 70″ (203 cm x 180 cm). Pieced. Cotton. From a private collection.

Mary Glynn Coulson may have made this quilt around the time of her August 1890 marriage to Henry Coulson. Family tradition relates that she was a seamstress and she may have obtained some of the fabric scraps from her business. The colors and prints are typical of the late 1870s through the late 1880s suggesting that she may have saved some of the older fabric from the time she was a young girl. The diversity of red-brown and tan prints is typical of dress goods in the 1870s. Fabrics fashionable ten years later include sporting prints. These figurative, as opposed to floral, prints have realistic motifs such as the coiled ropes, horseheads, and anchors that appear in Mary Coulson's quilt.

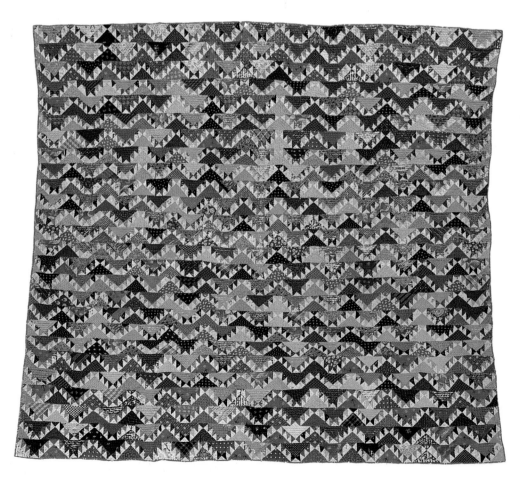

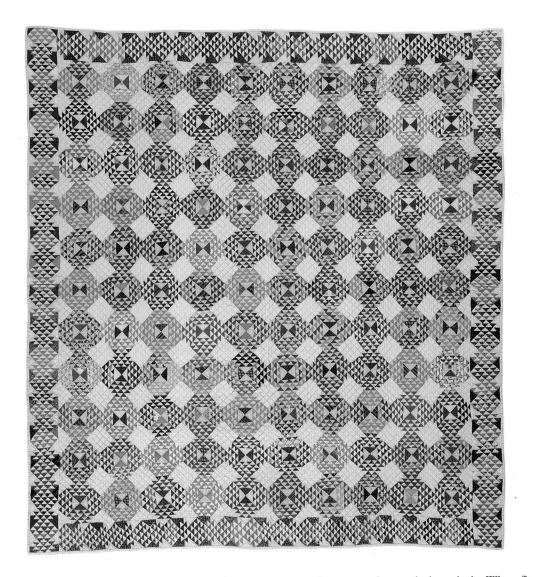

[88] *Old Maid's Puzzle.* Annie Hart Beal (1861–1867), Bedford Township (Meigs County), c. 1876. 84" x 77" (213 cm x 196 cm). Pieced. Cotton. Collection of the Ohio Historical Society.

According to family records, Annie Hart was fifteen when a prize was offered by a county fair to the person who could make a quilt containing the most pieces. She began this quilt, which she called Old Maid's Puzzle and is known now as an Ocean Waves pattern, in response to the announcement. She was unable to finish in time, and another woman won with a quilt of more than seven thousand pieces in it. When finished, Annie Hart's quilt contained 110 blocks composed of 14,572 pieces, and requiring 20 spools of thread, each 250 yards long. Apparently, the quilt was regarded as special and was never used. The pencil quilting lines are still evident, and visitors to the Hart-Beal house remember asking to see it. When Annie Hart Beal's son gave the quilt to his son, he composed a poem to mark the occasion.

■

L. A. C. WISHES to know how to wash a black calico dress to prevent fading.

Put one gill of salt in a tub; pour one gallon of boiling (hard) water over it; put in your dress immediately; thoroughly saturate it, stirring occasionally until cold; then wash in a good suds as you would anything else. Always iron on the wrong side, and your dress will be as nice as new. H. Homer, Ohio

Another: Take clear, soft water, put in salt and alum; wash quickly, and hang in the shade to dry. Omit soap in washing, if possible. Warsaw, Ohio   Mamie
The Farm and Fireside
October 1, 1882

■

For instance, some of the soft tan or brown shades present in older cotton quilts today may have initially been green or red (see illustration 194 on page 76). Natural dyes, on the other hand, usually fade to a paler version of the original color.

Both natural and synthetic dyes, particularly brown and black, sometimes injured the fabric. The damage is most often seen in red and green cotton prints, when small brown or black figures deteriorate, leaving tiny holes in the background color. Cellulose fibers (cotton, and linen) do not dye as readily as protein fibers such as wool and silk.

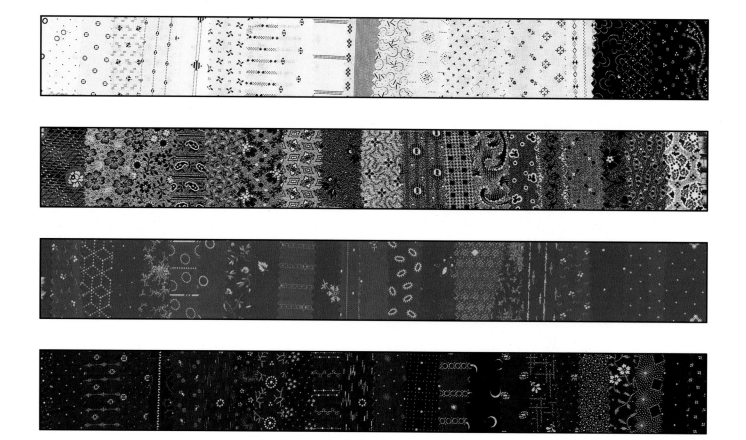

[89] Printed Cotton Dress Fabrics, 1890–1915. Courtesy of
Anita Schackelford and Ellen B. Hess.

Turn-of-the-century work dresses and wrappers were often made
in one of these two-color combinations. The small, stylized
floral and geometric patterns continued to be made for years in
these darker hued colors, as well as in pinks and lighter blue
shades. Shirting prints added a lighter color range during this
time period. These white-background fabrics, designed in one
or two colors in a variety of tiny motifs, were often used in
place of plain white fabric in pieced quilts.

The new shades available were reflected in the quilts
made from the dress scraps. Rich, red browns and coppery hues printed in stripes, dots, and small floral sprigs,
as well as larger paisley designs, were popular from the
1870s through the mid 1880s (see illustration 87). This
array of shades and prints may have inspired the fad of
"charm" or "scrap" quilts. Thousands of tiny squares
and triangles were cut out and sewn together to make
these mosaic creations (see illustration 88). Improvements in black dyes for cottons in the 1890s led to a decline in the copper brown and red prints of the 1870s and
1880s. Black prints, along with other darker colors, deep
maroon, navy blue, and grey, became popular dress fabrics and gave turn-of-the-century Ohio quilts a somber
hue (see illustrations 89 and 90).

These late-nineteenth-century quilts, as did their
earlier counterparts, reflected fabrics available to Ohio
quiltmakers and showed the progress of the textile industry and the impact changes in technology had on
quiltmaking.

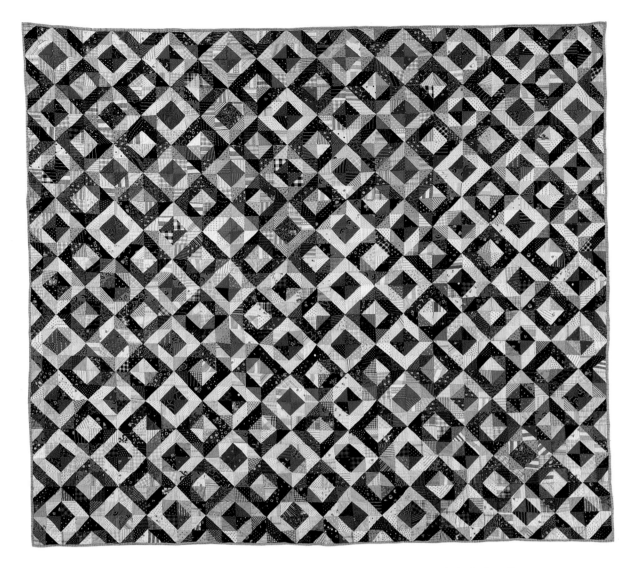

[90] *Light and Dark*. Mary Ettie Bailey Carey (1870–1938), Careytown (Highland County), c. 1900. 83″ x 76″ (211 cm x 193 cm). Pieced. Cotton. Collection of Mary Jane Burgess.

Mary Ettie Bailey Carey lived her entire life in the Samantha/ Careytown/Highland area of Highland County. At the age of twenty-two she married Benjamin Conrad Carey, the first neighbor boy to kiss her (she was a week old, and her future husband was four years old).

They farmed outside of Careytown and had four children, three of whom survived to adulthood. Her granddaughter and namesake remembers two things about her grandmother: her gingerbread cookies and her stark white wraparound apron.

The dress scraps Mary Ettie Carey used in this quilt display the color palette available at the turn of the century. These include indigo and double pinks, still popular after several decades of use, and newer shades of cadet blue (a grey blue shade) and wine-colored reds. Many of the light tones are small-figured shirting prints and stripes. Typical of this period are the black background cotton prints and white and black prints, which appear to be grey. All these fabrics were widely available in Ohio at this time, and possibly by trading with friends, Mary Ettie Carey was able to obtain this extensive variety of fabrics.

[91] Mary Ettie Bailey Carey

BATTING AND WADDING

A quilt can be regarded as a textile sandwich, the top, back, and filling held in place by the quilting stitches. This filling or batt provides insulation and creates a warm bed covering. It is often hard to determine a quilt's batting material unless a quilt is frayed or worn in places that allow a peek inside. While Ohio quilters preferred cotton as a filler, we found wool, cotton, silk, flax, woven blankets, and worn-out quilts used as batting.

The invention in 1793 of the cotton gin, and its widespread use by the beginning of the nineteenth century, eliminated the time-consuming task of cleaning seeds and debris from the raw cotton. As with all textile-working machines, production quality varied, and cotton batts with bits of debris should not be assumed to predate 1793.

Before the advent of manufactured batting, people produced filler at home. Small amounts of unspun cotton or wool were individually carded into batts. These batts were, in turn, laid side by side to cover the quilt lining. The top was then put in place and the three layers quilted together. For instance, in 1827 John Johnson, in Piqua (Miami County), bought two pounds (the right amount for a quilt) of unspun ginned cotton for 14.5 cents a pound. Because factory-spun cotton thread was available, cotton such as Johnson's may have been made into batts for quilts.

Among the technological improvements in the textile industry, the appearance of ready-made batting must have been greeted with great enthusiasm. One of the first companies to produce it was Stearns and Foster of Cincinnati. George S. Stearns and Seth C. Foster perfected a

[92] William's Dayton Directory, 1856

method of commercially producing cotton batting in the mid 1840s. The result was a strong, thin sheet (under thirty-six inches wide) with a glazing of starch paste to keep the fibers from stretching.

Batting was not the only Stearns and Foster product advertised in mid-nineteenth-century Cincinnati directories. From at least 1849 they produced wadding as well as batting. The entries do not make it clear which came first. Both batting and wadding are sheets of carded cotton. Wadding, however, was usually thicker and was used in clothing as well as upholstery.

Williams' Cincinnati Directory
1860

BATTING, N, cotton or wool in masses prepared for quilts.
Wadding, N, 2. A kind of soft stuff of loose texture, used for stuffing garments.
Noah Webster, *An American Dictionary of the English Language*
1845

Batting, N, 2. Cotton in sheets, prepared for quilts or bedcovers.
Wadding, N, Suitable for stuffing or lining garments & c; as, wadding materials.
Noah Webster, *An American Dictionary of the English Language*
1860

The fashionable mid nineteenth-century silhouette called for a round-shouldered appearance. Wadding, properly placed, could fill out the hollows of the chest. Many men's frock coats and vests from 1830 through the Civil War contained a layer of cotton wadding between the outer fabric and the lining, quilted or tacked into place. Even some women's dresses were padded, tapering from the shoulders to the breast. These pads were either tacked in, as in the men's garments, or were removable pads, as in the case of an 1855 wedding dress in the Ohio Historical Society collections.

Wadding and/or batting was used in other garments to provide warmth. Quilted hoods, cloaks, and petticoats that date from the first half of the nineteenth century are found in Ohio textile collections (see illustration 93). In hoods and petticoats the quilting forms a decorative pattern similar to that found on quilts. The linings in capes are often quilted in a simple pattern of diamonds.

NOV. 28, 1832   Wrought on my canton [a ribbed cotton or silk fabric] quilt in company of Mr. Hamilton an old Revolutionary 76er
Nov. 29, 1832   Sewd at crape quilt . . . walked down to my mothers, wrought at q [quilted] peticoat putting in frame.
Nov. 30, 1832   Quilted [the petticoat] & 31 [?] do [quilted]
Dec. 1, 1832   (Saturday) finished with my mothers help too my quiled [quilted] peticoat
    Eliza Wilson, diary
    Steubenville (Jefferson County)
    1832
    Ohio Historical Society
    Courtesy Adrienne Saint-Pierre

---

[93] Quilted cotton print petticoat, c. 1850. Quilted silk hood. Quaker, Ohio, 1845–1860. *Courtesy of the Ohio Historical Society.*

After cotton, the second most common type of batting found in Ohio was wool. It was a logical choice because of its greater insulating properties and the fact that Ohio ranked third among the states in wool production, according to the 1840 census, and first in the next three censuses. However, judging from the quilts we saw, pre-Civil War woolen quilts were the most likely to have wool batts (see illustrations 66 on page 48, 68 on page 72, and 98 on page 80). A few late-nineteenth-century and early-twentieth-century comforters had wool batts, but only one cotton quilt documented by the project from this later period had a wool batt.

It is possible that quilts made for heavy, utilitarian purposes were filled with wool because of the warmth factor, and in these sparsely stitched quilts its disadvantages were not of concern. Wool does not compress as much as cotton and creates a puffy appearance, obscuring the detail of the quilting pattern. Especially in cotton quilts, there is the problem of the wool shrinking and felting when cleaned. A pieced cotton quilt with a wool batt would not gracefully survive the rigors of the nineteenth-century wash tub.

Silk and flax are of minor importance for batting in Ohio quilts. We found silk batting in a mid-nineteenth-century silk lap throw and flax batting in another mid-nineteenth-century quilt. This flax-filled quilt was worn out and used as filler for a much later quilt (see illustration 94). Old blankets and scraps of woolen cloth also made economical filling for quilts and were documented in a few Ohio quilts.

A new type of batting appeared on the market in the early 1960s. A product of the synthetic fabric industry, polyester batting has become standard among many of today's quilters. Compared to the cotton batting it replaced, polyester batting is easier to push a needle through and does not have the tendency to shift when washed. Because the batting remains in place, the need for close quilting is eliminated. Its widely spaced rows of stitching and resilient puffy qualities create a different appearance from that of cotton-filled quilts.

The last several years have seen a renewed interest in the flat, densely quilted look achieved with cotton filler. Batting companies, like Stearns and Foster of Cincinnati, have responded to the demand, and cotton batting is once again widely available.

[94] *Streak of Lightning*. Detail. Mary Groseclose Sheets (1857–1937), Guyan Township (Gallia County), 1875–1890. 79″ x 71″ (200 cm x 180 cm). Pieced. Wool, cotton, and flax. Collection of Jackie Graham.

Fascinating histories accompany not only quilts in excellent condition, but also some in worn condition. In Mary Groseclose Sheets's quilt, the worn and frayed edge reveals information that would have remained inaccessible in a less-used piece. An old quilt with blue stripe fabric is used for batting. It dates from the late 1840s to the 1850s, and the worn edge reveals its flax batt.

Domestic linen production was becoming uncommon by the mid nineteenth century, but some families continued the tradition. The flax may have been grown for the seeds, which were crushed to make linseed oil. After the seeds had been stripped, the stem could then be processed to produce the flat, shiny fibers used for filler in the inner quilt.

The census reports for Ohio in 1850 and 1860 list production of 223 tons and 441 tons of flax respectively. Much of this was grown in the middle and southwestern counties of Ohio. Cincinnati had a large linseed oil mill, and Dayton records crushing 200,000 bushels of flax seed annually.

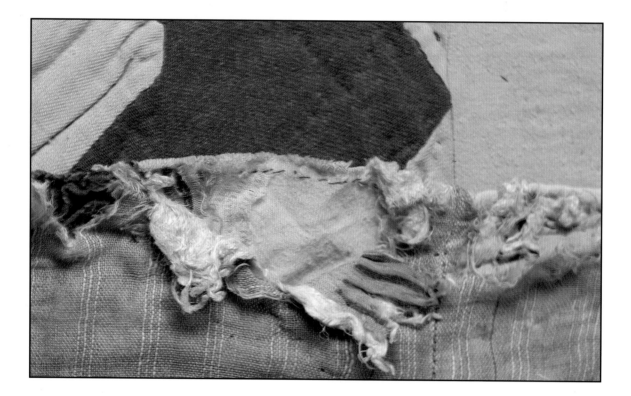

THE COLOR ORANGE AND NINETEENTH-CENTURY DRESS GOODS

Historical research sometimes raises as many questions as it answers. One such question is the relationship between costume, quilts, and the bright yellow-orange (marigold orange) cotton fabric that appears as an accent color in quilts. In almost all cases, the fabric is a solid color, not a printed pattern, woven stripe, or plaid. A vibrant color, this shade first appeared in the 1840s on appliqué quilts, in flower buds or the center circle of a multilayered flower. It was used on floral appliqué quilts throughout the nineteenth century and adds a touch of brightness to mid- to late-nineteenth-century piecework quilts (see illustrations 77 on page 63, 89 on page 72, 95 and 101 on page 84). Bright orange is found in twentieth-century quilts as well, but the larger color palette and the tendency toward lighter, brighter hues minimize the impact of this color in post-World War I quilts.

Surprisingly, orange rarely appears in surviving nineteenth-century costume. Solid-colored cotton was little used as dress fabric. Cottons intended for dress goods or furnishing fabrics were usually printed in floral or geometric patterns or woven in plaids and stripes. Wools and silks, however, were often a solid hue: left the natural cream color; dyed tones of blue, brown, gray, and black; or tinted the less common pale shades of pink, yellow, and green. After the Civil War, wool and silk dress goods were also available in varying hues of red, green, purple, and mustard.

As with the orange fabric, solid red and green cotton fabrics are found in nineteenth-century appliqué quilts, beginning in the 1840s. Because these colors are not found in existing cotton dresses of the same period, it is concluded that they may have been produced especially for quiltmaking (see page 85 for an 1849 Cleveland, Ohio, advertisement mentioning prints made especially for quilts).

◼ ORANGE DRAPERY—Orange is too brilliant to be elegant; it makes fair complexions blue, whitens those who have an orange tint, and gives a green hue to those of a yellow tint.
Godey's Lady's Book
August 1855 ◼

Orange, however, remains the most fascinating color because, unlike the red and the green, the shade is rarely found in cotton dress prints; bright yellows and oranges are unflattering to most, caucasian skin tones. Loud colors were also considered vulgar and immodest.

We may here properly observe that American women would be a great deal better dressed if they would more carefully consult simplicity and sobriety in the colors and arrangement of their costumes. . . . Let our fair readers then be aware that the well dressed lady is one who appears in the street or public places in the fewest, simplest, and least conspicuous colors, choosing of course such of the neutral hues as are most suited to her complexion and having every part of her attire the most scrupulous fit, neatness and propriety.
—*Godey's Lady's Book*, March 1854

There is only one orange dress out of approximately 150 women's cotton print dresses in the Ohio Historical Society's collection. It is a woven orange plaid dress worn in the late 1860s in Trumbull County.

The examination of orange in quilts illustrates one of the ways improvements in technology affected quilts. Until the early 1840s, vegetable dyes such as fustic, black oak bark, peach leaves, and goldenrod were used to produce the spectrum of yellows. Oranges could be made by overdyeing yellow with red. Many early dye goods either faded rapidly or produced colors in the yellow/brown family.

◼

IN PRODUCING certain results, advantage is taken of that affinity or attraction by which one substance A unites with another substance B in preference to a substance C; so that if C be dissolved in A, the addition of B would cause C to leave A in order to unite with B; as, when resin is dissolved in spirits of wine, the addition of water will throw down the resin as a precipitate, because the spirit has a stronger affinity for the water than it has for the resin. The coloring matter is produced in or upon the cloth in the form of an insoluble precipitate by mixing two solutions, in neither of which does the color exist separately. The advantage of this method is, that the cloth can be impregnated with one solution, and then, upon immersing it in the other, the insoluble coloring matter is formed within the elongated cell or tube which forms the fibre of the cloth, so that the resulting precipitate being, as it were, imprisoned within the fibre, is rendered incapable of being removed by washing. In this way mineral colors, such as chrome-yellow, prussian-blue, iron-buff, and manganese-brown, may be applied to textile fabrics. In all these cases, the proper coloring matter is insoluble in water, and is precipitated whenever the two solutions proper for its formation are mixed. Thus, when an aqueous solution of bichromate of potash is mixed with an aqueous solution of acetate of lead, an insoluble precipitate of chromate of lead (chrome-yellow) is produced. In the processes for dyeing cloth with mineral colors, the fastness of the colors is supposed to be entirely a mechanical effect, in no way referable to a chemical attraction of the fibre for the coloring matter. A piece of white cotton cloth, moistened with either a solution of bichromate of potash or of acetate of lead, may be easily cleared of either of these salts by washing it in water; but if the cloth be first impregnated with one solution, and afterwards with the other, the precipitate of chrome-yellow produced within the fibre can never be removed by washing with water. The chrome-yellow that is afterwards washed away is merely attached loosely to the exterior of the fibre.
Godey's Lady's Book
April 1853 ◼

According to James Liles in his article, "Dyes in American Quilts Made Before 1930" (*Uncoverings* [1984]), it was not possible to produce a bright, clear yellow or orange that would not fade on exposure to light until the chemists perfected the potassium dichromate dye process about 1840. This multistep procedure involved soaking the cotton fabric in lead acetate, then in potassium dichromate to produce lead chromate, a chrome yellow. Chrome orange was achieved by placing the yellow cotton fabric in a hot alkaline solution. Even with the discovery and marketing of synthetic dyes in the last half of the nineteenth century, this formidable chemical procedure is the only recipe for yellow and orange colors given over and over in housekeeping columns and cookbooks. It was not until after World War I that synthetic dyes finally replaced this process.

■ ───────────────────────────

TO COLOR YELLOW on cotton—For five lbs. of goods, dissolve one pound of sugar of lead with water enough to thoroughly saturate the goods, and one half pound of bi-chromate of potash in the same quantity of water in a separate vessel. Dip the goods well, and drain in each alternatively until the desired shade is secured, then rinse and dry. If an orange is desired, dip the yellow rags into strong, hot lime water before rinsing.
   "Directions to Dye 5 lbs of Cotton Carpet Rags"
   The Farm and Fireside
   December 15, 1881

──────────────────────────── ■

[95] *Wheel of Fortune.* Made by members of the Edwards family, Ansonia (Darke County), 1850–1875. 76" x 76" (193 cm x 193 cm). Pieced, appliquéd. Cotton. Collection of Elaine Dugan Miller.

Mary Elizabeth Edwards was born in 1849 near Ansonia, the youngest by twelve years in a family of five girls. Two of her older sisters made this quilt, and, as they never married, it was given to Mary Elizabeth. By using bright orange in this amount, it becomes a major color component of the quilt. Thirty-six points surround each wheel, and the eighteen center sections are pieced on the bias. A needleworker must be skilled to avoid stretching fabric cut on the bias and to achieve flat, round wheels such as these.

THE RELATIONSHIP BETWEEN INDIGO COVERLETS AND QUILTS IN NINETEENTH-CENTURY OHIO

One of the unexpected findings of this project was the scarcity of blue and white quilts in the central and western regions of Ohio. It was not until the project held Quilt Discovery Days in the southeastern counties that we saw these quilts in the quantity that we had anticipated (see illustrations 4 on page 13, 8 on page 15, and 176 on page 137). Popular patterns found in the blue and white quilts were Star, Jacob's Ladder, and Pinwheel. Some of these quilts also exhibited the eastern Ohio characteristic of wide outer borders and narrow, pieced inner borders.

A major reason this crisp color combination appealed to quiltmakers was the abundance of dark blue indigo cotton prints available from the mid nineteenth to the early twentieth century. Another reason might be the blue and white quilts' resemblance to woven coverlets of the pre-Civil War period.

Indigo, a vegetable dye used to produce various shades of blue, is one of the oldest known dyes. Even though it was costly, indigo was one of the most widely used dyes in America. Properly dyed, it was unusually colorfast and fade resistant. During the eighteenth century farmers in North and South Carolina, Louisiana, and Georgia cultivated indigo; but by 1800 cotton had replaced it as a more profitable crop. Therefore, Ohio merchants imported indigo, as well as other dye stuffs, from the Far East and South America. Barr and Keys of Chillicothe advertised in the *Scioto Gazette* on March 10, 1814, that they had logwood, indigo, madder, and redwood available for purchase, which supplemented native dyes such as walnut hulls and goldenrod.

[96] *Goose in the Pond.* Catherine Wilson Cain (1826–1916), Houston (Shelby County), 1898. 85″ x 85″ (216 cm x 216 cm). Pieced. Cotton. Collection of Josephine Royon Feth.

Fay Akin received this quilt the Christmas she was eight years old. Her grandmother, the maker, stitched this inscription in a stem stitch on the face of the quilt: "A Merry Christmas to Fay Akin by her Grandma C.V. Cain A 1898." Catherine Wilson Cain's grandparents were early setters in Shelby County. She taught school there until her marriage to David Cain shortly before her twenty-ninth birthday.

The quilt contains eight different blue and white printed cottons and has remained in the family unused.

[97] Catherine Wilson Cain

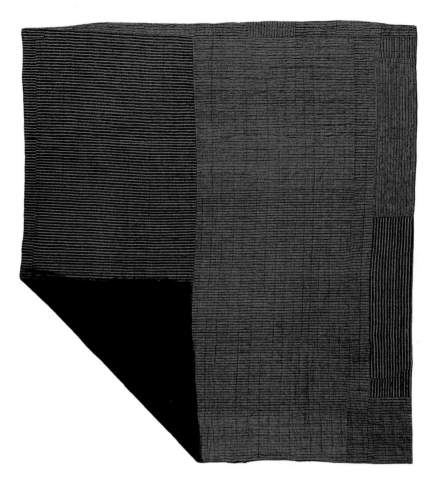

Some dye processes are simple and could be accomplished at home; but others, including indigo, are long and complex. Early Ohioans could employ professional dyers to color their domestically produced thread or cloth. The resulting indigo-dyed thread was woven as solid, striped, or plaid cloth and used for clothing, blankets, and quilts (see illustration 98). It was also used in blue and white or multicolored coverlets.

Blue Dyeing

MRS. LOOKER informs her old customers that the
BLUE DYEING BUSINESS
Is again commenced, at the old establishment, in the Brick building with a White Porch, back of a Frame House, on the north side and nearly opposite to the middle of the new Market House. COTTON or WOOLEN YARN and CLOTHING will be colored Deep Blue, Half Blue or Pale Blue as may be required, at a short notice and on reasonable prices. Half the price of coloring will be taken in such country produce as may be agreed on.
   Liberty Hall
   Cincinnati (Hamilton County)
   April 8, 1816

One of few women proprietors, Mrs. Looker had a dye business in Cincinnati. Her offer to dye clothing was not unusual. Stained, light-colored garments were commonly dyed a darker color to extend their wear.

[98] *Whole Cloth*. Detail. Rana Jones Stiles, Miami Township (Champaign, now Logan, County), 1813. 80″ x 84″ (203 cm x 213 cm). Wool. Collection of the Ohio Historical Society.

When Rana Jones Stiles made this quilt in 1813, the Miami Township area had been settled for seven years. The area was still considered wilderness, and she may have had to travel miles to obtain the indigo to dye the thread she spun. She did not cut the handwoven fabric into small pieces, but sewed the large rectangular pieces together, selvage to selvage. The dense wool filler is held in place with a two-ply linen thread, stitched in a 2″ x 2½″ grid.

It is difficult to judge how common this type of quilt was in Ohio, since so few remain. When the wool cloth was made domestically, these coverings were inexpensive to produce and may have been regarded as solely utilitarian, worn out and discarded instead of saved.

We documented no blue and white quilts made before 1860, for several possible reasons: printed cotton dress goods were expensive before 1840, resulting in few cotton quilts of any type, and earlier examples may have worn out. Also, professionally woven wool and cotton coverlets were very popular (see illustration 99). In the Ohio Historical Society's collection, doubleweave and Jacquard coverlets outnumber quilts of the same time period five to one. Often purchased as gifts for family members, they were then passed down as family heirlooms. Coverlets were expensive and considered more decorative than utilitarian.

Franklin County Probate Court records illustrate the price differences in bedding. The average price of coverlets listed in the records from 1844 to 1848 was $5.60. The average blanket was appraised at 86¢. Quilts listed were difficult for us to judge because the values ranged widely and the descriptions were not consistent. The most expensive quilt, described as cotton, listed for $3.33. Other quilts, also described as cotton, were listed for as little as 12½¢. Condition may have been the determining factor. The popularity of quilts and coverlets reversed after the Civil War. The increase in factory-produced yard goods supplanted handweaving and the professional weaver, and quilts became the preferred bed covering in many parts of Ohio.

[99] *Jacquard Coverlet.* Edward W. Marshall (1813–1891), Steubenville (Jefferson County), c. 1840. 80″ x 87″ (203 cm x 221 cm). Two-piece, doubleweave. Blue wool and white cotton. Collection of the Ohio Historical Society.

Edward Marshall, a weaver originally from Windsor, Connecticut, moved to Steubenville in the late 1830s with his wife, Julia. There, according to family records, he wove this coverlet before relocating to Knox County in 1840. The strong design similarities between coverlets and quilts can be observed when comparing this coverlet with the quilt made by his wife, Julia, and daughter, Frances (see illustration 31 on page 25). The overflowing footed urns, grapevines, and arching branches were motifs used in both pieces.

The design similarities of these two pieces mask the fundamental differences between coverlets and quilts. In general, professional male weavers produced wool and cotton doubleweave and Jacquard coverlets for sale during the first half of the nineteenth century. Quilts were sewn together, using layers of cotton fabric, by women in a domestic setting in the second half of the nineteenth century.

[**100**] Blue and white printed cotton fabrics, 1880–1910.
Courtesy of Anita Shackelford and Ellen B. Hess.

It has been suggested that the color combination in blue and white quilts in the latter part of the nineteenth century was an attempt to re-create the look of the earlier blue and white woven coverlets. A more likely reason for the popularity of these quilts may be the profusion of indigo-dyed cotton prints available at the turn of the century. East Coast fabric mills produced literally hundreds of different styles in this color (see illustration 100).

The Sears-Roebuck Company catalogue published in the spring of 1902 lists: "Full standard genuine old indigo blue dress prints at five cents a yard, best heavy Dutch indigo blue dress prints at six cents a yard, German indigo blue dress prints at eight cents a yard and extra heavy strong Dutch indigo blue prints at 10 cents a yard." All four types were offered in a selection of prints including stripes, polka dots, floral, and scroll designs, and small, medium, or large flowers. These prints were only offered as a white figure in a dark blue background. Other sources offered similar prints with the addition of an orange figure.

Synthetic indigo was introduced to the market in the late 1890s; but, according to Victor Clark in his 1929 edition of *History of the Manufacturers in the United States*, the United States was still importing $1.5 million worth of natural indigo in 1904. A satisfactory synthetic indigo was not perfected until after World War I, which may explain why fabric descriptions stressed that these were indigo prints and not a fugitive synthetic blue dye.

Other shades of blue prints were produced throughout the nineteenth century. A lighter, brighter blue, closer to prussian or azure blue, was fashionable from the second quarter of the nineteenth century to just after the Civil War. Another shade, gray blue, called "cadet blue" in the 1902 Sears, Roebuck Company catalogue, was available for 5½¢ a yard. The gray blue prints featured many of the same white in colored background patterns as the indigo blue prints. Still, the indigo blue prints remained a popular choice for ladies' wrappers, blouses, aprons, children's clothes, and quilts. In the same 1902 catalogue, girls' wash dresses and ladies' wrappers were always offered in blue, and many specified indigo blue.

This quotation from the September 20, 1894, issue of *The Ohio Farmer* illustrates the popularity of blue and white quilts: "Many housekeepers intend to piece quilts this coming winter. . . . One of the prettiest quilts I have is made of scraps of indigo blue calico and white muslin. As most families use a great deal of the blue calico, it would not take long to save enough for a quilt."

OHIO RED AND GREEN FLORAL APPLIQUÉ OF THE NINETEENTH CENTURY

Quilts were not made in isolation, their makers laboring over them uninfluenced by the outside world. The quilting network of the early nineteenth century, unaided by the printed word, succeeded in spreading the latest style quickly and accurately. The clearest evidence of this was the simultaneous appearance throughout Ohio in the early 1840s of red and green floral appliqué quilts, Ohio's first statewide quilt style. These quilts consisted of a center field of repeated, appliquéd blocks, surrounded by a wide border, usually decorated with a vine. Motifs in the blocks were floral; the color scheme was consistently red and green on a white background. While floral appliqué quilts were made throughout the second half of the nineteenth century, the greatest number were made between 1840 and 1870.

Although quilts were made in Ohio prior to 1840, the project saw very few. Those we did see were either quickly made, pieced, utilitarian quilts, or highly decorative quilts appliquéd with motifs cut from printed chintz and sewn to the background (see illustrations 72 on page 55 and 75 on page 58).

In the 1840s two identifiable quilt styles appeared concurrently in Ohio. The first was the album block, a regional style imported from New England and found primarily in the Western Reserve (see "Early Migrants to Ohio," pages 9–20, for further discussion of album block quilts and their strong New England antecedents). Album blocks were usually signed and dated by many people, with each person writing in ink on a different block although sometimes one person wrote the names because it was very difficult to write on cloth without making a blot. They were often made to mark a special occasion, such as a birth, marriage, or departure. Although a few album block quilts were appliquéd, most we documented were pieced and comprised the most popular pieced style made before 1870 (see illustrations 14 on page 18 and 77 on page 63). The second, more widely popular, quilt style that began in the 1840s was the red and green floral appliqué quilt (see illustration 101). Like album block quilts, floral appliqués were often signed and dated, although usually be only one person. Inscriptions were either embroidered or inked. Like album block quilts, floral appliqués were often made to mark special occasions.

Floral appliqué quilts share a number of distinctive characteristics: color, subject matter, overall design, and outstanding needlework techniques. The most noticeable characteristic of quilts in this style is the consistent palette. The vast majority of appliqué quilts from this period is red and green on a white background, often with details in yellow, orange, or pink, and, occasionally, blue (see "Germanic Aesthetics, Germanic Communities," pages 23–48, for additional discussion of floral appliqué quilts). By contrast, we found no consistency of color combinations in pre-1840s quilts, either decorative or utilitarian.

An attempt to explain the source of the popular red and green color combination by looking at new developments in dye techniques, dress fabrics, or interior decorating schemes was inconclusive. There were no recent gains in green dye methods, which continued to be a two-step process, yellow on blue or vice versa, until a synthetic green dye appeared about 1875. This one-step dye process was not a distinct improvement, since the green often faded to a soft tan. Nor had the method of red dyeing changed. By the middle of the eighteenth century, European dye houses had discovered the secret of producing a rich, true red from madder, commonly called turkey red. This multistep process originated in the eastern Mediterranean area, and specialty dye houses produced these color-fast, vibrant reds throughout the nineteenth century (see illustration 102).

Costume is another possible source of the red and green color scheme of floral appliqué quilts, but this, too, was inconclusive. While both red and green printed cottons are found in dresses and children's garments in the late 1830s to early 1840s, they were less common than tans, blues, and pinks (see illustration 76 on page 61).

A more possible source of the color scheme was interior design, in which deep red and rich green were fashionable colors for drapery and upholstery. Window coverings in crimson red were recommended for dining rooms and parlors, although rarely were red and green mentioned in household guides as being used together. Other recommended decorating colors were dark gold and blue. Many American portraits and paintings of interiors executed between 1800 and 1850 depict red drapery swagged across openings, with gray green as a background color; but it is impossible to determine whether this use of complementary colors was an accurate depiction of American interiors or artistic license. Whatever the design inspiration, Ohio's quiltmakers obviously introduced these strong colors into their bedrooms in the form of floral appliqué quilts.

■————————————————————

THE CUSTOM of buying new calico, to cut into various ingenious figures for what was called handsome patch-work, has become obsolete.
Eliza Leslie
Miss Leslie's Lady's House-Book
1853
Although possibly becoming obsolete in the East, this "custom" continued in Ohio for the next fifteen or more years.

————————————————————■

[101] *Rose*. Anna Emma Feldner Young (1836–1859), Adams Township (Washington County), before 1859. 84″ x 84″ (213 cm x 213 cm). Appliquéd, pieced. Cotton. Collection of Ruth Young Campbell.

Anna Emma Feldner married William John Young in 1855 and completed this quilt sometime before her death in 1859. Elaborately quilted, it displays many of the characteristics of mid-nineteenth-century Ohio appliqué quilts. Red and green floral motifs are accented with yellow-orange and are placed on a white background. The edges are finished with a swag border centered between pieced sawtooth borders.

[102] Cotton Swatches. Nineteenth century. Courtesy of Arnold Savage.

Small prints and solid colors such as these are difficult to date as they were produced for years. The pink, often referred to as "double pink," is found in mid-nineteenth-century children's dresses, as well as in turn-of-the-century pieced quilts. Similar prints are available today. The red and green prints have as long a history. Used for dresses and linings since the early nineteenth century, they remained virtually unchanged until after the Civil War. Red and green prints similar to these were used extensively in appliqué quilts. Problems with dye rot can cause small, regular holes in these prints.

The solid red and yellow-orange swatches are examples of madder and chrome orange dyes.

After the red and green color scheme, the most obvious characteristic of floral appliqué quilts was the consistent subject matter in the design motifs: stylized flowers, foliage, swags, floral wreaths, and flower-filled urns were the predominant choices. Design possibilities were limited only by the shapes the scissors could cut and the seamstress's imagination. Shapes that were difficult to turn (folding the raw edges under before stitching to the background fabric) were usually sewn down with a buttonhole stitch. Few nineteenth-century Ohio appliqué quilts deviated from the popular floral theme. The exceptions were often notable (see illustrations 154 on page 127, 188 on page 145, and 192 on page 146).

A third characteristic found in a significant percentage of these quilts is the arrangement of design elements: repeated blocks surrounded by a prominent border design, usually a vine. The floral appliqué style was the earliest instance we found of appliqué used in a repeated block format. In many cases, appliquéd blocks alternate with solid white ones, providing the maker an opportunity for elaborate quilting, the final characteristic of these quilts.

Quilted designs in the plain white blocks are often unique, displaying additional techniques of stuffed work and cording. Such elaborate handwork is rarely found on pieced quilts or on later-nineteenth and early-twentieth-century appliqué quilts. The women who created the intricate needlework on mid-nineteenth-century floral appliqué quilts may not have been aware that their quilts were among the last examples of such skill. In the 1840s and 1850s fine hand sewing was still regarded as a desired accomplishment. With the mid-nineteenth-century invention of the sewing machine and its growing acceptance by the late 1860s, sewing by hand became outmoded. The decorative emphasis switched from exquisite hand sewing, as employed in appliqué and stuffed work, to the surface embroidery used in the lavishly decorated crazy quilts, table covers, and novelties so popular in the late nineteenth century.

Several conditions in early-nineteenth-century Ohio probably account for the popularity of mid-nineteenth-century floral appliqué quilts. The first factor was economic. During the first decades, advancements in the cotton manufacturing and textile printing industries reduced the prices and increased the amount of cotton print fabric available (see illustration 103). By 1840 Ohio was no longer a frontier (except in its northwest corner). Log structures and virgin forests had been replaced by frame and brick houses on established farms or in settled communities. Although the majority of Ohioans still lived in rural areas, among states Ohio ranked third in population, with over 1.5 million residents. Vast improvements in transportation were achieved with the advent of the canal system in the late 1820s and the completion of the National Road from Wheeling to Springfield in 1838. These routes increased access to goods while they also decreased transportation costs.

The second reason, closely related to the large growth in population, although difficult to document, was the rise of the middle class, with a related increase in leisure time. Frontier lifestyle and the struggle to provide all the essentials of survival—shelter, food, and clothing—diminished as Ohio became more settled. By 1840 the average woman living in Ohio could buy, at reasonable cost, almost everything that had once been produced at home. The woman's role in the home gradually changed from producer to consumer, especially in the more urban areas. Many could afford to hire others to help with such time-consuming tasks as laundry, cooking, and sewing. Relieved from the burden of constant household chores, these women had time to produce decorative appliqué quilts.

[103] Raymond & North Newspaper Ad

The last line under "dress goods" lists prints sold for quilts, an indication that manufacturers and merchants were conscious of the popularity of quilts.
Cleveland Herald
May 7, 1849

The same period saw a proliferation of popular magazines and domestic advice books. *Godey's Lady's Book*, first published in 1830, and Catharine Beecher's *A Treatise on Domestic Economy*, published in 1841, were among the publications aimed at educated middle-class women. Many of these writings promoted the concept of "women's sphere," which held that a woman's duty was to create a home that would be a haven from the outside world in which she would raise her children as morally upright citizens and inspire her husband to the same lofty goal. An attractive and comfortable home was essential; and rooms embellished with the products of her hands, including elaborately worked quilts, were considered symbols of successful attention to this domestic duty.

The popularity of the floral appliqué style decreased after the 1870s. Beginning in the 1880s, farm periodicals and women's magazines began to publish patterns for pieced quilts, as well as suggestions for crazy work; but seldom were appliqué patterns illustrated. Tastes changed with each succeeding generation, and the daughters and granddaughters of earlier quiltmakers may have found floral appliqué quilts stark and unadorned in contrast to the rich embellishment and embroidered detail of crazy quilts and the popularity of quilts made from thousands of tiny fabric scraps. When the appliqué technique was revived in the early twentieth century, the red and green color combination was only a minor element of the new style.

WHITEWORK QUILTS, STATE FAIR CATEGORIES, AND WOVEN MARSEILLES QUILTS

Making a whitework quilt gives the quiltmaker an unparalleled opportunity to show off her needlework skills. The success of the design depends completely on the quilter's ability with a needle. Whitework quilts share design characteristics with other early-nineteenth-century quilts, although the making of whitework and whole-cloth quilts uses only one fabric for the face of the quilt. Whitework quilts consist of all-white cotton or linen fabric; the whole-cloth quilt can be of solid-colored wool or a printed cotton furnishing fabric.

During the project, we did not find any whole-cloth quilts of printed cotton, nor did we document any of the elaborately quilted solid-colored wool quilts, commonly but erroneously called "linsey-woolsey." This linen and wool combination fabric did not appear in the other quilts we saw and is not represented in the Ohio Historical Society's textile collection of fifteen thousand predominantly nineteenth-century Ohio items. The term *linsey-woolsey* seems to have survived the original fabric and now is used to mean any coarsely woven wool and cotton or wool and linen material.

While both whitework and whole-cloth quilts feature elaborate quilting designs, it is the whitework quilt that is notable for the stuffed-work technique. A sculptured effect is achieved by padding or stuffing selected areas of the design (see illustration 104). After outlining the motifs with quilting, the threads in the loosely woven back are pried apart and small bits of batting inserted; when the quilt is washed, the threads realign. Sometimes a small slit is cut in the back and the batting inserted through it. To produce long, thin lines, two parallel rows are stitched; then cording is drawn or pulled through the created casing.

These techniques appear in all six Ohio whitework quilts documented during the project. Two of the quilts were stuffed and corded only; the areas between the designs were left unquilted and without batting. The rest have batts and were closely quilted in the unstuffed areas. Since whitework quilts were not constructed for warmth, when there was a batt, it was quite thin. The amount of leisure time needed to produce the design and the use of cotton instead of linen in the earliest pieces are also

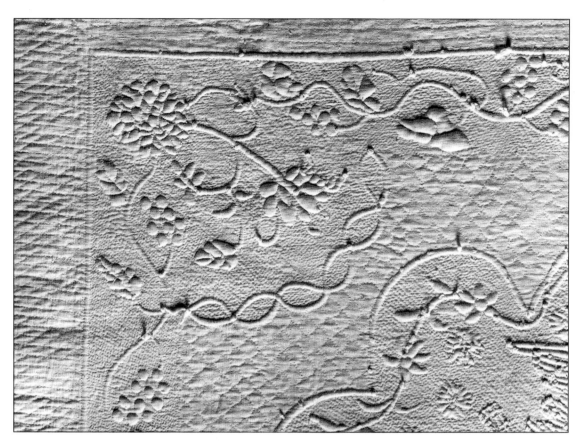

[104] Stuffed whitework quilt (detail of back), Washington County, c. 1817. Stuffed, corded, and quilted. Bits of the cording can be seen. *Courtesy of the Ohio Historical Society.*

indications that these were made for nonutilitarian reasons.

The mass production of high quality cotton sewing thread had great impact on nineteenth-century sewing, including elaborate quilting. Prior to the early nineteenth century, cotton, wool, and linen thread were domestically produced and used judiciously in the simple clothing and household textiles worn and used by the majority of Americans. Decorative needlework was primarily the province of the well-to-do until the production of manufactured cotton thread in the early nineteenth century. The marketing of three-ply cotton sewing thread by Samuel Slater of Rhode Island and the Clark Brothers of Paisley, Scotland, around 1810 and 1812 respectively, gave impetus to the nineteenth-century embroidery fad. Quilting uses a great deal of thread and, freed from producing thread and having it available inexpensively, women began making elaborate, thread-consuming pieces such as whitework quilts.

COTTON SEWING THREAD usually called sewing cotton has of late been made so beautiful by machinery, and its utility and cheapness are so well known, that it has, in a measure, superseded, the use of linen thread formerly used.
    Thomas Webster and Mrs. Frances Parkes
    An Encyclopedia of Domestic Economy
    1848

Three of our six documented quilts were made before 1820 and were dated by reliable family history, which corresponded with the style and fabric type. The others had dates in the stitching, one from 1856 and two from 1867 (see illustration 105). All of the whitework quilts had cotton, rather than linen, tops.

This use of cotton is significant because before 1820 almost all other household textiles were made of linen. Sheets, towels, and tablecloths made of linen were standard in early-nineteenth-century Ohio. Certain articles of clothing, such as men's shirts and women's undergarments, were also made of linen. Linen or flax could be locally produced in Ohio, whereas cotton had to be imported. The Ohio Historical Society has examples of early white linen shirts and women's linen chemises (a basic undergarment) with finely woven cotton ruffles on the cuffs and neck edges, the areas which would show when these garments were worn. Beginning in the 1820s, cotton replaced linen as it became cheaper and more available through improvements in the cotton spinning and weaving industries.

Another factor to consider when examining whitework quilts is the strong link these quilts have to the classical design elements of the federal style and to other white needlework of the first half of the nineteenth century. All six quilts we documented are similar to the framed medallion quilts with design elements arranged

[105] *Whitework Quilt*. Catherine Ehret (1836–1902), Rome (Richland County), 1867. 85″ x 86″ (216 cm x 218 cm). Quilting, stuffed work, and cording. Cotton. From a private collection.

Christian H. Ehret, Catherine Ehret's father, emigrated from Germany in 1817 at the age of nineteen. Stopping first in Pennsylvania, he was living in Blooming Grove Township (Rome) by the early 1820s. Her mother, Catherine Pifer, was born in Pennsylvania in 1813 and moved to Richland County with her parents at age fourteen. She became Christian's second wife in 1836 and bore her namesake, Catherine, the same year. Catherine, the daughter and maker of this quilt, never married. A schoolteacher, she stitched her name and date, "Kate Ehret 1867," in the center. The surface design is produced by tiny rows of stitches, one thirty-second of an inch apart. In other areas there are thirty-two to sixty-four stitches per square inch. The cotton twill tape binding is machine stitched.

around a central motif (see illustration 72 on page 55). Urns, eagles, and inscriptions are surrounded by vines and garlands with balanced geometric borders.

There is another, more subtle, relationship to the other types of needlework produced at the same time. The influence of classical design was felt even at the domestic level. Rejecting the previous ornate ornamentation, architecture and interior design adopted a simplification of form incorporating classical elements. The new unembellished shapes influenced furniture, and subtle decoration was the mode. In textiles this subtle surface was achieved by using white-on-white needlework. Fashionable women gave up elaborate silk gowns in the late eighteenth century and began wearing simple, slim white cotton dresses. Of course, extremes of fashion then, as now, were embraced by few; yet their influence was widespread.

WE USED TO HAVE spinning bees. . . . A neighbor would send flax enough around the neighborhood to spin twelve cuts for each one, and send an invitation for us to come on a certain day and bring our dozen of thread, and partake of a good dinner, and a good time in general. The men would have log-rollings, and house raising, and corn-huskings, we would have our wool-pickings, and quilting . . . we could and did ride on horseback for miles to meeting or to market or visiting, and thought it only a pleasant recreation. We could pull flax, scutch it, spin it, weave it, bleach it, and make it up into shirts for the men.
 "Early Recollections of Mrs. Sarah M. Moore" [c. 1812]
 The History of Champaign and Logan Counties
 1872

White needlework on white cotton or linen abounded in early-nineteenth-century Ohio; for, regardless of one's economic standing, a small amount of fabric could be turned into an embroidered cap or an infant's dress. These garments, as well as white stuffed work stand covers and embroidered candlewick bedspreads, are well represented in the Ohio Historical Society's textile collections. By the mid nineteenth century, collars, cuffs, and undergarments were lavished with white embroidery (see illustration 106).

OUT HERE IN THE DELL, the embroidery fever is raging as bad as the yellow fever ever did in New Orleans. Such hen-pecked collars as some of the novices do wear are awful; and then the poor things haven't got the city style of raising the dress just enough to display a hen-pecked skirt, but they are learning very fast, for the school master's wife has been to New York, and she is instructing them.

There was an application made to the trustees of our town lately, to have an infirm old mother taken to the poor house, because the daughters were unable to support her by their own labor. The very next Sabbath afternoon I saw her daughters at Church, and all their apparel that could be embroidered, was neatly and heavily wrought, while their sleepy sunken eyes, sallow faces, and round shoulders, told of midnight stitching and weariness and worn out spirits. Poor girls! walking exhibitions they were of overtaxed and mistaken exertions, and of neat embroidery too! The collars on their tired necks, the chemisettes, the petticoat, that showed just a hand's breadth, the dainty chemise sleeve, that showed *accidentally* through daintier lawn, and the gossamer handkerchief, that wondrously often wiped a nose as dry and lifeless almost as a powder horn, and the pinky, sorry looking eyes! Oh they all told of busy, busy months of intense stitching. . . .

Had they done their duty, and thrown this fashionable mania to the idle, and worked at varied and healthful employment, and received wages, that mother would have had no cause to weep over the serpent-sting of a child's ingratitude, their consciences had been clear, their health unimpaired, their spirits buoyant; God would have blest them, and their end been perfect peace.
"The Rage for Embroidery"
The Ohio Cultivator
September 1, 1856

It is interesting to note that while embroidered white candlewick bedcovers were made in Ohio between 1820 and the mid nineteenth century, there is a gap of most forty years between the last of the early-nineteenth-century Ohio white quilts we documented and the first of those from the mid nineteenth century (1820 to 1856). Because so few quilts of this type have been documented, more questions are raised than conclusions drawn.

One of the most frustrating things about researching material culture like nineteenth-century quilts is the scarcity of primary source material. Letters and diaries are not indexed, so it is only through luck or chance that one stumbles on the mention of a quilt. The reference is often teasingly short, such as, "Sewed on quilt today," leaving the reader with questions. What was the pattern? What were the colors? Was silk, cotton, or wool used? It is the same with probate and inventory records: "Bed quilt," "old quilt," "flannel quilt," "calico quilt," may all be listed for the same estate without distinction.

Another primary source is state fair records that Virginia Gunn examined carefully in her article, "Quilts at Nineteenth Century State and County Fairs: An Ohio Study" (*Uncoverings* [1988]). Agricultural fairs were started for educational purposes and helped advance new farm technology. These events were considered family affairs, and women were encouraged to study the prize-winning exhibits in the Floral and Domestic halls as examples of good taste. According to the 1856 Annual Report of the Board of Agriculture for the State of Ohio, "taste is both created and refined, and many rustic homes are better adorned year after year for the thoughts and feelings which spring up from a visit of children and adults to the fair."

[106] Hem of white cotton petticoat. Eyelet embroidery. Made by Mary Stone Shipman. Marietta (Washington County), 1855–1870. Embroidered infant cap. Tambour work on muslin. Worn in Ohio, 1832. *Courtesy of the Ohio Historical Society.*

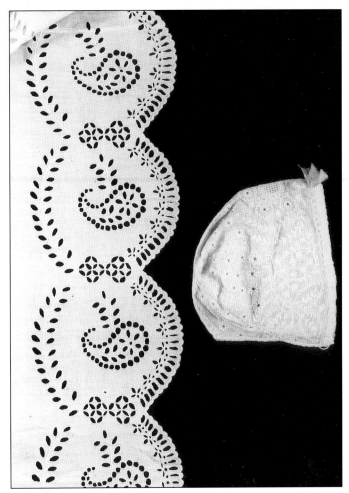

If this were true and women did emulate the prize winning quilts, why did we not document more quilts of whitework and silk, which were continual categories at the state fair? This question is further complicated by the confusing nineteenth-century terminology. For the years 1850 to 1852, the term *worked quilt* is used as one of the three categories at the fair, the other two being *white quilt* and *silk patchwork quilt*. In 1853 and 1854, *worked quilt* was dropped and the term *patchwork* appears. Do they have the same meaning? By 1855 both *patchwork* and *worked quilts* are categories. The term *appliqué* never appears, yet we documented two appliqué quilts that won prizes at the state fair during these years.

Patchwork— 1. Work composed of pieces of various figures sewed together. 2. Work composed of pieces clumsily put together.
Work— n. 5. Embroidery; flowers or figures wrought with the needle. 6. Any fabric or manufacture.
Noah Webster, *An American Dictionary of the English Language*
1845 and 1860

In these dictionaries, the terms *worked* and *appliqué* did not apply to quilts.

When studying Ohio State Fair records from 1850 to 1900, it is apparent that the fair board recognized many types of quilts, including whitework quilts, every year for the fifty years examined. Why did we document only three white quilts made during this period, and why were they all made between 1856 and 1867, when the fair category for white quilts existed until 1900?

One possible explanation is that only a few quilts were entered under each classification. The 1856 State Fair Division of Needle, Shell, and Waxwork, which had twenty-two categories, including four for quilts, recorded 210 entries, an average of fewer than ten items for each of the twenty-two categories. Another explanation might be that younger relatives of the quiltmakers continued to enter the same whitework quilts as antiques in Ohio fairs.

This discrepancy between the state fair quilt categories and quilts we documented during research for the project occurs again when examining the silk and velvet quilt categories. Beginning with Ohio's first state fair in 1850, silk quilts were listed, first as *silk patchwork*, and then in 1872 as just *silk quilts*. In 1886 *silk* is listed again as a patchwork category, and as *silk quilt, not embroidered*. The term *crazy quilt* is not used, and we can only guess under which category these embroidered silk quilts would have been entered. *Velvet quilts* appears in 1879 and remains as a category through the end of the nineteenth century. Despite the fact that silk and velvet quilt categories appear year after year at the state fair, we documented very few non-crazy silk quilts and only two velvet quilts.

CATEGORIES OF QUILTS at the Ohio State Fair 1850–1900

1850–52: worked quilt, white quilt, silk patchwork quilt
1853–54: patchwork quilt, white quilt, silk patchwork quilt
1855–69: patchwork quilt, worked quilt, white quilt, silk patchwork quilt
1870–71: patchwork quilt, worked quilt, white quilt, silk patchwork quilt
1872–77: patchwork quilt, fancy-worked quilt, worsted quilt, white quilt, silk quilt, cradle quilt (1874–77)
1878–80: patchwork quilt, fancy-worked quilt, white quilt, silk quilt, cradle quilt, velvet quilt (1879–80)
1881–85: patchwork quilt, fancy-worked quilt, white quilt, silk quilt, velvet quilt, cradle quilt
1886–90: patchwork quilt—silk or worsted, patchwork quilt—calico, white quilt, silk quilt—not embroidered or embroidered, velvet quilt, cradle quilt
1891–93: patchwork quilt—silk or worsted, patchwork quilt—calico, white quilt, silk quilt, embroidered quilt, velvet quilt, cradle quilt
1894–97: log cabin quilt, worsted quilt, patchwork quilt, white quilt, silk quilt (crazy), silk quilt (not crazy), velvet quilt (large), cradle quilt, cotton comfort, worsted comfort
1898–1900: Same as previous group with the addition of: silk comfort and in "old ladies" category: fancy quilt
Virginia Gunn, "Quilts at Nineteenth Century State and County Fairs: an Ohio Study"
Uncoverings (1988)

All this leads to questions about the state fair categories which, according to Gunn, were mirrored at the county fair level. How accurately do they reflect what was being made in Ohio? It would be interesting to examine entries in the Ohio State Fair Arts and Crafts division today and determine if those items are an accurate reflection of the tastes of a majority of today's Ohioans.

No study of whitework quilts in nineteenth-century Ohio would be complete without examining their similarities to the woven Marseilles quilts (see illustration 107). These white cotton bed covers were originally

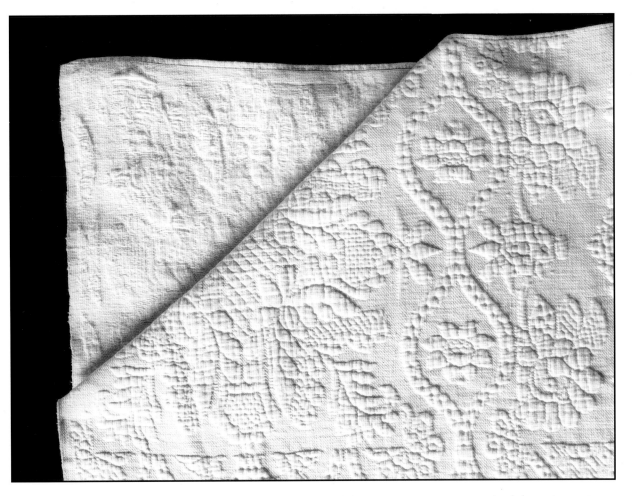

[**107**] Detail of Marseilles spread, showing face and reverse. 1860–1885. *Courtesy of the Ohio Historical Society.*

MARSEILLES QUILTS are a more elegant kind of bed-quilts, and lighter than common white counterpanes of cotton. This fabric is a double cloth with a thread of softer material between, which is kept in its place by the quilting done in the loom.
   Thomas Webster and Mrs. Frances Parkes
   An Encyclopedia of Domestic Economy
   1848

---

hand-quilted and originated in Marseilles, France, during the seventeenth century. England and America imported these French white bedcovers and petticoats. However, by the mid 1760s, English weavers were producing loom-woven fabric in imitation of the French hand quilting. By the late eighteenth century, Americans imported these woven Marseilles to use as both yard goods for men's vests and bedcoverings. Marseilles vestings were listed in the estate inventory of merchant John B. Johnson of New Haven (Huron County) in 1826.

Pink, blue, and buff, as well as white "strip Marseilles vesting," were valued at forty cents per yard, placing it in the price range of silks and velvets. These English woven imitations of French hand-quilted bed covers could have inspired the whitework quilts produced in this country.

Extant examples of woven Marseilles quilts are constructed entirely of cotton. They have finely woven tops with coarse backs and heavy, unspun cotton roving in between, creating a three-dimensional, stuffed effect. Characteristic of woven Marseilles spreads, like the hand quilted whitework quilts, is a central medallion design.

AMONG SOME half dozen [quilts] which were exhibited, it was difficult to decide which was really the most beautiful. The one presented by Mrs. Rappee, to which we awarded the first premium, is in imitation of Marseilles. It, in our opinion, is quite as handsome as any imported article of the kind.
   Report of the first Stark County Fair.
   5th Annual Report of the Ohio State Board of Agriculture
   1850

Patchwork Quilts & Mental Cultivation

FARMERS WIVES have little enough spare time at the most & any woman who desires to have an intelligent & well informed mind will prefer to spend her leisure hours in trying to get wisdom, instead of wasting them in making patchwork quilts, especially as a clean, white spread for the outside covering of a bed, looks nicer, & is in better taste, than all the patchwork quilts in existence. . . .

C. Wood
Western Rural, March 31, 1870

Patchwork Quilts—Tied Comfortables

Nothing . . . is neater in my opinion than a neat scrap quilt, to say nothing of economy. . . . I save every scrap left from my dresses & aprons, & have often remarked to Mother, what a great loss would occur if there were no scrap quilts made. If we sold them for paper rags we could get only 2 cents a pound, while at the very least we would pay 12½ cents a yard for calico to make comfortables.

Hass
Western Rural, April 14, 1870

Patchwork Quilts—A Ghost Raised

If it is a waste of time to make quilts, it is a greater waste to throw away or sell, for 2 or 3 cents a pound, all the remnants of new chintz & calico which will accumulate in most families; & if they are to be sewed together, it shows no little skill & handiwork to put them in some form that will please the eye and make of them a thing of beauty.

Many elderly ladies there are . . . whose habits of industry will not admit of their being idle. . . . And many a little girl's fingers can be just as usefully employed in forming designs out of bits of calico, as in that common way of spending time, crocheting.

Aunt Sally
Western Rural, April 28, 1870

Patch-Work Quilts—Working Man

I do not think it takes as much time to piece quilts as it does to wash spreads & keep them clean. . . . I would like to ask C. Wood how she would keep spreads clean where there are farmers & threshers to sleep in the beds. I suppose she would say, have them put on clean shirts at night. Very well, but whoever saw threshers that were at that trouble? . . . I never did, & I have lived on a farm a great many years . . . if farmers wives want to save labor, *piece quilts,* so they will not have to work so hard washing spreads for 6 beds every week.

Young Housekeeper
Western Rural, May 5, 1870

There is abundant evidence that Marseilles quilts were available in Ohio. They were advertised by Kelley and Company as "a genuine article" in the *Cleveland Herald* on April 30, 1849. The woven spreads were highly acclaimed by the 1853 Ohio State Fair reporter in the October 1 issue of the *Ohio Cultivator:* "A number of unusually pretty patchwork quilts were shown, but none of them are so tasteful and elegant as the white Marseilles quilts, which can now be purchased at a very low price, and save weary eyes and fingers, and prevent the sad waste of time now bestowed upon patchwork." Mid-nineteenth-century whitework quilts may have been an attempt to unite the fashionable white bed coverings and the somewhat maligned art of quilting.

Woven Marseilles quilts have outlasted the hand-quilted versions. With the decline in popularity of elaborate needlework, whitework quilts, along with similarly stuffed work appliqué and candlewick white bed coverings, were no longer popular. Our documentation uncovered no white-on-white quilts after 1867, but Marseilles quilts were described in the 1881 Lord and Taylor catalogue as being "chosen in preference to the various fancy colored bed coverings in use for the last few years. . . . A fine-light quality Marseilles is now used and new patterns are still in graceful flower and leaf designs." The prices ranged from 75¢ to $13.50 in sizes 36" by 45" to 96" by 100". By 1895 Montgomery Ward and Company offered imported "Marseilles toilet quilts" priced from $1.50 to $4.25, depending on the weight of the spread. Finally, to illustrate their lasting popularity, the Bates Mills on the Androscoggin River in Lewiston, Maine, still produces Marseilles spreads.

LOG CABIN QUILTS AND THE SPREAD OF QUILT PATTERNS AND TECHNIQUES

Because Americans today feel an urgent need to name and categorize, identifying quilt patterns was important to many owners of the quilts brought into the project's documentation days. Learning that there are often two or more names for the same pattern or, worse, no known name, disappointed them.

With so much information available now through the proliferation of quilting magazines and pattern books, as well as workshops and televised quilting shows, it is difficult to comprehend how nineteenth-century women achieved their consistent results without detailed instructions or patterns. However, their knowledge of new styles and techniques is not surprising when we examine how nineteenth-century women were accustomed to dealing with fashion changes. Not until the early 1870s were full-size paper dress patterns available. These were supplemented by various drafting systems, as dress bodices became more tailored and form-fitting. Before these guides appeared, fashion illustrations in magazines like *Godey's* had specific information on types of fabric to use, various methods of trim, and fashionable colors, but few construction details.

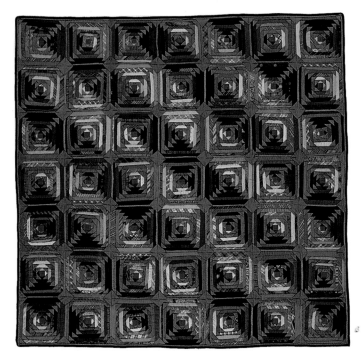

[108] *Log Cabin.* (Pineapple Variation, Straight and Furrows Set). Marietta Hickox Humiston (born c. 1818, died before 1900), Burton (Geauga County), 1870–1880. 72″ x 72″ (183 cm x 183 cm). Pieced. Wool. Collection of Geauga County Historical Society.

Marietta Hickox Humiston's mother's family, the Umberfields, were among the first settlers of Burton in 1798. Her father, Eleazer Hickox, arrived shortly after and by 1838 had built the brick house that is now part of the Geauga County Historical Society. Marietta Humiston made this quilt in this house, possibly while caring for her father. She had lost both her husband, Samuel Humiston, and her mother, Stella Hickox, in the fall of 1855, and, according to the 1860 census, was the head of the household, which included her eighty-three-year-old father. The *Geauga County History*, published in 1880, stated that she "kindly cared for [her father who] though suffering much from the fall of the colt, lived to [the] very ripe old age [ninety-one years]. . . . She is keeping house on a part of the old farm, just east of the square."

[109] Detail of illustration 108 shows the rich variety of colors available in woolen dress fabrics. The soft lavender grey wool had been originally a bright purple, possibly one of the "new" (post-1856) synthetic dyes that were not yet colorfast. Plaids were quite popular for both women's and children's dresses. Small boys wore dresses up to the age of four or five and mid-nineteenth-century photographs of these young boys often show them wearing wool plaid dresses with simple braid trim.

Dressmakers offered their services, but an article in the June 1854 issue of *Godey's* noted: "It is not always economically feasible to employ them for anything but a very special dress." One method of obtaining a pattern was to take apart an old bodice and use it as a guide, altering waist heights and increasing or decreasing sleeve fullness as needed to achieve the current style.

■

EVERYBODY IN A COUNTRY town has been annoyed by being obliged to loan dresses, mantillas [mantle or cloak], etc., often of fine or easily soiled materials, to have the patterns taken.
   Godey's Lady's Book
   April 1853

■

Women borrowed neighbors' and friends' home-made patterns and exchanged ideas on fitting and constructing the current fashion, both in clothing and in quilts. Most were competent seamstresses, adept in following vague instructions; they would be astounded at the profusely diagrammed quilt guides available today.

Published quilt patterns were not common until the 1880s when they began to appear in farm magazines like *The Farm and Fireside*, published in Springfield, Ohio. Barbara Brackman, author of the *Encyclopedia of Pieced Quilt Patterns*, recorded about four thousand published designs and over six thousand names, the vast majority of which came into use (or print) after 1885. In statistics compiled for her 1983 *Uncoverings* article, "A Chronological Index to Pieced Quilt Patterns," she documented 86 pieced patterns in 1825, 200 in 1850, and 380 pieced patterns in 1875. In 1975 Brackman recorded approximately four thousand patterns in print.

Researching the origins of a particular pattern can be an exercise in futility. Even if the name occurs in the literature, one is never certain without a diagram that the names from the late twentieth century and the mid nineteenth century are describing the same pattern. The history of the log cabin quilt is a good example of the complexity of such research (see illustration 110).

Before widespread use of printed patterns, word of mouth and personal observation were the methods of obtaining new designs such as the log cabin. Although log cabins were mentioned in print for a commendation at the Ohio State Fair in 1863, the earliest ones we documented, dated from family histories and fabrics, were from the late 1860s through the early 1870s. The majority were made between 1870 and 1895. The unique construction of these quilts is a testimony to the nineteenth-century quilting network.

Using the foundation method of construction, log cabin quilts seem to have appeared spontaneously from Maine to Georgia, and as of now no pre-1882 instructions for this new technique have been discovered. S.F.A. Caulfeild and Blanche Saward's English publication *The*

[**110**] Occasionally more than one name was used to describe the same pattern.

Log Cabin, *The Farm and Fireside*, March 15, 1887

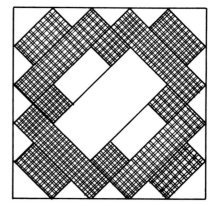

Album, *The Farm and Fireside*, April 15, 1887

Standard Log Cabin Block

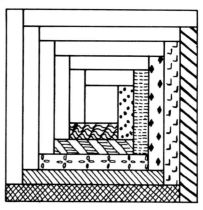

Dictionary of Needlework, an Encyclopedia of Artistic, Plain, and Fancy Needlework (1882) gives instruction for what the authors call an "American log house patchwork" of silk ribbons worked on a cotton foundation. How widely Caulfeild and Saward's influence was felt on this side of the Atlantic is not known, but their inclination to English tastes and techniques would seem to have limited the book's influence in the United States.

Japanese [Crazy] Patch-work

THIS IS a new style in which to piece silk, and one which wastes but little of the material. Cut a lining of calico, or cotton, of about thirteen inches square, and if you remember how the log cabin quilts were pieced you will have the idea, only in that you had a square for the centre.

The Farm and Fireside
October 1, 1882

This foundation technique was first used extensively in log cabin quilts and later in the creation of the crazy quilt, which made them different from other piecework quilts. Starting with a square of muslin, a smaller square, traditionally a darker color, usually red, is tacked to the center. A strip of fabric is then placed, right sides together, on one edge of the center square, the seam sewn and the strip turned right side up. More strips are added, concentrically working out from the center, alternating two dark, then two light strips. Strong graphic results are created by diagonally dividing the square into light and dark configurations.

The log cabin quilts we documented also differed from previous quilts because they used dress weight wools and wool mixtures (see illustration 111). Advancements in the woolen industry and improvements in sheep breeding had led to the production of lightweight dress woolens by the third decade of the nineteenth century. Beginning in the 1840s and continuing through the 1870s, woolens or wool-and-cotton or wool-and-silk mixtures, such as challis, cashmere, mousseline de laine, and alpaca, were popular for dresses. These fabrics were often printed in floral designs or woven in plaids or twills.

The fabrics in the surviving wool or wool-mixture dresses dating from the 1840s through the early 1860s are finely woven and supple enough to accommodate the full, gathered skirts. As dresses became more tailored toward the end of the 1860s, the fabrics became stiffer, with more body; yet they retained their fine texture. Since wool was considered a year-round material during the nineteenth century, it is not unusual to find spring and summer wool wedding and graduation dresses from the mid nineteenth century.

Another dress component found in log cabin quilts is the narrow wool braid sometimes used as binding. Known as hem tape, it is most often found on the hem of dresses from the mid 1850s through the 1870s to protect the edge of the skirt from dirt and abrasion.

Wool dresses maintained their popularity through the turn of the century. However, during the last decade, the heavier wool used in the new separate skirts and jackets did not lend itself to the narrow strips of the earlier log cabins. As the century drew to a close, log cabins began to appear with wider strips of lighter colored cotton prints.

The majority of log cabin quilts differed from other

[111] Skirt hems showing dress weight wools and wool mixtures. Worn in Ohio, 1850–1870. Narrow woolen braid protects hem on skirts second from each end. *Courtesy of the Ohio Historical Society.*

Description of Fashion Plate

DRESS OF MOUSSELINE [mousseline or mousseline de laine: wool or wool and cotton fabric, often printed], printed in a disposition pattern, the corsage, sleeves, and upper part of the skirt being plain, and the flounces in wreaths of spring flowers in bright and tasteful grouping.

Walking dress of camel's hair cashmere, a white ground, with small, French-blue figure, simply a knot of leaves.

Dress stuffs have a great variety. The first opened this season were chintzes of the usual neat patterns, brilliantees [brilliantes or brillantine: a fine weave of silk and wool, later cotton and wool], the best article of the kind, and, in the end, the cheapest . . . as they will outwear muslins, and even chintzes. . . . They come nearly a yard in width, of white grounds, with small figures at regular intervals in all the delicate spring shades, blue, buff, fawn, green, purple, etc. . . . The favorite mousselines, which are always needed at this season of the year as "a go-between," merinos [merino: woven from wool of Merino sheep, sometimes with the addition of silk] and muslins, or bareges [a gauze weave of wool and silk], are also in these shades, the newest being a waved or watered pattern on a white ground.

Godey's Lady's Book
April 1853

quilts in another way: they were tied and not quilted. All the earlier quilts we documented had been quilted, which in one respect is surprising. Tying the top, batting, and backing together is much less time consuming than stitching the layers. It would be a quick way to provide warmth if the utilitarian aspect of the quilt were the only point being considered. One of the earliest references to tying quilts was found in the September 1854 issue of *Godey's*. The article concerning English pieced quilts advised, "Quilt it in any pattern you please, so as to keep the lining and the cover tied together; or it may be knotted in the center of each star, with any bright colored floss, silk or Berlin wool."

Quilting the narrow pieces of a log cabin was impractical. If one followed the seam lines, the quilting would not show, and one would encounter seam after seam if attempting to work across the strips. Tying or tacking the quilt top to the backing was the practical solution. Some quilters eliminated the batting altogether because it would shift unless the ties were placed quite closely.

■

Scrap Worsted Quilt

THERE IS NO prettier way of using up scraps of worsted [a woolen fabric] for quilts than the log cabin style.
The Farm and Fireside
April 15, 1887

■

In general, the earliest log cabin quilts we documented were wool, or predominantly wool, made between the late 1860s through the early 1890s. Cotton log cabin quilts overlap the wool quilts beginning in the mid 1880s, and all quilts in this pattern appear to have fallen from favor in Ohio by the turn of the century. Delicate silk log cabin quilts were found, but not in the quantity we expected. While it is often mentioned in the period literature and is listed as a category at the Ohio State Fair, the frail nature of late-nineteenth-century silk may account for the small number of these quilts recorded.

Although other state projects documented heavy woolen log cabin comforters, we did not see any in Ohio. We also found few log cabin quilts made in the pastel cottons of the second quarter of the twentieth century. It was not until the quilt revival after the bicentennial that the pattern became popular again. Constructed without a foundation layer, these new versions were made of wide strips of cotton and cotton blends in the then popular shades of rust, tan, and brown.

PRINTED COTTON FEED AND FLOUR SACKS

When we were documenting quilts made in rural areas during the 1930s and 1940s, the owners often pointed out feed sack materials used in the quilts. We did not encounter any other fabric for which the source was so clearly identified. One possible reason for this identification is that many of these quilts were made during the owner's lifetime. Also, there is a romanticized view of feed sacks today, perhaps because of their association with a rural childhood and the Great Depression.

During the early part of the nineteenth century, individuals made their own feed and grain sacks. A farmer would send his grain to the mill in sacks labeled with his name. After the corn or wheat was ground, it would be packaged and transported home in the same sack. Around 1875, heavy, coarse, seamless cotton grain sacks were commercially produced. The 1894–95 Montgomery Ward catalogue offered these seamless sacks in the two-bushel size from twelve to seventeen cents each. Nineteenth-century feed sacks were used until they were worn out. The fourteen late-nineteenth-century feed sacks in the Ohio Historical Society's collection are faded and patched (see illustration 114).

Food stuffs were not usually packaged individually until the turn of the century when animal feed, sugar, flour, salt, and corn meal became available prepackaged in white cotton sacks. Once they were empty, the homemaker would open up the sacks and soak, scrub, boil, and bleach them to remove the printed ink label. The fabric could then be used for toweling, undergarments, pillowcases, quilt backings, or foundations for log cabin or crazy quilts.

■

IN APRIL OF 1822, Eleanor Worthington, wife of Gov. Thomas Worthington, sent the following note to Isaac Green, a miller in Chillicothe (Ross County):

Sir,
I send Joseph Randal to the mill for corn meal and bran; will you please to let him have seven hundred weight of flour and grind the bag he brings with him. I send some flax; will you please to send it to Biddy McLaughlin and tell her to spin it the same size as she did that last fall. Mr. Worthington wishes you if you please to rent the place at the mill to as good a tenant as you can get. I would have sent sooner but the waters has been so high I did not expect you could grind any.
Respectfully,
E. Worthington

Thomas Worthington Family Papers
The Ohio Historical Society
Courtesy Adrienne Saint-Pierre

■

According to oral tradition, these sacks were dyed by the homemaker and used in quilts. We documented only one quilt composed of dyed sacks. Quilts made from dyed feed sacks have been documented more commonly in the South.

In the early twentieth century, bag manufacturers began switching to water soluble inks that were easier to remove. Some companies printed removal directions on the sack, recognizing that the sacks were being put to a multitude of household uses. Glued-on paper labels that would soak off were another labeling technique.

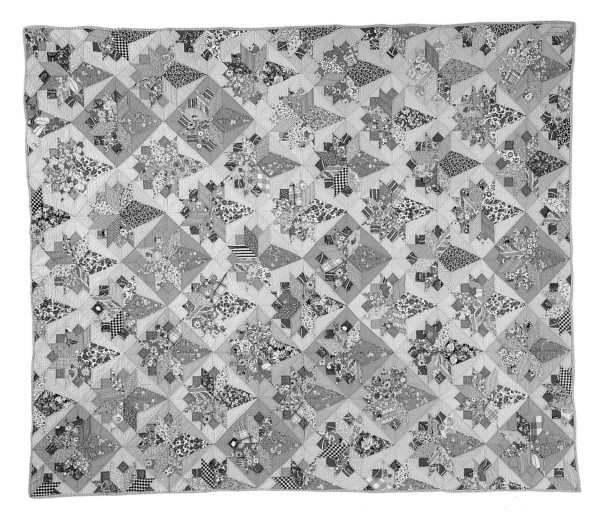

[112] *Bridal Bouquet.* Anna Elizabeth Stewart Aikin (1870–1962), Bloomfield (Muskingum County), 1950. 84″ x 73″ (213 cm x 185 cm). Pieced. Cotton including printed cotton feed sacks. Collection of Janet Patton Doyle.

By the late 1930s, feed and flour were widely available in colorful printed cotton sacks. The Bemis Bag Company, headquartered in Minneapolis, was the largest manufacturer of cotton feed sacks in the United States. In August 1942, the company newsletter, *Bemistory*, stated: "Although the idea was conceived during the Depression, it has only been in the last four or five years that the demand has been so great. Demand has steadily increased until in 1941 bag manufacturers were turning out approximately 50 million of these colorful bags. . . . It is chiefly in the South, Southwest, and Middle West that the bright print bags are sold. . . ." Although Bemis and other bag companies employed their own fabric designers, their prints are hard to differentiate from the yard goods found in stores (see illustration 115). Some former feed sacks are slightly rougher than regular dress goods. The August 1942 *Bemistory* describes the fabric as "linen-like." Occasionally one can positively identify former feed sacks in a quilt by the telltale holes left from the sewn opening.

During an interview in the spring of 1990, Ted M. Stults II of Buckeye Feed Mills, Inc., situated in Dalton (Wayne County), Ohio, indicated that the feed sacks of the 1930s and 1940s were made of a coarse fabric. His company ordered bales of these "dress bags" from southern

Anna Elizabeth Stewart Aikin surprised her twelve-year-old granddaughter, Janet Patton, with the gift of this quilt in 1950.

An active seamstress who never wasted anything, she used clothing scraps from dresses, shirts, and sunbonnets as well as printed feed sacks to make the quilt. After graduating from business college, she raised five children and helped her husband, John Alexander Aiken, on their farm and in the family's general store. Her granddaughter, Janet, recalls her grandmother's use of feed sacks from the store and from the Patton dairy farm in Madison County:

"The white feed sacks in which soup beans, white sugar, brown sugar, and tea plus animal feed came in were of two qualities. The heavier quality was used for quilting as background and backings. The other type was used by boiling out the print, dyeing the fabric, and then making clothes for the children, mostly dresses for her four daughters.

"The printed feed sacks from our farm came from the man who ground the feed for us before we had our own grinder. If we paid extra for them, it was not stated as such on the bill. Supplement came in those sacks and was added to our own grain, which we raised."

factories. Stults thought the printed sacks were a marketing ploy to boost sales and were well received by Ohio dealers (see illustration 116). Buckeye bags were tagged, not labeled, and printed cottons were used until the 1960s when paper and plastic packaging became cheaper alternatives. The company sold the last of the empty Buckeye sacks to dealers in East Cleveland who in turn sold them to immigrants from Eastern Block countries for fifty cents each. The immigrants sent these unused feed sacks to relatives in Eastern Europe.

From the 1920s until the early 1950s, both the Textile Bag Manufacturers Association and the National Cotton Council published booklets with instructions for making household items from cotton sacks. Some of the ideas suggested were curtains, aprons, tablecloths, quilts, and dresses. Opened up, the 100-pound sacks measured approximately 38″ x 47″. Two to three would make a child's dress; five or more, a woman's.

According to our informants, printed sacks were traded among households, to achieve sufficient matching fabric. After construction of clothing and other household projects, the trimmings could be recycled into a scrap quilt. Quiltmakers achieved this style by combining a wide variety of prints and colors, unifying them with one solid color, usually white. Many of the quilt patterns we found with identified printed cotton sacking typify the scrapbag style. These patterns, Grandmother's Flower Garden, Bridal Bouquet, Double Wedding Ring, and Appliquéd Butterfly, have remained Ohio favorites throughout the years.

■

WE LIVED ABOUT 9½ miles from town [on a large turkey farm] and I remember our neighbors would see our truck go by [loaded with feed in printed sacks] and call us on the telephone before the truck arrived and request the print feed sacks. . . .

Then by the time I left for college in 1943, it was during the war and [we] couldn't get good sheets, so Mama worked hard to bleach out four to make one nice sheet. The waddle of the turkey, red you know, was real hard to get white. . . .

Even in 1948 when I started teaching, the beginning Home Economics girls would bring in 3 or 4 feed sacks to make a dirndl skirt—or the advanced girls a pinafore. We even padded old cut down chairs and tried to make little padded bedroom chairs—covered buttons, cording and matching pillows.

The first day, we'd unravel the sacks, (put the straight stitch toward you—the chain stitch to the back and ravel from the right) roll-up the string in a ball—go behind the school house and shake out the remainder of the feed—then we'd wash them.

The next day we'd pull a weft thread to straighten them—Oh! How they would complain.

Sacks would usually sell for 25 cents each—but of course, that would be more than one square yard of fabric. . . .

Quilts were made from feed sacks too—we made the sunbonnet pattern—used feed sacks for the body, but our Aunt gave us plain scraps for the sunbonnet—she was a dressmaker.

Feed sacks required a lot of ironing to make them look nice (home-boiled starch or the water left from cooking rice is what we used) but they really withstood many, many washings—yes, the old wringer, clothesline and all.

Emily Marks, Reminiscences from Knox County
Letter to the Ohio Quilt Research Project 1990

■

[114] Early nineteenth-century through mid-twentieth-century feed, grain, and salt sacks. *Top row, left and right:* late-nineteenth-century cotton grain sacks used by the Haus family near Lancaster (Fairfield County). *Top center:* early-to-mid-nineteenth-century linen tow grain sack. Spun, woven and used by the Downey family of Noble County. *Center:* early-twentieth-century cotton salt sack. The Ohio Salt Company, Wadsworth (Medina County). *Bottom:* printed cotton feed sacks, 1945–1960. *Printed cotton feed sacks courtesy of Madelyn Horvath. Remainder courtesy of the Ohio Historical Society.*

[115] Detail of illustration 112

[116] Not every feed sack was a printed cotton fabric. Some, as seen in this photograph, were white cotton with a printed label. Farmers often purchased several types of feed; laying mash, dairy feed, and various other supplements. According to two of our informants, both of whom grew up on farms during the late 1930s through the mid 1950s, the different sacking materials made it easy to distinguish between types of feed. *Courtesy of Ted M. Stults II, of Buckeye Feed Mills, Inc.*

RURAL AND URBAN QUILTMAKING TRADITIONS: THE PUBLISHED QUILT PATTERN AND TWENTIETH CENTURY STYLE CHANGES

As we reviewed the quilts documented during our research period, we saw an unanticipated pattern developing. Many of the quilts, we discovered, fell into two categories, each associated with a particular population group: decorative bed coverings made by urban women and the more practical utilitarian quilts made by their rural counterparts.

The rural and urban traditions merged and separated throughout the nineteenth and early twentieth centuries, uniting after World War I in the familiar pastel quilts in such popular patterns as the Double Wedding Ring and Sunbonnet Sue.

The two types of quilts, one created as a decorative bedcovering and the other, the more practical counterpart, made for warmth, were produced concurrently throughout Ohio's history. However, many quilts were used both for decoration and for warmth, and it is rarely possible for a researcher to identify a quilt made solely for one purpose or the other. The majority of the quilts recorded fell somewhere in between the two types.

One way to differentiate the rural and urban traditions is to examine the literature of the period and its intended readers. When quiltmaking became a popular topic in the 1880s and 1890s, these publications placed different emphases on practicality and fashion, appealing to specific groups of women.

Although we documented few of what we termed utilitarian quilts and comforts, references to them abound in nineteenth-century periodicals. These quilts were subjected to heavier use and had less chance of survival than their more decorative counterparts.

The first styles of decorative quilts in Ohio were the framed medallion and cut-out chintz quilts. Although we found fewer than ten of these early quilts in Ohio, they did occur in greater numbers throughout other states, most notably the southern ones. In general, makers of these quilts lived in more populated areas and had the leisure time, the knowledge of the latest styles, and the financial means to purchase the imported cotton prints needed to produce these bedcoverings. Why so few of these early fashionable quilts were found in Ohio remains a question. Was it because the majority of Ohio women were not aware of early-nineteenth-century decorative styles? Or did they lack the means to produce them?

Thick, warm quilts of coarse wool were still being made as fashionable framed medallion and cut-out chintz quilts waned in popularity during the 1830s and 1840s. Then the two traditions merged briefly when women from all areas of Ohio made appliqué quilts from the less expensive red and green printed cottons. While red and green floral appliqué quilts continued to be made into the

> **PATCH-WORK QUILTS** of old calico are only seen in inferior chambers; but they are well worth making for servants' beds. . . . Quilts are now made entirely of the same sort of dark calico or furniture chintz; the breadths being run together in straight seams, stuffed with cotton, lined with plain white or buff-dyed thick muslin, and quilted simply in diamonds, shells, or waves. It is usual to have a quilt or bedspread of the same chintz as the curtains.
> *Miss Leslie's Lady's House-Book*
> 1853

1870s in the less populated areas, their popularity was short-lived in the urban areas. A quotation from the October 1855, *Godey's Lady's Magazine* illustrates this point: "Patchwork quilts, unless in silk, are rarely seen in cities, the glory of our grandmothers having passed away."

The traditions grew further apart as the century progressed. Silk crazy quilts briefly revived urban interest in quiltmaking in the 1880s, but it was the rural women and possibly the less affluent women who continued to make utilitarian cotton or wool quilts throughout the second half of the nineteenth century.

> **JUST THINK** of the work a poor farmer's wife does in a year, compared with our town sisters: We must carry on all the household machinery, even to laundrying, baking, bringing in our wood and coal, water—perhaps from a distant spring—making and working a garden, and care for a family of children.
>
> Our town sisters hire their laundrying, buy their bread, no milking or churning, their afternoons spent in calling or receiving calls. They can make fancy work but, my dear sisters, let us not pattern after them. I believe in plain things. Make quilts of plain muslin, not quilted very close. Save ourselves all the stitches we can, and employ the spare time in improving our intellects.
> *The Ohio Farmer*
> August 9, 1894

To better understand the separate traditions, it is important to examine the phenomenon called the colonial revival, which is commonly acknowledged to have begun with the Philadelphia Centennial Exposition in 1876. The centennial inspired increased feelings of national pride. The last decades of the nineteenth century were also years of deep concern about changes in America. The increasing number of immigrants, especially from southern and eastern Europe, and growing industrialization and related urbanization caused many to fear a loss of their America, the America of a "simpler" past.

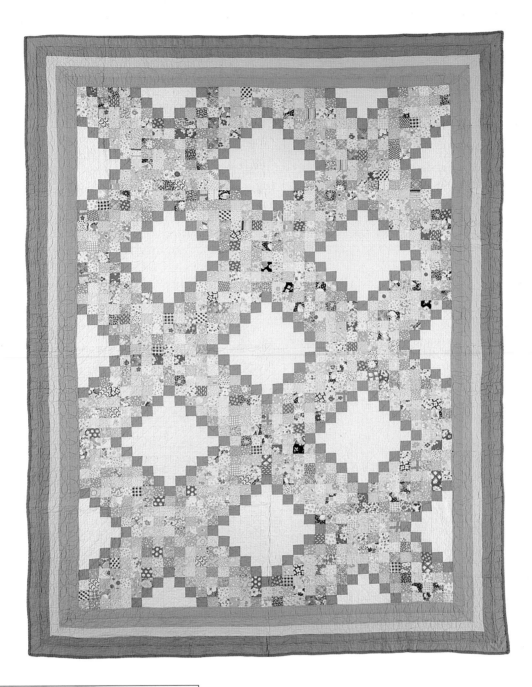

[117] *Stepping Stones to Grandmother's Garden*. Marge Agnes Colwell Bly, Cleveland (Cuyahoga County), 1930–1936. 92″ x 70″ (234 cm x 178 cm). Pieced. Cotton. Collection of Marge Bly.

Marge Colwell began her quilt in 1930, the summer she was sixteen. While she was visiting her aunt and uncle, Annie and Walter Venable, "Aunt Annie" took her to the Euchre Club at Eleanor Parker's house. Marge admired the quilt Eleanor Parker was piecing. Mrs. Parker suggested that Aunt Annie teach her niece to piece a quilt. The next day aunt and niece went to J.C. Penney's (Marge's first visit to a Penney's store). There they selected nine patterned fabrics and purchased four inches of each, a total of one yard. Marge's uncle made her a template by gluing sandpaper to sheet metal. Marge finished piecing the top in two years. Eleanor Parker added the rainbow border and quilted it. She called this pattern Stepping Stones to Grandmother's Garden. The pattern is traditionally known as Irish Chain and was a popular nineteenth-century pattern.

[118] Marge Agnes Colwell (Bly)

Ohio had changed. In 1860 just over four hundred thousand people in Ohio lived in urban areas, while almost two million people lived in rural areas or small towns. By 1900 the urban areas had caught up. The population was divided evenly, with about two million in each area.

SEVENTY-FIVE YEARS ago the world moved more slowly, and they had to find things to occupy their time. With a complete reversal of conditions, we now have to search for time to accomplish those things we want most to do. If, more than anything, you'd like to hand down to posterity a patchwork quilt, you can very easily do so by purchasing the patches ready cut, and sewing them together on a machine. The one in Figure 11 was made in that way in a single day, and you would, I think, like it immensely. Put together by hand, and further enhanced by quilting, it is as fine as anything your grandmother could have made. This is called the churn-dash pattern; it is made of two different shades of pink printed calico (sunfast) and unbleached cotton cloth. Finished, it measures 75″ x 89″. The unbleached cotton is supplied for the binding but not for the back, for it can be purchased anywhere. The price of the patches, ready cut, is $7.50, postpaid!—Patchcraft Corporation, 233 Fourth Avenue, N.Y.C.
House Beautiful
January 1929

In an era of increased mechanization, hand-crafted objects like pieced cotton quilts reflected the simpler time (see illustration 119). The actions of the daughters and granddaughters of the founding families of Marietta, Ohio, illustrate this idea. To help celebrate the centennial of Marietta in 1888, members of the Women's Centennial Association organized a "relic room" of curios and artifacts from the founding families. Historical accuracy was not the aim of this display; but, as stated in their November 12, 1888, "Request for Relics," it was to "foster sympathy in pioneer matters in the minds of the young and serve as a touching reminder of the aged." Included among these items on display were quilts only fifty years old, spinning wheels, and pieces of handwoven linen. Were these women's lives so far removed from those of their parents and grandparents that these quilts seemed a product of the past? Can we then assume that quilts were not a common form of bedding in their homes?

THE PIECED COTTON quilt, which has not been a possible bed-covering within the memory of the woman of to-day, has now become a most modish dressing for beds. The reappearance of the furniture of our forebears has quite naturally brought about a rehabilitation of the long-despised coverlets with which bridal chests were once so well plenished. The modern housewife, casting a keen glance quiltward, has discovered that nothing, save perhaps the old hand-woven bedspread, so effectively drapes a mahogany four-poster as one of these gay quilts. She has also seen them used with effect upon brass, iron, or even modern wooden beds.
The Ladies' Home Journal
April 1902

Objects that reflected the past quickly became a new home decorating trend. Women's magazines urged readers to recreate grandmother's quilts to match their fashionable colonial bedroom decor. Writing in the October 1894 issue of the *Ladies' Home Journal*, Sybil Lanigan declared: "The decree has gone forth that a revival of patchwork quilts is at hand, and dainty fingers whose owners have known only patches and patchwork from family description are busy placing the blocks together in new and artistic patterns, as well as in the real old time order."

It is important to note who read the *Ladies' Home Journal*. Titles of articles in the September 1899 issue indicate to whom the magazine was directed. "The Young Man and the Professions" details such professions as law, medicine, dentistry, veterinary medicine, electrical engineering, and architecture, as possible vocational goals for the readers' sons. Another article entitled "Hiring a Trolley for Special Excursion Occasions" suggests that children's parties and theater parties be held on a rented trolley car. There is also a romantic article on harvesting wheat entitled "Bringing in the Sheaves" in which the readers were warned that "the modern concentration of men in cities has done much to undermine the oneness of feeling between man and the earth on which he lives." The article goes on to discuss in very romantic terms the threshers' clothes, the food on their dinner table, and the life of farm families.

Another article illustrates "the prettiest country homes in America," including President McKinley's substantial home in Euclid Heights (Cuyahoga County), Ohio. The same issue includes an article entitled "Twelve Designs for Patchwork Quilts," which was introduced with this paragraph:

> The time was when patchwork quilts were seen only in farm houses, when they were brought out when extra bed covering was required, and redolent of sweet lavender, formed the most comfortable and satisfactory of bed coverings. But recently, the city housekeeper has discovered how much more easily kept in order than either blanket or comforter is the patchwork quilt, which repeated visits to the laundry neither thickens nor fades, and she has made up her mind to add a few of these serviceable articles to her stock of winter bed coverings. For her, as well as the woman in the country, to whom the making of patchwork quilts represents many pleasant moments, this page has been prepared.

These articles were written for an audience of urban women who were sophisticated or aspired to be, with time and money on their hands, and who were far removed from rural traditions. Rural women also had publications such as *The Ohio Farmer* and *The Farm and Fireside* (published in Springfield, Ohio), that appealed to their interests.

The differences in lifestyles of the *Ladies' Home Journal* readers and the farm magazine readers were underscored by the widely diverse topics covered by the two

[119] *Star Upon Stars*. Elizabeth Alter Calhoon (1826–1903), Zanesville (Muskingum County), 1903. 96″ x 96″ (244 cm x 244 cm). Pieced. Cotton. Collection of Robert and Ann Nicholas.

Possibly inspired by the renewed interest in quilts, Elizabeth Calhoon, with the help of her daughter, pieced this quilt in the spring of 1903. This quilt, a copy of one she made in 1847 during the first year of her marriage, was the last quilt she made before her death in July 1903. The original quilt had been given to her granddaughter, Edna Calhoon, sometime before Edna and her family moved to Cripple Creek, Colorado.

[120] Elizabeth Alter Calhoon (center front), with her husband, Matthew, and members of her family. Edna is on her father's lap to the left of her grandmother.

types of publications. To readers of the former, quilting was undergoing a revival; to the rural homemaker, quilting was a continuing tradition.

Rural readers of the September 20, 1894, issue of *The Ohio Farmer* received practical information on how to cut down Papa's socks for the baby, a pattern for a practical loose-fitting cape, and instructions for canning and pickling tomatoes in an article entitled "Now That the Tomatoes Are In." Another story is entitled "The Country Young Man in the City," and a report on the 1890 census details the extraordinary population growth in the cities and towns. This issue also includes five unnamed quilt patterns with suggestions on color selections (blue and white or red and white), and a recommendation to use wool scraps in a crazy quilt. Women too busy to quilt are advised to make tied comforts with a sewing machine.

■

PATCHWORK QUILTS may not be fashionable but they are good, comfortable articles still, as we can any of us prove on a cold winter night.
The Farm and Fireside
February 1, 1882

■

A very important part of the gradual style change in early-twentieth-century quilts can be linked to the publication of quilt patterns. An examination of *The Farm and Fireside* and *The Ohio Farmer* shows illustrations of quilt patterns in the early 1880s (see illustration 121). Before this, farm periodicals rarely had pictures, and articles focused on housekeeping and child rearing hints. However, women's fashion magazines had a much older tradition of illustrated needlework projects. Although quilt patterns appeared in both types of journals, magazines for the urban readership had a greater variety of decorative needlework instructions, while farm magazines featured mostly quilt patterns.

Mass marketing of quilt patterns began in the 1880s during the crazy quilt fad, with the sale of commercial embroidery patterns, machine embroidered appliqués, and advertised sources for silk scraps. By 1882 patterns for traditional cotton pieced quilts began to appear in farm magazines, such as *The Farm and Fireside*, approximately six or seven years before periodicals like *Ladies' Home Journal* featured quilts.

■

LIKE JENNIE JOSLIN, I am a great hand to piece quilts, although I am not an old maid, but a farmer's wife and the mother of two children. I saved the pieces of my little boy's dresses and aprons until he was large enough to wear pants, then I pieced him a quilt of the pattern called "true love's knot." He thinks his quilt is very nice, and that he had very pretty dresses when he was little. I am saving pieces of baby's clothes for the same purpose, but as baby is a girl I think I will give her the task of piecing her quilt when she is old enough.

Licking Co., Ohio   J.L.
The Farm and Fireside
May 1, 1882

I WISH TO SAY to J. L. Licking County, Ohio that I like her idea of piecing quilts, for little ones out of the scraps of their dresses. If she will send me the pattern called "True Lover's Knot" I will send her "The Cross and Crown" pattern, if she wishes it, and will give me her full name.
Mrs. V. B. Randolph
Kent's Stove, Fluvanna County, VA.
The Farm and Fireside
August 15, 1882

■

Rural readers exchanged patterns through farm periodicals, some writing to share favorite patterns, others requesting certain ones. The earliest account we found was in the February 18, 1882, issue of *The Farm and Fireside*. Mrs. F. A. Warner of South Saginaw, Michigan, writing under the name of Jennie Joslin, offered six patchwork patterns and a year later had fifteen different patterns for sale.

■

SEVERAL HAVE ASKED me if I was the "Jennie Joslin" who offered the quilt patterns last winter. Yes; and in reply to your inquiries I will say that I have a number of new quilt patterns that were sent me by kind friends whom I have made through these columns. Here are the names of a few I have selected as being the prettiest and most useful in using up small bits: Wheel of Fortune, Box, Maple Leaf, Hay-stack, Devil's Puzzle, Old Maids' Puzzle, Dutchman's Puzzle, the Puzzle of Puzzles, King's Crown, Moon and Stars, Road to California and Back, Coffin, Star, Bear's Paw, Hit and Miss, and Sunflower. I will send you any one pattern for two stamps; six patterns for 25 cents; or the whole fifteen patterns named for 50 cents—enough to last one a lifetime, if they die in any kind of season. With every pattern I will send a paper block so you may see exactly how a block looks before commencing your work.

Again, another thing I wish to say: The name, "Jennie Joslin," is only a nom de plume which I am tired of using, as it looks too much like sailing under false colors. So I will now, and in the future, give my correct name.
Mrs. F. A. Warner
South Saginaw, Mich.
The Farm and Fireside
February 15, 1883

■

By the late 1880s and continuing well into the twentieth century, commercial concerns like the Ladies Art Company of St. Louis were publishing catalogues of quilt patterns. A more recent pattern source remembered by older Ohio quiltmakers was the syndicated column that appeared in many Ohio newspapers. From the late 1920s through the 1950s, these newspapers responded to the growing quiltmaking market by including a sketch of the pattern with suggestions for fabric and colors (see illustration 122). Ohio quiltmakers also used the premiums offered by Stearns and Foster with the purchase of their Mountain Mist batting (see illustration 123).

Hundreds of different quilt patterns are illustrated in these various sources. However, late-nineteenth and early-twentieth-century Ohio quiltmakers favored a relatively small number of patterns: Bow Tie, Ocean Wave, Double Irish Chain, Feathered Star, Lone Star, Eight-pointed Star, Shoo-fly, Monkey Wrench, Pinwheels, Four- and Nine-Patch, and Churn Dash. Difficulty of construction may account for the unpopularity of some of the published patterns.

Appliqué patterns were attracting renewed interest at the turn of the century. As a subscription incentive, in 1905 the *Ladies' Home Journal* advertised the forthcoming publication of a series of appliqué quilt patterns designed by famous artists. The designs appear formidable to construct, and neither patterns nor instructions were included. The circus quilt (see illustrations 143 on page 122 and 147 on page 124), made in 1935, was a modification of a design by Maxfield Parrish published in the March 1905 issue.

Not until the mid-to-late 1920s were more successful appliqué quilts designed by such women as Anne Orr and Ruby McKim. They were designers, not traditional quiltmakers, and worked as art/needlework editors for *Good Housekeeping* and *Better Homes and Gardens* respectively. Their appliqué quilts appear very different from their nineteenth-century forerunners. They feature solid pastel color schemes in realistic floral motifs, often in a medallion format, surrounded by well-defined borders, which are often scalloped.

The earliest quilt the project recorded in this new style was made around 1915 in a modification of a Marie Webster pattern, and it won a medal at a Cleveland Museum of Art show (see illustration 168 on page 000). Quilts we documented in this style were usually made by younger, more urban women, many as their first quilting project (see illustration 124).

By the early 1930s, Ohio quilts looked very different from those made a quarter of a century earlier. There were three major reasons for this change. First, a multitude of updated traditional patterns like the hexagonal pattern arranged in Grandmother's Flower Garden, as well as new appliqué patterns, were widely available. The latter included such well-known patterns as Sunbonnet Sue, Butterflies, and Dresden Plates, which are still quite popular with traditional Ohio quiltmakers.

The second difference is more obvious: the appearance of new pastel colors, greens, lavenders, blues, yellows, and pinks. This dramatic change in colors took place after World War I, in part because the war disrupted the domination of the German dye industry in American textile manufacturing. As a result, American chemical manufacturers began to develop synthetic dyes to replace the unobtainable German dyes. Through research and experimentation they enlarged the color palette to include many colorfast pastels (see illustrations 125 and 127).

A third factor influencing the appearance of these quilts was the changed nature of printed designs. Gone were the busy squiggles or the tiny one- or two-figure prints on dark grounds so popular at the turn of the century. Now, clear, light-colored backgrounds featured larger, simplified prints of stylized flowers and art-deco-influenced geometrics.

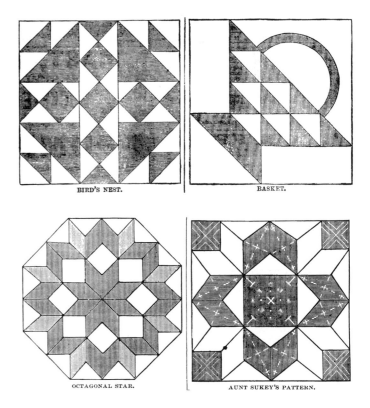

BIRD'S NEST.   BASKET.

OCTAGONAL STAR.   AUNT SUKEY'S PATTERN.

[121] Quilt patterns from *The Farm and Fireside*, March 15, 1883, and February 1, 1886.

[122] Sample Blocks. Mary Mitchenor, Lebanon (Warren County), 1930s. From a private collection.

The patterns for these sample blocks were published in syndicated columns in Cincinnati newspapers. Mary Mitchenor pieced and appliquéd more than three hundred blocks designed by Nancy Page, Ruby McKim, and others, recording the pattern name on each block. Her scrapbook contains the clipped columns.

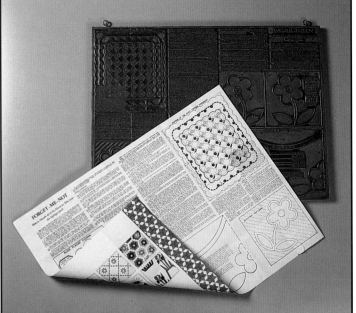

[123] *Forget Me Not #61.* Mountain Mist pattern printing block and paper pattern, 1931.

The Stearns & Foster Company of Lockland (Cincinnati), Ohio, offered free patterns with their Mountain Mist cotton quilt batting. Patterns were printed inside the batting wrappers, together with colored pictures of other available patterns and a coupon entitling the quilter to a discount on her next pattern purchase.

In an advertisement for "Mountain Mist quilt cotton" in *Good Housekeeping,* April 1937, the Stearns & Foster Company offered patterns for thirty-five cents, or twenty cents with a coupon. *Printing block courtesy of Kay Doerner. Paper pattern courtesy of Irene Goodrich.*

[124] *Tiger Lily.* Alice Virginia Smith Moody, Zanesville (Muskingum County), 1938–1941. 88″ x 76″ (224 cm x 193 cm). Appliqué, embroidered. Cotton. From a private collection.

Alice Smith Moody was employed as a schoolteacher in 1938 when she chose a kit for her first quilt. She was attracted to this kit by its colors and lily motifs and purchased it at the Lazarus Department Store in Columbus, Ohio.

The top was completed in 1940, and after her marriage in 1941 she quilted it with help from her mother-in-law and sister-in-law.

According to quilt historian Cuesta Benberry, kits for quilts were developed in the first decade of the twentieth century and were widely available by the 1920s. The kits provided color-coordinated fabrics stamped with cutting lines for each piece and directions for color placement. In later kits, quilting lines were stamped on the quilt top. In the late 1930s, kits were available in the three- to five-dollar range, with some available for as little as one dollar.

These new colors and prints reflected the revolutionary change during the 1920s in women's fashion. The new look of short hems and loose fitting dresses was expressed in brighter colors produced for these garments. Of course, the changes did not occur overnight, and the shift from traditional patterns to modern patterns and pastel colors was gradual. However, by the mid 1930s, the quilts we documented incorporated these new colors and patterns.

After World War II quiltmaking declined in urban areas. Newspapers and magazines less frequently syndicated quilt patterns, and fashionable decorating magazines embraced the new sleek, modern look in which quilts seemed out of place. In Ohio, however, the rural quiltmaking tradition continued. In fact, quiltmaking probably never declined in Ohio farm communities, as indicated by the large number of quilts we documented in rural areas, as many quilts made in the last two decades of the nineteenth century as in the first two decades of the twentieth century. The project documented many Dresden Plate, Sunbonnet Sue, Grandmother's Flower Garden, Periwinkle, Bow Tie, Irish Chain, Butterfly, and Double Wedding Ring quilts made during World War II and into the 1950s and 1960s (see illustration 128).

The saying, "History repeats itself," can never be more appropriate than when applied to quiltmaking. Hand crafts and self-sufficiency were part of the alternative lifestyles practiced by the disenchanted youth of the 1960s, and the interest in handmade items exploded into mainstream America during the U.S. bicentennial. Quilts are once again being made by women of all ages, in every region of Ohio, urban, rural, and small town.

[126] Alice Spies Harsha

[125] *Flower Garden*. Alice Elizabeth Spies Harsha (1896–1948), Marietta (Washington County), 1935. 106" x 76" (269 cm x 193 cm). Pieced. Cotton. Collection of Ruth Young Campbell.

Alice Harsha volunteered to make quilts for her two nieces if they paid for the fabric. They purchased fabrics for the flowers, and after Alice made them, colors were chosen for the borders. Alice Harsha then completed the quilts and gave them to her nieces.

The hexagon was one of the earliest patchwork patterns; in fact, it was the first pattern *Godey's* printed, although it was not until the 1930s that it became known as Flower Garden. Earlier, patterns using hexagons were called Honeycomb or Mosaic, and colors were usually arranged in bands or chevrons of light and dark.

In 1931 the *Oklahoma Farmer Stockman* published its pattern of Old Fashioned Flower Garden recommending a yellow center, solid-colored ring, printed ring, and white "path." This configuration became extremely popular and has become one of the classic twentieth-century quilt patterns.

[127] Sears, Roebuck and Company Catalog. 1928–29 Fall and Winter, page 204.

Four years later, in 1933, Sears offered pastoral cloth as "the best quilting fabric. . . . Many a prize winning quilt will be made from this fine cotton. The colors were chosen with blending in mind. . . ."

These coordinating solid colors enabled the quiltmaker to add subtle shading to floral appliqué quilts.

[128] *Star of the Bluegrass.* Alice Brown Layne (1870–1965), Ironton (Lawrence County), 1955. 85″ x 59″ (216 cm x 150 cm). Pieced. Cotton. Collection of Gloria Hogsten.

In a 1960 newspaper interview just before her ninetieth birthday, Alice Brown Layne listed sewing as one of her favorite occupations. While she was being interviewed, she sewed quilt pieces together.

Friends remember Alice Layne as "a very sweet lady [who] always had a quilt ready for all the new babies in the neighborhood." Widowed in 1918, Mrs. Layne used her quiltmaking to supplement her income. She charged "$2.00 to piece a top and $8.00 to quilt it."

Mrs. Layne made hundreds of quilts during her lifetime, working at her quiltmaking until her death in 1965. Many Ohio women continued quiltmaking after World War II, although quilting did not have the general popularity it had before the war years.

[129] Alice Brown Layne

QUILTING FROLICS

While reading nineteenth-century women's periodicals, Ohio newspapers, and county histories, diaries, and letters, we encountered an array of contradictory material on quilting bees. We also discovered a shift in the purpose, atmosphere, and group dynamics of nineteenth-century Ohio society. Two possible reasons for this were the change from frontier settlements to established communities and religious influences.

The earliest sources described events conforming to our romantic notions of an old-fashioned bee: women forming a community support system by helping to provide warm bedding for friends and neighbors. After the quilting was finished, men would join the women for a feast (the types and quantities of food served were carefully recorded in many accounts), followed by lively games and dancing far into the night. These gatherings reflected the nature of the community: small, somewhat isolated, settlers dependent on one another for survival. The greatest chance of community success lay in cooperation among all residents. Any possible social distinctions were overlooked for the sake of common interests.

Morris Schaff, in his 1905 book *Etna and Kirkersville* (Licking County), pointed out the egalitarian character of frontier living:

> There was no class founded on wealth, no one distinguished by either learning, ancestry, achievement, or pretentious estate,—we were all on the same level, wore the same home-made clothes, read or studied in dimly lighted rooms or by the light of wood fires, looked each other in the face when we met at each other's doors, all unconscious of that restless kingdom known as society, and in blessed, happy ignorance of what is now called refinement and culture.

The descriptions of these frolics fitted our preconceived notions, but we began encountering repeated accounts lamenting the passing of these community gatherings (quiltings, huskings, house raisings) as early as 1837. These recollections of past customs continued through the nineteenth century, many prefaced with explanations of quilting bees or huskings for uninformed readers, the younger generation, and urban dwellers.

We began to see a pattern that offered a possible explanation for the seemingly rapid demise of the quilting bee, or "frolic," the more common nineteenth-century term. The old-fashioned frolics were a practice of the early settlers; and, as frontier areas became settled farms and communities, these high-spirited customs faded. Communal activities like house raisings, corn-shuckings and quilting frolics were no longer necessary to ensure community survival. These communities were now accessible to other towns and villages, and the basic necessities were readily available for trade or cash. Social distinctions separated neighbors who had previously joined together, collectively accomplishing the task of building homes in the wilderness. The former sense of community was gone and in its place came a different type of community based on income, breeding, and education.

So, with the gradual passing of the frontier community—in some areas as early as 1820—and with the rise of an established social and economic order, survival kinship between neighbors disappeared. With the demise of this type of kinship, a new one based on common religious beliefs took its place.

Religion, always a pervasive force in American society, may have had a role in the changing mission of group quiltings. Beginning in the late 1820s, a religious revival swept the United States. Congregational and Presbyterian churches had been active in Ohio since statehood, attempting to civilize the new settlements. Now, newer churches, such as the Methodists and Baptists, saw Ohio as an opportunity for growth. All the churches gained numbers and influence in the revival in the late 1820s and 1830s, and by the mid nineteenth century there was a strong religious impetus for reform in many fields, including establishment of higher moral standards of behavior.

■

LAMENTING the degeneracy of the church and the deplorable condition of our perishing world . . . the undersigned covenant together under the name of the Oberlin Colony, subject to the following regulations. . . . We will eat only plaine & wholesome food, renouncing all bad habits especially the smoking chewing and snuffing of tobacco unless it be necessary as a medicine & deny ourselves all strong & unnecessary drink, even tea & coffee . . . . We will renounce all the world's expensive and unwholesome fashions of dress particularly tight dressing and ornamental attire. . . . We will strive to maintain deep-toned and elevated personal piety, . . . and to glorify God in our bodies and spirits, which are His.
Covenant of the Oberlin Colony
Lorain County
1833

■

This coincided with the period when Ohio was changing from a frontier state to a predominantly settled state. The settlement pattern and the growth of evangelical Protestantism and its allied reforms were connected. The organization of churches in the frontier helped facilitate the passage to established communities, although it was not an overnight change, nor did it happen at the same rate statewide.

Religious duty had a sobering effect on lifestyles. Dancing, intemperance in both food and drink, attending the theater, and rollicking quilting frolics did not conform to the strict moral standards of evangelicalism.

By the Civil War many group quiltings in settled areas such as the Western Reserve seem to have become plain and solemn single-sex affairs. Often church related, these groups encouraged conversation about Christianity and God while making garments and quilts for charity.

Even if the nature of quilting groups was not affected by religious beliefs, the motivations and functions changed. Women involved in the old-fashioned quilting frolic provided bedding for friends and family. A frolic was an occasional, festive event to benefit those in their immediate community. The later church-related quilting groups had a different purpose. These women met regularly and were concerned with a broader definition of community. In addition to families and neighbors, they were concerned with people they might never meet. Many of the quilts produced by these organizations, often known as Ladies' Aid Societies, were sent to strangers in foreign missions, as well as to charitable organizations in other states. In addition to bedding, church-related sewing societies also provided garments for the needy. The 1849 photograph of the Ladies' Benevolent Sewing Society of Strongsville (see illustration 130, page 114) depicts women making a quilt for a homeless mission in New York. Other quilts were made for departing missionaries.

By 1885 the objective of Ladies' Aid Societies had expanded to fill a new role: fundraising. They paid for church roofs, organs, and new buildings with money earned from quilting tops for others, raffling completed quilts, and making signature quilts. Many Ohio church sewing groups produced fundraising quilts in the popular color scheme of red embroidery on a white background. Church and community members paid to have their signatures embroidered on the quilt, and additional money was raised when the finished quilt was raffled. Church-related quilting groups continued their former mission of providing quilts for charity purposes throughout the twentieth century, sending quilts overseas to disaster areas as well as to the needy closer to home.

A different type of quilting group was established in the late 1970s. These quilting guilds (of which there are now over eighty in Ohio) were founded as idea and learning exchanges among novice quiltmakers. The emphasis is on individual projects rather than on group-made quilts. Good food, caring friends, and friendly advice play an important part in these group sewing activities today, and in a small way they keep alive this part of Ohio's past.

■

A MORE GENIAL and fraternal citizenship and neighborhood never existed than were the early settlers of Logan County—ready and willing at all times to lend a helping hand in every case of necessity. . . .

Many of the gatherings of the early settlers at the house-raising, barn-raising, rail-splitting, corn-shucking, and ect. [sic] were seasons of great joy and hilarity among all classes, and especially with the young people. . . . The men working hard all day at the out-door work and the women picking wool, scutching flax or quilting all partaking of a hearty dinner and a supper of corn bread, venison or wild turkey, coffee made from rye or wheat browned, or milk and pumpkin pie, and then at early evening came the inevitable dance, four and eight-handed reels and jigs, which would be kept up to the music of the fiddle with little cessation, till near the "break of day" the next morning.

In some neighborhoods it was not at all unusual to see several pairs of girls and boys comfortably ensconced in the corners with a silk or cotton handkerchief thrown over their heads indulging in whispers over their love affairs; or it might be that a few couples would recline across the beds in the room indulging in similar (to them) delightful entertainments. These practices and customs were of so frequent occurrence that no one of course ever thought of any impropriety in, or indulged in any invidious remark upon, such innocent amusements.

Judge N. Z. McColloch, "Pioneer History"
[Recollections of boyhood in Logan County just after the War of 1812]
The History of Champaign and Logan Counties
1872

It should be remembered that fond reminiscences of hard work and humble living conditions are usually held by those who have risen well beyond their modest beginnings.

■

THE LADIES of the Union are great workers, and among other enterprises of ingenious industry, they frequently fabricate patchwork quilts. When the external composition of one of these is completed it is usual to call together their neighbours and friends to witness, and assist at the quilting, which is the completion of this elaborate work. These assemblings are called "quilting frolics," and they are always solemnised with much good cheer and festivity.

Frances Trollope, *Domestic Manners of the Americans*
1832

Frances Trollope, an English author, spent the years 1825 through 1830 living in Cincinnati.

■

■

Husking Party

Farewell the pleasant husking night—
   its merry after scenes.
When Indian pudding smok'd
   beside the giant pot of beans;
When ladies joined the social hand,
   nor once affected fear,
But gave a pretty cheek
   to kiss for every crimson ear!

WE LIKE TO RECUR occasionally to the customs and pastimes of our ancestors. Talk as we may of the gay masquerade, and the fashionable ball, where beauty, and elegance, and refinement float down the dance, the soft music, like the lovely creations of a dream—who is there that will not turn a longing and a lingering glance upon the simple amusements of other times—when pastime went hand in hand with usefulness! We know that these may, at first view, appear rude and forbidding—that the sensibilities of the fashionables of the present generation would be shocked at the bare idea of a Quilting Frolic—an Appleparing, or a Husking Party.

The Husking party takes place in those long, bright evenings of autumn. A group of happy and kind-hearted beings, of all ages and sexes, from the fair young girl to the grayhaired old man, are assembled around the fruits of their neighbor's industry—the long and heavy pile of Indian corn, gathered from the field with its covering of husks. The whole length of the ample barn floor is lined with huskers, who after a few preliminary jokes, betake themselves zealously to their task.

The presence of females in such a group will no doubt be objected to. But wherefore? Ask the gray-haired yeoman, if, in the days of his boyhood, it was deemed improper, or inconsistent with the dignity and delicacy of their character, for his female companions to join their brothers and their neighbors, in an evening's amusement of this nature. They would smile at the idea of impropriety. The assembly is not one of strangers, where doubt and apprehension must seal every lip and fetter every movement, but of those who have lived together as children of one family, and have met each other, at all times, and at all places—in the kitchen or in the parlor—the field or the workshop, with the same frank smile of welcome. And pray where is the harm of mirth and pleasantry, tempered as they are here with pure, unstudied natural modesty? There can be none. The parties have not mingled in the hollow world, and learned to curl the lip at sincerity, and betray with out a scruple the confidence of the artless and unsuspecting.

The huskers ply their tongues as busily as their hands, while engaged in their pleasant task. Stories are related—songs are sung—jokes are passed—and soft words spoken. Imagine to yourself, reader, the sight of a long row of fine, healthy looking girls, with glowing countenances, and bright eyes, and sweet smiles. Depend upon it there is nothing like a sensible, good-natured romp of a country girl—one who will play "hide and seek," and "blind man's buff," with you, but, who would cuff your ears in indignation should you address

her in language which more refined and fashionable ladies would listen to with complaicence [*sic*]. During the process of husking, if a red ear of corn is found by any one of the ladies, she is liable to receive a kiss from some of the company. She, of course, hands the ear to her favorite beau, who readily understands the signal and acts accordingly. The red cheek is sure to be redder before he leaves it.

After the task is finished, the company adjourn to the house—a supper is provided—and after partaking of it, the parties separate for their respective homes—the girls being all provided with "fellows" to accompany them. But the genuine Parties, we grieve to say it, are now rarely heard of. They have lost the spirit which enlivened them—a false refinement has broken in upon their pleasant amusement; and bright eyes and fair hands no longer figure at a Husking.

Western Courier and Enquirer
Piqua (Miami County)
November 18, 1837

The above description of the husking party is included as an example of what the church leaders might be objecting to (the immodest mingling of the sexes) and what the aging writers were remembering with such fondness (that same mingling).

■

A YOUNG LADY attended a 'quilting'—those who were then present might not understand what he meant—but in the country it was known as a scene of great joyousness and there was also some extraordinary eating and drinking. The young lady . . . had been a good deal engaged and excited, and thus she sat down in the circle and rapidly drank some strong tea. She was immediately thrown into convulsions and died, the Physician testifying that her death was occasioned by drinking strong tea rapidly.

Professor Whipple, Oberlin Collegiate Institute (Lorain County)
"Address to the 2nd American Health Convention"
The Graham Journal of Health and Longevity
1839

The fact that Professor Whipple felt the need to explain a quilting to his Boston audience suggests that by 1839 the quilting frolic was not practiced in more urban areas. This quotation also reflects the beginning of the reform movements that swept this nation before the Civil War. Everything from diet, to dress, to slavery came under fire.

These various reform movements were closely related (the Oberlin Colony espoused all of them), and proponents often cited religious bases for their beliefs.

■

FEBRUARY 7—We have had deep snow. No teams passed for over three weeks, but as soon as the drifts could be broken through Mary Scott sent her boy Frank around to say she was going to have a quilting. Everybody turned out. Hugh drove on to the Center where he and several other men stayed at the Tavern until it was time to come back to the Scotts for the big supper and the evening. There were papers at the Tavern, and Hugh says they are full of the new Whig President [William Henry Harrison]. . . . I took six squash pies for Mary's supper. My pumpkins all froze. She had two big turkeys and her famous *bar le duc* [fruit preserves]. What wouldn't I give to taste some real cranberry sauce again—and oysters. But of course we don't have anything like that here. . . . One of Mary's quilts she called "The Star and Crescent." I had never seen it before. She got the pattern from a Mrs. Lefferts, one of the new Pennsylvania Dutch families, and pieced it this winter. A lot of Dutch are taking up land here in the Reserve. . . . Her other quilt was just an oldfashioned "Nine-Patch."

    Ruth E. Finley
    Old Patchwork Quilts and the Women Who Made Them
    1929

Efforts to determine the author of this letter have been unsuccessful. Possibly adapted for the modern reader by Ruth Finley, it was published as being written by a woman in Ohio (probably a member of Ruth Finley's family who were early settlers in the Western Reserve) to a relative in Connecticut in 1841.

■

RESOLVED: . . . to deny the pleasure, if pleasure it is, of preparing either rich food, or a great variety of plain food, particularly at or for the meetings of this Society. . . .

    No member of this Society, in providing refreshment at, or for the meetings of the same, shall exceed the following specifications: viz., either bread *or* biscuit—one kind of cake *or* pie—one kind of sauce *or* preserve—cheese *or* dried Beef. . .

    Records, Ladies' Benevolent Sewing Society
    Strongsville (Cuyahoga County)
    May 1849

By the mid nineteenth century, Strongsville was a settled community well past the frontier stage, with over one thousand residents and four churches. The Ladies' Benevolent Sewing Society of Strongsville, organized in 1848, provided quilts and garments for the needy and Christian fellowship for its members.

These women were no longer primarily concerned with their families' immediate needs. Spiritual considerations, both at the personal and community level, were emphasized. It was at this personal level that the denial of the "sensual appetite" was addressed in their regulations. For an 1849 portrait of this group, see illustration 130 on page 114).

■

JANUARY 15 1861
I quilted all day on Mrs. M's quilt & finished it. I worked 6 days on it for $2.
    Lucinda Cornell, Diary
    Franklin County
    1861

■

MARCH 3 Put quilt in to-day and quilted some on it
March 4 Sally French, Jane Starbuck and Beth Davis helped quilt some
March 5 I got my quilt out and worked at it 'til 8 o'clock
March 11 Finished binding my quilt
March 15 I helped wash this morning then put a quilt in
March 16 I've been busy all day with my quilt I got it out about 4 o'clock.
March 18 . . . then continued binding my quilt.
April 10 I finished Mary's quilt for her today.
    Lizzie Stanton, Diary
    Barnesville (Belmont County)
    1869

Not all quilting took place in groups, as Lucinda Cornell and Lizzie Stanton testify. Lizzie quilted two quilts in the month of March, 1869, with three friends coming to help one day. Other diaries and letters reveal that many quiltmakers worked alone in their homes with occasional assistance from relatives and friends.

The Cornell and Stanton diaries also indicate that some women quilted for others, sometimes earning a small income for themselves and their families. For a quilt made by Lizzie Stanton, see illustration on page 133.

■

■

A City Quilting Party

A FEW DAYS AGO I attended a "quilting party," and it was so different from any "quilting" that I ever attended before. I would like to tell the lady readers about it. We were requested to meet at half past one p.m., the gentlemen at half past seven in the evening. We were all assembled at the appointed time, and at two o'clock we (six of us) sat down to the quilt. . . .

It was all marked when we sat down to it and our hostess kepts [sic] the needles threaded.

Part of the time we were entertained by a young lady who played very nicely on the piano. At half past three o'clock, a servant brought in some cake and chocolate. After this dainty lunch, finger bowls, filled with perfumed water, were passed, and when the wiping of fingers was over we went back to our work. At a quarter to six the quilt was ready to be taken from the frames. Very pretty it looked and the quilting was nicely done.

We went to the dressing-room to smooth down the ruffles, frills, and laces, and make ourselves look "pretty" for the half past six o'clock dinner. The dinner consisted of roast beef, mashed potatoes, sweet potatoes baked, boiled turnips, cabbage salad, mixed pickles, lemon pie, cocoanut pudding, bread, butter, tea and coffee. The table looked very pretty. The tablecloth was white damask, napkins to match. The carrying and tray cloths were white, embroidered with white silk. The centerpiece was cream-colored silk embroidered in the center filled with beautiful flowers. The dishes were china, all white.

The gents were all on time and at eight the tables were placed and whist was played until half past ten. Then ice cream, cake and lemonade were served on the card tables. At a little after eleven we started for home, and as our hostess bade us good night she put in the hand of each lady guest an envelope containing a block, worked with her initials and date of the quilting. That block was to be the center for a quilt started by each of the quilters and we are to see which will have the next "quilting."

We had a very pleasant time, but to my taste there was far more enjoyment in the "old-fashioned quilting-bee," than the one of the present time.

The Ohio Farmer
August 9, 1894

This quilting frolic, held at a time of renewed interest in quiltmaking during the late nineteenth century, is tame and formal, when compared with the high-spirited frolics held in frontier Ohio.

■

THE WOMEN also had "bees"—sewing bees, wool-picking bees, and quilting. These were royal times. A supper of short cake, sweet cake and stewed gooseberries constituted the bill of fair. . . . All were on a level—no kid glove or codfish aristocracy among them. . . .

As the settlements increased in size, morality and religion increased and a disposition to dispense with whiskey at raisings and bees also increased, until the better portion of the settlers discarded its use altogether.

"Pioneer Life in Lorain County"
The Ohio Farmer
August 30, 1894

■

THE DAYS of quilting, save at church sewing societies, are well nigh over, though the cotton quilt of our grandmothers is in very good form, provided one has luckily been inherited.

Judith Gould, "Household Hints"
House Beautiful
February 1903

■

IN TALKING at length with seventeen older traditional quilters, most of them born in the first decade of the twentieth century, some observations can be made. . . .

. . . most of these quilters as well as their older relatives, had quilted alone all their lives or with just one family member or interested neighbors. Although some were now quilting in groups . . . they were recent exceptions. When group quilting had occurred, it was usually connected with a fundraising event for a church, library or civic organization. Many felt strongly that the results were usually better when one quilted alone.

Jeannette Lasansky
In the Heart of Pennsylvania . . .
1985

Interviews with older quilters in Ohio echoed these sentiments. We were told of quilters surreptitiously removing the unsatisfactory stitches of other quilters. Group quiltings were fine for fund raisers, but if one were particular it was best to select one's fellow quilters carefully. If these traditional older quilters did participate in group quiltings on a regular basis, it was for various church-related ladies' aid organizations.

■

[130] *Ladies' Benevolent Sewing Society,* Strongsville (Cuyahoga County), 1849. These relatives, fellow Christians, and migrants from New England met regularly to meet human needs and reform society through their needles. This quilt was sent to the Home for the Friendless in New York. From the collection of Stella Mallory Dickerman. *Photo courtesy the Ohio Historical Society.*

SISTERS, SAINTS, AND SEWING SOCIETIES: QUILTMAKERS' COMMUNITIES

RICKY CLARK

T he Ladies' Benevolent Sewing Society of Strongsville (Cuyahoga County), founded in 1848, is a useful metaphor for all of Ohio's quiltmaking communities (see illustration 130). On the surface, it was founded to provide the Christian women of Strongsville with an efficient means to produce quilts and clothing needed by various missionary outposts. Beneath the surface, however, the society provided the opportunity for women to bond together from a wide variety of communal interests and concerns.

As with many Ohio women in the nineteenth century, these Strongsville ladies were deeply involved in issues of family, religion, and social reform. Such women shared experiences within their families, then broadened their definition of family to include female relatives, friends, and fellow church women with whom they worked to fulfill their socially prescribed roles as protectors of the home. As they encountered social situations that threatened the home and victimized women and children, they fought these evils, at first within their families and religious institutions and then by the twentieth century through increasingly secular social agencies. The sewing society produced goods that met genuine needs; but perhaps more importantly, it served to nourish the sense of community and mutuality of interests of those who attended. Research into the Strongsville society reveals this dramatically.

well as a desire to fight an assortment of social ills. The society's founders belonged to the Free Congregational Church, a splinter group organized in 1842 by antislavery Congregationalists. Membership in the society was open to any Christian woman in Strongsville, however; and Keziah Pope, whose husband had organized the Free Congregational Church and whose parents had established Strongsville's Methodist church, drew in most of her female relatives. By the end of the first year, one-quarter of the society's members were Popes; by the time it disbanded in 1882, seven of its ten board members were women in the Pope family.

The Popes, along with most charter members of the society, were among the earliest settlers of Strongsville. Their family of ten had migrated from Massachusetts in 1818, two years after the town's first settlers. Strongsville was in the heart of the Western Reserve, a three-million-acre tract in northeastern Ohio settled almost entirely by New Englanders or New Yorkers with New England roots. "New Connecticut" is still dotted with orderly communities surrounding town commons and bearing New England names and was once described as "more like New England than New England itself." Less visible than town planning and architecture, however, were the values the region's settlers brought with them, most conspicuously respect for hard work, high moral values, religion, social justice, and education.

When the society organized in 1848, the members already shared familial, religious, and geographic ties, as

Quilters in the Ladies' Benevolent Sewing Society were as intensely involved with the people they helped as they would have been with relatives. They sent quilts and garments to mission stations in Canada, China, and the Sandwich Islands and read the missionaries' letters aloud at society meetings. When they completed the quilt in illustration 130 in March 1849, society members "proposed to have a Daguerreotype of the scene taken and sen[t] with the Bedquilt to the Home in N. York," just as they might have had daguerreotype portraits made to send to distant relatives.

Ladies in the Benevolent Sewing Society were members of several "communities": transplanted New Englanders, patriotic Americans, relatives, friends, church members, and social reformers. Their activities caused them to reach out and create new communities. Sometimes these communities existed accidentally and independently; in other instances, they coalesced in fascinating hybrids. It is remarkable that Ohio quilts, as these pages demonstrate, reflect and distinguish these communities through their intended use, design, materials, and patterns of preservation and inheritance. For discussion purposes, the communities are broken out in their three broadest categories—family, church, and reform societies—although the quilts themselves often cut across these classifications, and many reflect interesting, specific subthemes.

FAMILY HEIRLOOM QUILTS

Whatever the utilitarian or decorative purpose served by a quilt, certainly most of the quilts documented in Ohio went far beyond utility in the values assigned them by their makers and subsequent owners. Many quiltmakers used their quilts to affirm kinship bonds, a function not always articulated but nonetheless recognized by quiltmakers and their descendents up to the present. We found strong traditions of family inheritance, intra-family collaboration and commemoration of family history, personal relationships, and rites of passage. This issue of kinship-bonding persisted throughout the nineteenth and twentieth centuries and in all areas of the state.

Probably the most consistent tradition discovered during our documentation of almost seven thousand Ohio-made quilts was the pattern of quiltmakers and subsequent owners passing their quilts on through the family and within the family, through women. We discovered this tradition everywhere in Ohio, regardless of the region, ethnic group, or time period. And the tradition continues, as owner after owner testified that her quilt will eventually go to a daughter.

When there were no daughters in the family, quiltmakers often gave their quilts to other women in the family: daughters-in-law or, in the case of unmarried quiltmakers, nieces. Sometimes the recipients were namesakes, as well as relatives. Less frequently, quiltmakers gave quilts to friends, but even then the tradition continued of passing the quilt on down the distaff side of the quilt's new family.

Jennie Brunton's quilt, almost 130 years old, is a case in point. Jennie Brown Brunton made her Rose quilt in 1862, while her husband was away fighting in the Civil War (see illustration 131). The Bruntons lived in Camba (Jackson County), just a few miles north of the Kentucky border. Her quilt has been passed from daughter to daughter through three generations. Jennie Brunton's great-granddaughter, the current owner, has already decided that the quilt will eventually go to her own daughter.

While Jennie Brunton was making her quilt in southern Ohio, the only part of the state invaded by Confederate forces, Emily Ball Welch was making a Double Irish Chain quilt in Vermilion Township (Huron, now Erie, County), on Ohio's northern border (see illustration 132). Although military action during the Civil War never reached northern Ohio, Emily's family had suffered during the American Revolution. Her grandparents were among the residents of nine Connecticut towns wantonly burned by the British in the latter days of the Revolution. As "fire sufferers," they were granted reparation by Connecticut in the form of a land grant in the western portion of Connecticut's Western Reserve, a 500,000-acre tract known as the Firelands. The Ball family settled in Vermilion Township around 1818, and Emily, the youngest of eleven children, was born there in 1835. Emily's quilt, like Jennie Brunton's, descended from mother to daughter and eventually will go to the daughter of its current owner.

We found countless imaginative variations on this theme of matrilineal descent. Tina Snyder of Benton (Holmes County) gave her 1860s wedding quilt to her oldest daughter, and it has continued to descend through the oldest daughter in each generation. Therese Keller Springlemeier of Cincinnati (Hamilton County) gave hers to her oldest granddaughter, and it has been passed on to the oldest granddaughter in each generation ever since. Jane Linke of Woodville (Sandusky County) pieced her Lily quilt in 1878 when she was sixteen, and it has been presented to subsequent oldest granddaughters in the family on their sixteenth birthdays.

The passing on of quilts was usually informal. Until the passage of a Married Women's Property Act in 1846, each married man owned all family property, including any his wife may have brought to the marriage, purchased with her own earnings, or created by her own hand. At the husband's death, all property, including quilts, became part of his estate. Thus the early inventories list quilts as a part of a man's estate at his death, even though they had been made by his wife and daughters. David Abbott's estate, for instance, included fourteen quilts when he died in Huron County in 1824. They were undoubtedly made by women in the Abbott family, who might very well have wanted some of them to go to daughters. However, those quilts would have been sold, along with other household items, to settle any debts Abbott might have had. Before 1846 the only way for most quiltmakers to ensure that their quilts went to intended recipients was to give them away during their lifetimes.

Even after 1846 there is little evidence that women made wills leaving quilts to specified people. Those wills we did discover, however, were notable. Christina Keener, along with her husband and eight children, emigrated from Germany to Thompson (Geauga County) in 1880. Her will, written in 1924 when she was seventy-five, is extremely detailed and even specifies that her funeral be held "in the Lutheran Church at Geneva, Ohio, with Pastor Else to preach and the four verses of song No. 409 . . . be used." Her will indicates the value she assigns various items in her household. After bequests of furniture and a "zither harp" to two of her sons, Christina bequeaths "to my grand-daughter May Keener one of my fine quilts, which I direct that she keep unused for seven years before putting it to regular use as she will value it more after that lapse of time." An identical bequest to another granddaughter, Esther Keener, follows. Her final bequest, "the pony which I have usually driven," is to a grandson.

In an interesting variation, Eliza Denney, the last of three unmarried sisters who lived together in Gallipolis (Gallia County), "sold" her quilts after she died in 1941. In the sisters' attic was a trunk full of "things" destined to go to their younger relatives, as they told a twelve-year-old grand-niece during the 1930s. The things were quilts, and Eliza's will stated that each surviving family member would receive one quilt, provided he or she paid one dollar for the privilege. Since the family genealogist estimates that there were at least twenty-six eligible heirs, the quilt collection must have been enormous.

For some quilt owners, a break in family ownership was a wrenching experience. Maria Harper Southwick's quilt, made in New Bloomington (Marion County) during the 1860s, descended through women in the family until 1970, when her relatives decided to sell it. Before it left the family forever, the oldest female descendent dictated the quilt's history to its new owner while her relatives wrote down the story for their children (see illustration 133).

[131] *Rose*. Jennie Brown Brunton, Camba (Jackson County), 1860–1865. 76″ x 74″ (194 cm x 189 cm). Appliquéd, pieced, embroidered: embellished with reverse appliqué and machine chain-stitch. Cotton. Collection of Charlotte Davis Sprecht.

Jennie Brown Brunton made this quilt in southern Ohio while her husband was fighting in the Civil War. Extant Ohio quilts made during the war are rare; many were given to the United States Sanitary Commission to be sent to Union hospitals. Except for the colors, this quilt is related to the floral appliqué style discussed in chapter 2. An unusual feature is the early machine chain-stitch used as an embellishment.

Since it was made, this quilt has descended through women in the family. All the women in the current generation appreciate it particularly, as all are quiltmakers and quilt collectors.

Another quilt, made in Huron County during the 1890s, was given to the maker's only son and daughter-in-law, who moved to California. The couple divorced; yet the significance of quilts as bonds between women in the family was so respected that, in spite of the divorce, the wife returned the quilt to her former mother-in-law.

Another tradition important to Ohio's quiltmakers was working with other family members on quilts. Although the popular image of quiltmaking in the nineteenth century is of neighborhood quilting bees, we found more instances of collaboration between smaller groups of relatives: mothers and daughters, sisters, even husbands and wives.

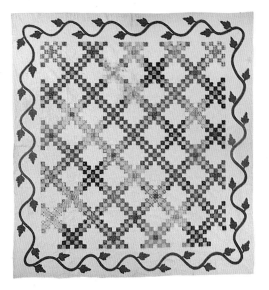

[132] *Double Irish Chain with Leaf Border.* Emily Ball Welch (1835–1891), Vermilion Township (Erie County), c. 1860. 95" x 88" (241 cm x 224 cm). Pieced, appliquéd. Cotton. Collection of Patricia S. Thayer.

Emily made her quilt on Ohio's "north coast" at the same time Jennie Brunton was making hers. As "fire sufferers" during the American Revolution, Emily's grandparents were granted land in Ohio by the state of Connecticut. Emily's parents lived there in 1835 when Emily was born. Emily married Thomas Welch in 1864, about the time she made this quilt. The pattern she chose has been a favorite of Ohio quiltmakers throughout the nineteenth and twentieth centuries. Emily lived all her life in Vermilion Township.

Since Emily's death, her quilt has been passed down from mother to daughter and is still with Emily's descendents.

■──────────────────────────────

WEDNESDAY, FEBRUARY 3, 1875
I quilted all day aunt Betsy helped me this after noon this was
a very cold & windy day
        Elizabeth Arnold
        Dayton (Montgomery County)
        1875

──────────────────────────────■

Learning to quilt was often an occasion for family collaboration, usually between mothers and daughters. One pair of sisters, however, decided to learn on their own. In 1925, when they were seven and ten years old, Helen and Margaret Hess of Mount Cory (Hancock County) found a series of Ruby McKim embroidery designs in *Childlife* magazine and decided to make a quilt from them (see illustration 134). They purchased muslin for the back from Woolworth's but decided to embroider the designs on sugar sacks, which they first bleached to remove the printing. They worked their embroidery in the red floss recommended by the magazine.

Although they completed the embroidery, the sisters lost interest in the project and set the quilt blocks aside.

Fifty-five years later they rediscovered them and resumed work on the quilt, completing it in 1980. Now, in 1990 Helen is replicating the quilt in contemporary materials.

Other quiltmaking sisters sometimes made identical quilts, perhaps in the spirit of competition (see illustration 6, page 14). Alma Donaldson Rockey of Continental (Putnam County) was a prolific quiltmaker. Born in 1877, she made quilts in a variety of techniques and in all the styles popular until her death in 1947. Her quilts form a wonderful record of styles and techniques current during the first half of the twentieth century. Her collection also includes several of the patterns found to be favorites throughout Ohio between 1870 and 1940, including Single Irish Chain, Feathered Star, and Grandmother's Flower Garden.

Alma Rockey's masterpiece was an appliquéd Whig Rose (see illustration 136). The pattern, a variation of one popular in the 1850s, apparently impressed her sister, Belle, who made a masterpiece quilt identical to Alma's.

[133] *Civil War Quilt.* Maria Harper Southwick, New Bloomington (Marion County), 1860–1870. 74" x 67" (188 cm x 170 cm). Pieced. Cotton. Collection of Marjorie Scott Fagan.

Maria Southwick made this quilt during the Civil War while she was awaiting her soldier-husband's return. He never came home; while he was with the Union troops in Nashville, Tennessee, he died of illness.

Maria Harper Southwick descended from one of the earliest settlers of the Western Reserve. The Harper family settled Harpersfield (Ashtabula County) in 1798; their historical home is now maintained by the Western Reserve Historical Society. Maria's quilt was passed down through women in the family until the family sold it in 1970. Before it went to its new owners, Maria's descendents documented its history.

[134] *Childlife Quilt*. Margaret Hess and Helen Hess, Mount Cory (Hancock County), 1925, 1980. 105″ x 86″ (267 cm x 218 cm). Embroidered, pieced. Cotton. From a private collection.

In 1925, seven-year-old Margaret Hess and her ten-year-old sister, Helen, decided to make a quilt. They chose patterns from *Childlife* magazine and embroidered the designs on sugar sacks, then lost interest in their project. In 1980, with renewed interest they joined the embroidered squares and completed the quilt.

[135] The Hess sisters and their mother, Hancock, Ohio, c. 1926. Ethel Hess stands behind her daughters, Margaret (*left*) and Helen.

[136] Alma Lee Donaldson Rockey

[137] *Whig Rose*. Alma Lee Donaldson Rockey (1877–1947), Continental (Putnam County), c. 1900. 75″ x 74″ (190 cm x 187 cm). Cotton. Collection of Phyllis Rockey Lloyd.

Alma Rockey's Whig Rose is only one of many quilts she made. This quilt, however, inspired her sister, Belle, to make one identical to Alma's. Belle's replica is equally masterful.

QUILTS AS FAMILY RECORDS

Kinship-bonding was affirmed not only in the way in which the quilts were made and passed on, but in their specific designs as well. Some were structured as family records, illustrating domestic history through words or images. The earliest we found in this category dates from 1839; the most recent (we saw several), 1979. Reflecting the current interest in finding our roots, some of the new quilts are literally decorated with genealogical charts. Regardless of age, those we saw were in remarkably fine condition, suggesting that they were made primarily as family records, rather than for warmth.

Rebecca Abercrombie was a masterful quilter at age twenty-seven when she finished her extraordinary quilt "July 24, AD 1839/County Green/Ohio Xenia," recording the information on it in minute quilting stitches (see illustration 138). She also quilted her name and the initials of her parents and eleven sisters and brothers in the centers of elaborate and apparently original quilting designs. Her crisp, bright red pieced design may also be original, according to the quilt's owner (who told us she is "not a blood relative" of Rebecca but a "soul-sister").

Although this is the only quilt we saw attributed to Rebecca Abercrombie, it displays such extraordinary skill that she must have made many others before she began this one. Its fine state of preservation suggests that she treasured it as a family record and rarely, if ever, used it as a bed cover.

The family record Emme Hulse Ayers created in 1869 is quite different from Rebecca Abercrombie's made thirty years earlier, although both quiltmakers lived on farms less than forty miles apart and each was twenty-seven when she quilted her family record (see illustration 139).

Known as "Emme," Loretta Emeline Hulse was the daughter of David Hulse and Ernestine Krouskopf Hulse. Emme's father was four years old when his family came from New Jersey to Pisgah (Butler County) as pioneer settlers in 1815. Her mother, Ernestine, was two when her parents emigrated from Germany to Butler County. David and Ernestine married in 1840 and moved immediately to the farm on which Emme was raised. David Hulse was a blacksmith as well as a farmer and, according to a Butler County historian, Ernestine "probably rendered as much service to the sick as many a physician with college diploma," specializing in obstetrics and diseases of women and children.

Emme's "pictorial quilt," as she labels it, is a signature quilt whose pieced blocks are inscribed with inked names, dates, and sentiments. All the names are of Emme's close relatives: parents, siblings, nieces, and nephews. To underscore their kinship to Emme, she frequently noted specific relationships such as "your mother," "your father," "your little brother."

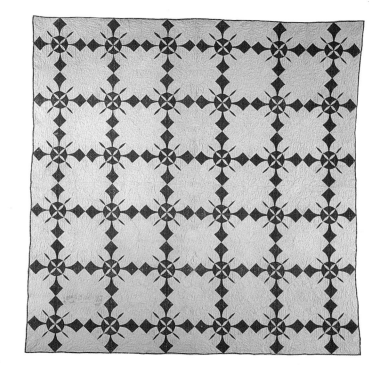

[138] *Unknown*. Rebecca Abercrombie (1811–1879), Sugar Creek Township (Greene County), 1839. 86″ x 85″ (218 cm x 216 cm). Pieced. Cotton. Collection of Gay Dell.

Rebecca Abercrombie's masterpiece is a quilted family record. In the white blocks alternating with the pieced blocks she quilted "Rebecca/Abercrombie/July 24 AD 1839/County Green/Ohio Xenia," as well as names and initials of her relatives.

Rebecca's parents, John and Jane Abercrombie, migrated from Pennsylvania to farm in Sugar Creek Township. Rebecca was born there in 1811 and lived there most of her life. She never married, but late in her life she moved to nearby Bellbrook to live with her sister, Kezia. They died within two weeks of each other in 1879.

Indelible Ink.

TAKE SIX CENTS' worth of lunar caustic, and having put it into an ounce phial full of vinegar, and a very little sap-green, cork it tight and hang it in the sun. In a couple of days it will be fit for use.

To make the preparation for the above, take a lump of pearlash, of the size of a chestnut, and dissolve it in a gill of rain-water.

The part of the muslin to be written upon is to be wet with the preparation, and dried and glazed with a warm flat-iron; immediately after which, it is ready for marking.

The New England Economical Housekeeper and Family Receipt Book
1845

Her quilt presents a much more lively and personal picture of Emme's family than is usually the case in quilted family records, as Emme decorated each block with drawings that vividly illustrate life on the Hulse family farm in 1869. She depicts her brother, David, hunting, riding his horse, and training his dog to sit; a woman, perhaps Ernestine, washing clothes, hanging them on the clothesline, and sweeping; brother William F. (who managed the family farm in later years), riding a "folded harvester," one of two pieces of farming equipment illustrated. Animals evidently played a large role in Emme's family. Jack, the family dog, is honored with an entire block all to himself and portraying him in five poses. In another block he towers over a tiny girl who tries to push him out of the garden while threatening, "Come Jack get out of the garden, or I'll take you by the Nape of the neck and . . ." (the dire consequences are concealed in the seam allowance, see illustration 140). Other animals include kittens, birds, kicking donkeys, and a trio of ostriches—a bird rarely found on Ohio farms during the postwar period and probably inspired by a published illustration.

The Hulse family had experienced the Civil War more directly than many Ohio residents. In June 1863 Confederate Col. John Morgan led his cavalry first into Indiana and then into Ohio, pillaging the southern and southeastern counties for over a month until captured in

[140] This detail of Emme's quilt (see illustration 139) shows a small girl attempting to push the enormous family dog, Jack, out of the garden. Two corner blocks portray Mother washing and drying the family's laundry.

[141] Detail of illustration 139. Emme's young brother, Lewis, died in the Civil War. This is one of two quilt blocks honoring the martyr. Such obituary blocks often read like gravestones, as this does, and have the same function of memorializing the dead. By including Lewis in her family quilt, Emme Ayers symbolically preserved her entire family, in spite of Lewis's death.

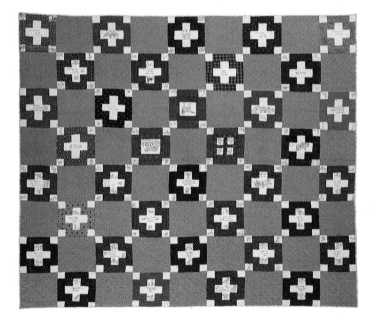

[139] *Pictorial Quilt.* Loretta Emeline Hulse Ayers (b. 1842), Pisgah (Butler County), 1869. 93" x 81" (236 cm x 206 cm). Pieced. Cotton. From a private collection.

Emme Ayers's quilted family record is quite different from Rebecca Abercrombie's. Emme has inscribed her quilt blocks with inked inscriptions and drawings depicting life on a Butler County farm just after the Civil War. The drawings provide unusually personal glimpses of Emme's family.

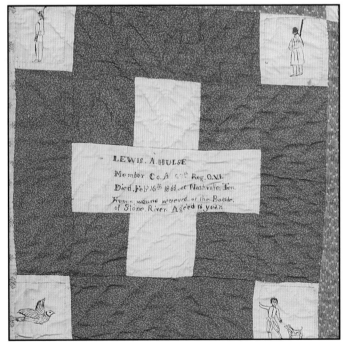

Columbiana County, the farthest north that any Confederate unit had penetrated. Morgan's Raiders plundered the Hulse farm, as Emme's father reported in a letter to his brother. "The Morgan raid created the greatest excitement that I ever seen," he wrote. "Citizens in every direction, were running off their horses into back hollows and thick woods. . . . There was much loss sustained by the train of thieves, which allways [sic] follows Armies in the disguise of soldiers."

More tragically, the Hulse family lost a son in the Civil War, and Emme included two obituary blocks on her quilt commemorating her young brother as a war hero: "Lewis A. Hulse/Member Co. A 69th Reg. O. V. I./Died. Feb' 16th 1863 at Nashville, Ten./From a wound received at the Battle./of Stone River. Age'ed [sic] 18 years" (see illustration 141). The other obituary block adds, "Honor the brave." Flags, shields, and Union soldiers decorate the quilt squares. Such inscriptions read like epitaphs on gravestones (see illustration 142); in fact, their memorial function is identical. Their inclusion on quilts otherwise recording living family members parallels an early-nineteenth-century tradition of including deceased relatives in painted family portraits: the dead were still considered part of the family and were therefore included in visual family records.

[142] This more traditional gravestone commemorates another Ohio victim of the battle that took the life of Lewis Hulse. Portions of the epitaph for Simon Huntington of Kelley's Island (Ottawa County) are almost identical to Emme Hulse Ayers's quilted memorial for her dead brother:

DIED
At Nashville Tenn., Jan. 19, 1863
From wounds Rec'd. at the battle of
Stone River Dec. 31, 1862

FAMILY GIFTS

In addition to quilting family records, some women made quilts as gifts for specially beloved relatives, again confirming the importance of family to Ohio's quiltmakers. A particularly warm relationship existed between grandmothers and their grandchildren, for we saw many quilts made by grandmothers. Most were gifts to young children, rather than to newborn infants. Some, from the 1890s on, were based on commercially available transfer prints published in magazines. The most charming and personal incorporate images based on the children's interests.

At the turn of the twentieth century, commercial textile design was strongly influenced by illustrations from late-nineteenth-century children's books. This interest trickled down to quiltmakers, not only through exposure to "sophisticated" furnishing fabrics incorporating storybook images appropriate for appliqué, but through magazine articles aimed at quiltmakers. Some, such as the 1905 *Ladies' Home Journal* series of quilts, designed by artists who had clearly never attempted to reproduce their designs in appliqué, were intimidating (see illustration 143). We saw only a few children's quilts from this time period. By the 1930s, however, when

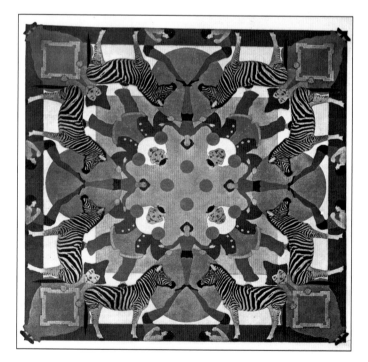

[143] *A Circus Bedquilt*, designed by Maxfield Parrish and published as one of a series of five quilts designed by professional artists, in the *Ladies' Home Journal*, March 1905. No patterns were provided.

[144] *Animal Caravan Quilt.* Leila Ada Cialdine Baker McDonald, Bellaire (Belmont County), 1935. 82″ x 63″ (208 cm x 160 cm). Appliquéd, embroidered, stuffed. Cotton. From a private collection.

Leila McDonald made this quilt for her granddaughter and namesake, Leila Ada Robinson, basing it on the child's favorite book, *The Animal Caravan,* by Frank R. Leet (1930). This is one of two quilts we documented that were inspired by the same illustrations by Fern Bisel Peat. The other quilt was made in Hancock County. In both cases grandmothers made the quilts. We documented more children's quilts made by grandmothers than by mothers, who were probably otherwise occupied when their children were young.

[145] Leila McDonald wanted to replicate the illustrations in the storybook, detail for detail. To find exactly the right fabrics, she ordered some from Wanamaker's Department Store in New York City. The quiltmaker's technical skill is admirable and unusual for the 1930s (note the stipple quilting).

[146] Leila McDonald holding her infant granddaughter and namesake, Leila Robinson.

many of the most outstanding children's quilts were made in Ohio, there was a more workable relationship among children's books, printed textiles, and quilts. Not only are there many children's quilts from this period, but also storybooks illustrated with children in quilt-covered beds or with animals made of patterned cloth. During this same period dress fabrics printed with juvenile themes and patterns for pictorial quilts were commercially available. Although many of the children's quilts we saw were made from commercial kits, some quiltmakers were inspired to design their own.

In 1930 Frank R. Leet wrote a children's book, *The Animal Caravan Book,* and illustrated it with pictures designed to look like appliquéd fabric animals. *The Animal Caravan Book,* published in Akron (Summit County), was the favorite of Leila Ada Robinson of Bellaire (Belmont County). In the mid 1930s Leila Ada McDonald, the grandmother for whom young Leila was named, made a quilt for her granddaughter, based on illustrations in Leet's book (see illustration 144).

Wanting to replicate the pictures exactly, Leila McDonald searched diligently for her fabrics, even writing away to Wanamaker's Department Store in New York City for exactly the right materials (see illustration 145). Grandmother Leila had grown up in a family of outstanding quiltmakers and had apparently inherited their skills. Not only is the quilt visually charming, but it is an extraordinary technical achievement for this period. She incorporated stuffed and three-dimensional forms in her blocks, and surrounded the figures with stipple quilting. She embroidered her granddaughter's name and the date on the quilt back and "L. A. R. 1935" on its front. Leila Robinson still cherishes both her favorite storybook and the quilt it inspired.

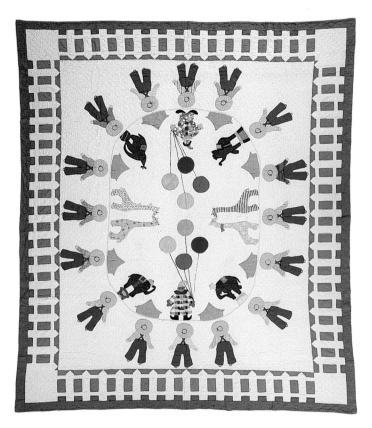

[MRS. FOSTER] does fine embroidery without the aid of glasses, and since her eighty-fifth birthday has pieced more than fifty quilts, bestowing them upon her children and intimate friends as souvenirs of her old age.
  Mrs. Amanda A. Sackett
  Amherst (Lorain County)
  1896

Another quilt, replicating exactly the same illustrations, was made by Maggie Mertie Baumgardner Neal of Mortimer (Hancock County) for her granddaughter, Carolyn Neal. Carolyn still remembers being ill in bed and spending hours making up stories about the animals on her quilt.

Dora Ann Major had no grandchildren; she had never married. She had a great-grandnephew, however; and in the 1930s, when she was in her late sixties, she made a Circus Quilt for eight-year-old Willis Godden (see illustration 147). Dora, daughter of Eber and Nancy McIlravy Major, was born in 1867 in Brown Township (Franklin County) and moved to nearby Columbus in 1912. Combining popular published quilt patterns, such as Overall Sam and a picket fence, with others apparently original with the quiltmaker, Dora appliquéd a charming circus scene for the lucky little boy.

When the top was finished, Dora sent it to Willis's great-aunt on the other side of the family, Edna Baker Smith, who quilted it for him. Older female relatives from both sides of the family thus collaborated on a quilt that reaffirmed their special relationships with a young child.

Children were not the only recipients of quilts made to underscore strong family relationships. One of the most remarkable quilts we discovered was made by Sarah Harper Wells of Lodi (Medina County) for her mother-in-law, Chloe Wells (see illustration 149). "Sadie" Harper was born in 1853 in Medina Township and in 1879 married Willard Wells, a jeweler from nearby Wayne County. In 1886 and 1887 Sadie made a quilt for Chloe Wells that is remarkable in many respects.

[147] *Circus Quilt*. Dora Ann Major (1867–1945) and Edna Baker Smith (b. 1883), Madison County, 1935. 108″ x 97″ (273 cm x 246 cm). Appliqué, embroidery. Cotton. Collection of Willis and Faith Godden.

Dora Major appliquéd this quilt for her great-grandnephew, Willis Godden, during the 1930s. She has combined familiar patterns (Overall Sam and Picket Fence) with apparently original circus figures. Dora may have been inspired by A Circus Bedquilt designed by Maxfield Parrish and published in *Ladies' Home Journal* in March 1905 (see illustration 143, page 122). The theme and organization of the two quilts are very similar.

After she had finished the top, Dora sent it to Willis's great-aunt on the other side of the family, Edna Smith, who completed the quilt.

[148] Dora Ann Major

[149] *Mother Wells's Quilt*. Sarah Harper Wells (b. 1853), Lodi (Medina County), 1886–1887. 71″ x 79″ (180 cm x 201 cm). Appliquéd, pieced, embroidered. Cotton, furnishing fabrics, novelty prints. Collection of Kenneth Coin.

Sarah Wells (Sadie) made this quilt as a gift to her mother-in-law, Chloe Wells. Although it appears to be a contained crazy quilt, it is actually a tile quilt, with irregularly shaped fabric pieces appliquéd to a white background rather than joined to each other directly. Sadie was interested in fabrics and selected many with realistic motifs.

[150] Detail of illustration 149. Sadie embroidered "Mother" Wells's portrait in the center of her quilt, as well as the jewelry store owned by Sadie's husband, Willard Wells, and countless other delightful motifs. The printed Santa Claus figure was designed by Thomas Nast, credited with creating our image of St. Nick.

[151] Sarah Harper Wells

Although decorated in the style of the crazy quilts popular at the time, this is a tile quilt with realistic figures and irregularly shaped fabric pieces appliquéd to white fabric and separated from each other by the background fabric in such a way that the fabric patches appear to be framed by the exposed ground.

This quilt contains a wealth of textile information. The fabrics are varied and include a number of novelty prints, including cheater cloth (fabric printed to imitate patchwork), fabrics depicting oriental scenes, and a large print of one of Thomas Nast's Santa Claus figures, similar to many produced as advertisements or Christmas souvenirs by the Oriental Print Works in North Adams, Massachusetts. Other printed material commemorates Gilbert and Sullivan's *The Mikado*, first performed in 1885. To the further joy of textile historians, two pieces of fabric are inscribed with helpful information: "This piece of calico over 100 yrs old when quilt made," and "This piece of calico bought in 1861 for .50 a yd." The quilt is edged with an unusual pleated commercial binding.

Sadie appliquéd human figures, oriental fans, farm animals, and Jumbo the Elephant. She also embroidered such homey objects as a cup and saucer, knife and fork, and rocking chair, along with cows, horses, and symbols of the Knights of Pythias, a fraternal lodge. The largest embroidered subjects are a portrait of "Mother" Wells and Willard Wells's jewelry store in Lodi, which sold "Silver Ware Watches" and "Jewelry," according to the signs embroidered on the windows (see illustration 150). Sadie finished her quilt on March 1, 1887, and recorded the event in embroidery.

The story of the quilt's adventures since that date are as remarkable as the quilt itself. At some point, it was sold out of the family and was eventually acquired by an antiques dealer in Tucson, Arizona, who advertised it for sale in a 1984 issue of the magazine *Antiques*. Sadie Wells's great-great-great grandnephew, who lived in Michigan, saw the advertisement and bought the quilt back into the family. In 1986 he saw in the magazine *Early American Life* a news release describing the Ohio Quilt Research Project and wrote us, kindly offering to let us document Sadie's quilt for our archives.

RITES OF PASSAGE: BIRTH

A significant subset of quilts emphasizing the importance of family are the many made to celebrate rites of passage in the lives of quiltmakers or their relatives. From the mid nineteenth century to the present, quiltmakers marked birth, marriage, death and (more recently) graduation with special quilts (see illustration 152).

When her daughter was born on November 9, 1869, Mary Elizabeth Duncan Lash made her first baby a quilt (see illustration 153). Considerably larger than cradle size, the quilt must have been intended for use after she graduated to a larger bed. There was no doubt, however, about the identity of the person being honored. In a precursor of computer alphabets, Mary decorated the border of the quilt with a legend recording the significant information: "Lavada/Idella/Lash born/November 1869."

Mary and her husband, Orange Scott Lash, descended from several generations of Coshocton County residents. Lavada was the oldest of their fourteen children. Although Mary was a prolific and talented quiltmaker, this is the only one of her quilts still in the family. A 1987 estate sale of the contents of the family home included many beautiful quilts. The quiltmaker's great-grandson, who hoped to purchase some of Lavada's quilts, found he could not compete with other bidders. He did buy a box of unfinished quilt tops overlooked by the bidders and found this quilt at the bottom.

One of the most spectacular quilts given to a newborn baby was made in 1872 by Phebe Cook of Gilead Township (Morrow County) for her granddaughter, Blanche Corwin (see illustration 154). Phebe Cooper Cook was sixty-eight when she made the quilt as a family record and gift to her new granddaughter. According to family tradition, she made a similar one for Blanche's brother.

Phebe and her husband, Abel, were both born in Washington County, Pennsylvania: Phebe in 1804, Abel a year earlier. They married in Knox County, Ohio, in 1822 and in 1857 moved to Gilead Township to an eighty-acre farm they had purchased four years earlier. In 1877 their daughter, Hattie Cook Corwin, died leaving three young children. Phebe and Abel undertook the care of their grandchildren; from age five Blanche was raised by her grandparents and maiden aunt, Amanda, who still lived with her parents. Blanche attended nearby Iberia College and taught school. For over fifty years, until she was in her nineties, she wrote poetry and feature stories that were published in the *Cincinnati Enquirer*.

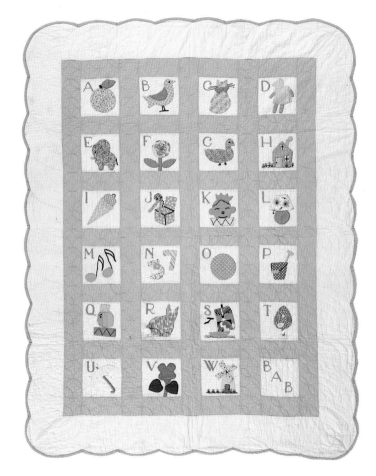

[152] *ABC Quilt*. Regina Wilhelm (c. 1860–1940), Massillon (Stark County), 1930–1931. 65″ x 49″ (165 cm x 124 cm). Appliquéd, embroidered. Cotton. Collection of Barbara Bauer Edmunds.

Regina Wilhelm made this quilt for her great-granddaughter, Barbara Bauer, when Barbara was born. Its colors and scalloped edge are characteristic of 1930s quilts.

Phebe's quilt portrays more than one hundred people and animals involved in social activities and farm chores. The appliquéd figures are enhanced with embroidered details, ruching, yarn hair, and clever manipulation of fabric (see illustration 156). The figures on the quilt represent family, friends, and neighbors of the Cook family. A man driving a horse and buggy, for instance, was a local physician, Dr. Britton. Both black and white figures are represented, an unusual feature reflecting the interracial character of the Mount Gilead community, which included a strong contingent of antislavery Quakers and was a stop on the Underground Railroad (see illustration 157).

[153] *New York Beauty*. Mary Elizabeth Duncan Lash (1850–1918), Coshocton County, 1870. 74″ x 74″ (188 cm x 188 cm). Pieced. Cotton. From a private collection.

Quiltmakers frequently made quilts to mark significant life events. Mary Elizabeth Lash made this quilt to celebrate the birth of her daughter, Lavada Idella Lash, whose name and birthdate are spelled out in block letters on the border of the quilt. Almost all the nineteenth-century quilts made for infants and documented by the project are either cradle- or full-sized. The familiar standard-sized crib, for which the quilt in illustration 152 (page 126) was made became popular after 1890.

[154] *The Phebe Cook Quilt*. Phebe Cooper Cook (1804–1891), Gilead Township (Morrow County), 1872. 93″ x 74″ (236 cm x 188 cm). Appliquéd, embroidered, embellished with dressmaking techniques. Cotton, silk. Collection of the Ohio Historical Society.

Of all the quilts we documented that were made for newborn babies, this is undoubtedly the most spectacular. Phebe Cook made it for her granddaughter, Blanche Corwin, in 1872. It records people and events in the quiltmaker's family and community.

[155] Abel (1802–1891) and Phebe Cooper Cook

[156] Blanche Corwin Kelly, for whom the quilt was made, seated under portraits of quiltmaker Phebe Cook and her husband, Abel.

RITES OF PASSAGE: MARRIAGE

The largest group of quilts made by Ohio quiltmakers to mark rites of passage were those made to celebrate weddings. Most date from the 1850s and 1860s, and many were red and green appliquéd quilts. Despite the oft-repeated myth that it was considered bad luck for a bride to make her own quilt, half of those we saw were in fact made by the brides themselves, the rest by relatives as gifts to the married couple. Approximately half of the quilts made for weddings were signed, initialed, and/or dated by the quiltmaker.

Lydia Melinda Blake of Cleveland (Cuyahoga County) was justifiably proud of the dramatic appliquéd and stuffed quilt she made to celebrate her wedding to Rufus Sproul (see illustration 159). Like an artist signing a painting, she embroidered her initials on the quilt's back. Born in Cleveland in 1827, Lydia was twenty-five at the time of her wedding. She had lived in Cleveland all her life; Rufus had come to Cleveland from New York.

Rufus was a sailor and captain of a Lake Erie sailing ship. After their wedding in 1852, they moved across the Cuyahoga River to a town officially called City of Ohio but always known as Ohio City, a fiercely independent community that tried unsuccessfully to compete with Cleveland's shipping industry and finally merged with Cleveland in 1854. Lydia and Rufus remained in Ohio City and raised four children there.

The design for Lydia's quilt is apparently original, although it incorporates familiar motifs of flowers and hearts. In addition to stuffing the flowers, Lydia quilted stars, wreaths, and hearts on her quilt. She used blanket stitch to apply her cutout motifs to the quilt blocks.

■ ——————————————————

FEBRUARY 19, 1869
[I] have been binding my quilt to-day. People are bound to have me married so I will get ready. Such talk!
    Lizzie Stanton
    Barnesville (Belmont County)
    February 19, 1869

—————————————————— ■

A year after the Sprouls married and moved to Ohio City, another newly married quiltmaker moved with her husband to Rockport (now Lakewood), the town adjoining Ohio City to the west. Serena Tucker was twenty

[157] Detail of illustration 154. Phebe Cook used dressmaking techniques such as braided thread for hair and separate flounces to enhance her figures.

[158] Detail of illustration 154. Phebe's quilt reflects the interracial nature of the Mount Gilead community.

years old when she signed and dated the quilt she made for her 1853 wedding to Francis Wagar (see illustration 161). She embroidered her inscription in elegant counted cross-stitch on a corner of the quilt (see illustration 163).

Serena was born and raised in Monroe Township (Richland County). After she married her schoolteacher husband, they moved north to Rockport, now Lakewood, (Cuyahoga County) where Francis's family had settled earlier. There is still a Wagar Avenue in Lakewood, named for her husband's family.

Although Serena's parents were New Englanders of English ancestry, her quilt reflects the influence of the Germanic county in which she was raised, as does the quilt made by Julia and Frances Marshall (see illustration 31 on page 27). Furniture, *fraktur*, towels, and other objects of north-central Ohio's German settlers are frequently decorated with pots of flowers and tulips, as is Serena's quilt. Her tulip border is reminiscent of those on Jacquard coverlets; a number of Germanic coverlet weavers lived in Richland County during the mid nineteenth century. Like Lydia Sproul, Serena finished her quilt with a colored binding that contrasts with the adjacent white border. This detail, unusual in quilts made in the Western Reserve, is a device much favored by Ohio's Germanic quiltmakers.

Serena's quilt has descended through women in her family and twice has served to commemorate weddings. In 1984 Eunice Tillotson, who had inherited the quilt, gave it to her granddaughter as a wedding gift.

[159] *Hearts and Flowers*. Lydia Melinda Blake (1827–1920), Cleveland (Cuyahoga County), c. 1852. 91" x 78" (231 cm x 198 cm). Appliquéd, stuffed. Cotton. From a private collection.

Lydia Blake made this quilt for her wedding to Rufus Sproul in 1852. Her design is apparently original. Many mid-nineteenth-century floral appliquéd quilts were made to celebrate weddings.

[160] Lydia Melinda Blake Sproul

Occasionally, men were the recipients of wedding quilts, as in the case of Joseph Crowell of Darke County (see illustration 166). In 1900 his friends and family made him a friendship quilt, which they presented to him as a wedding gift two years later.

[161] *Flower Basket*. Serena Tucker (1833–1915), Monroe Township (Richland County), 1853. 85″ x 80″ (216 cm x 204 cm). Appliquéd. Cotton. Collection of Ellen Tillotson Namestnik.

Another bride, Serena Tucker, made this quilt to celebrate her wedding in 1853 to Francis Wagar. Serena had lived all her life in Richland County, a strongly Germanic region. This may account for her choice of tulips to decorate her quilt; tulips were a popular design motif among Ohio's Germanic residents.

Although the tradition of wedding quilts was apparently strongest in Ohio in the mid nineteenth century, it has prevailed well into the twentieth century. In the early 1920s, Cornelia Clawson of Cleveland (Cuyahoga County) made a quilt as a wedding gift for her granddaughter, Hazel Stowe (see illustration 168). She entered it in the Cleveland Museum of Art's Fourth Annual Exhibition of Work by Cleveland Artists and Craftsmen (later known as the May Show) where she received the Penton Medal for excellence in the quilts and bedspreads category (see illustration 169).

[162] Serena Tucker Wagar and husband, Francis Wagar

[163] Almost half the mid-nineteenth-century floral appliquéd quilts we documented were signed or dated. Serena both signed and dated her quilt in counted cross-stitch embroidery. The locket holds photos of Serena and Francis Wagar.

[165] Four generations of McBride women. *Left to right*, Martha Jane Kelly McBride (1841–1922) for whom the quilt was made, her daughter Mary McBride Shepherd (1861–1947), quiltmaker Mary Duncan Kelly and Mary Shepherd's daughter Ethyl (d. 1888).

[164] *Pine Burr.* Mary Duncan Kelly (1814–1898), St. Clairsville (Belmont County), 1858. 100″ x 89″ (254 cm x 226 cm). Pieced, stuffed. Cotton. Collection of the Ohio Historical Society.

Mary Kelly made this quilt for the wedding of her daughter, Martha Jane, to William Harrison McBride. She quilted both names in the center, along with their wedding date. About half the wedding quilts we documented were made by the brides, and half by relatives, as this was.

[167] Wedding picture of Clara M. Henninger and Joseph D. Crowell, May 2, 1902.

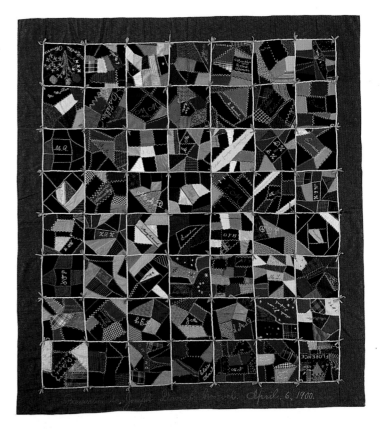

[166] *Contained Crazy Quilt.* Friends and family of Joseph D. Crowell, Darke County, 1899–1900. 78″ x 68″ (198 cm x 173 cm). Pieced, embroidered. Wool, silk. From a private collection.

Friends and relatives of Joseph D. Crowell made this signed friendship quilt as a wedding gift and "Presented [it] to Joseph Daniel Crowel [sic] April 6, 1900." They anticipated Joseph's wedding by two years; he married Clara Henninger May 2, 1902. The quilt blocks are outlined in baby ribbon, with ribbon bows at the intersections.

[168] *Poppy Appliqué*. Cornelia Slover Clawson (c. 1860–1935), Cleveland (Cuyahoga County), c. 1920. 89″ x 84″ (226 cm x 212 cm). Appliquéd. Cotton. From a private collection.

Cornelia Clawson made this quilt as a wedding gift to her granddaughter, Hazel Stowe. The pattern is a variation of one designed by Marie Webster in 1915 and published in her *Quilts: Their Story and How to Make Them*. Mrs. Webster's quilt style (center medallion orientation and appliquéd floral motifs worked in soft, solid colors) became nationally popular in the 1920s and 1930s. This is the earliest example brought to our attention.

[169] Cornelia Slover Clawson

[170] Detail of illustration 168. In 1922 Cornelia Clawson received the Penton Medal for excellence in the quilts and bedspreads category of the Fourth Annual Exhibition of work by Cleveland Artists and Craftsmen held at the Cleveland Museum of Art.

RITES OF PASSAGE: DEATH

Of all the rites of passage marked by Ohio women through their quilts, the most poignant is death. Although we found only a few mourning quilts in Ohio, we have learned that for quiltmakers the creation of mourning quilts is one way of coping with their loss. The earliest mourning quilt found was completed in 1851; the most recent is still in progress. Most were made by mothers to commemorate the deaths of children, a particularly tragic loss that inverts the natural order of life.

The process of making a mourning quilt deeply involves the quiltmaker in a continuing relationship with the deceased. Often the quiltmaker uses fabrics that were intimately linked to the deceased: scraps of the child's clothing, ribbons from funeral flowers, decorating materials from the child's room.

The quilt that marked the 1846 death of fourteen-year-old Laura Mahan of Oberlin (Lorain County) was begun by Laura herself as a friendship or signature quilt. Her stepmother, Sarah Mahan, who had raised Laura from the age of three, completed the quilt after Laura's death, "principally from fragments of her dresses." By completing the unfinished work of her stepdaughter, Sarah joined Laura in a traditionally female project in spite of her death; and by incorporating fabrics from Laura's dresses, she made the quilt an intensely personal symbol of the child. In a rare and remarkable inscription on the top center block of the quilt, Sarah directed that the quilt eventually go to Laura's collateral female descendents, thus keeping her memory alive and linking her to past and future generations (see illustration 171):

> This quilt, commenced by our dear Laura & finished by me, principally from fragments of her dresses, I give & bequeath unto her sister Julia M. Woodruff, or in case of her death to her sister Hila M. Hall, if she survives, otherwise to the oldest surviving granddaughter of their father, Artemas Mahan deceased.
> Oberlin Feb. 6, 1851
> Sarah Mahan.

Martha Fisher Cunningham was twenty-four when she died in 1865, a few days after giving birth to her only child, Riley Orlando, later to be called Landy. The mourning quilt made by her mother, Rachel Daniels Fisher, filled the same healing function for Rachel as Sarah Mahan's quilt did for her (see illustration 172).

John and Rachel Daniels Fisher were among the thousands of Americans who pressed westward during the mid nineteenth century. Descended from Quakers who had come from England with William Penn, John Fisher and Rachel Daniels were born in Pennsylvania. They married in eastern Ohio in 1839; and in 1843, when their first child, Martha, was two, they moved still further west to become pioneer settlers of Paulding County.

[171] *Sarah Mahan Quilt* (detail). Sarah Wadsworth Mahan, Oberlin (Lorain County), 1850–1851. 88″ x 77″ (224 cm x 196 cm). Pieced. Cotton. Collection of Allen Memorial Art Museum, Oberlin College, Oberlin, Ohio. Special Acquisitions Fund and Gift of Private Donors, 1985.

Sarah Mahan ensured that her deceased stepdaughter, Laura, would not be forgotten, by specifying the line of descent in the mourning quilt Sarah made from scraps of Laura's dresses. This inscription is in the center of the top row of quilt blocks.

[172] *Flower Basket*. Rachel Daniels Fisher (1839–1881), Pleasantville (Marion County, Iowa), 1866. 84″ x 71″ (212 cm x 180 cm). Pieced. Cotton. Collection of Gladys Cunningham Kohart.

The mourning quilt Rachel Fisher made after the death of her daughter, Martha Cunningham, was also made from fabrics connected to the deceased young woman. Rachel made the sashing from scraps left over from the wedding dress she had made for her daughter, a dress that also served as Martha's burial shroud. Thus both the clothing and the quilt were associated with rites of passage.

They built the first cabin in Paulding Township and had the first white child to be born there. Their remaining four children were also born in Paulding, where the Fishers lived until 1864 when they moved further west to Pleasantville, Iowa. Martha, now married to Charles H. Cunningham, remained in Paulding with her new husband.

When Martha died a few days after the birth of her son, her grief-stricken mother returned to Ohio and took the baby back to Iowa to raise. She also took back remnants of the material from which she had made the dress that was both Martha's wedding gown and her burial shroud. From these she created the Flower Basket quilt shown in illustration 172. As she worked on the quilt, Rachel told her neighbors, "Whoever gets Landy gets the quilt." Minnie Mae Johnston eventually "got" Landy and used the quilt throughout the fifty-seven years of their marriage. In 1892 Landy and Minnie Mae moved back to Paulding, bringing the quilt with them. When Minnie Mae died in 1939, Landy gave the quilt to his granddaughter, who still owns it.

WESTWARD EXPANSION

Although death was the ultimate threat to family ties, other occasions prompted Ohio women to affirm their family communities through their quilts. Like Rachel Fisher's, many of these quilts were made during the tumultuous period of westward expansion when families were uprooted and moved away from their communities of origin. This was the period of signature quilts, the textile equivalent of the autograph album popular at the same time and serving the same purpose of preserving memories and the ties of friendship. Several such quilts from the first half of the nineteenth century were signed by family members both in Ohio and the eastern communities from which the quiltmakers came (see illustration 14, page 18).

Sarah Mahan's quilt, already cited as a mourning quilt preserving the memory of the young Laura, also serves as an example of the quiltmaker's effort to preserve love ties with relatives and friends still alive. The specific impetus to complete it in 1851, five years after Laura's death, was Sarah's decision to leave Oberlin for the Minnesota Territory to teach in a mission school. In addition to Laura's relatives, Sarah had her own parents, friends, and fellow church members sign quilt blocks, which she then arranged on her quilt in family groups. Her quilt became truly a comforter as she carried with her this rich, appropriately female symbol of the communities she had left behind. When we first learned of it, her quilt had traveled as far west as Oregon. It had been passed to two of Sarah's descendents, each named Sarah.

Lizzie Stanton's quilt, begun in 1859, was another effort to reaffirm a community in the midst of upheaval (see illustration 173). In this case the community was religious: Stillwater Friends Quarterly Meeting in Barnesville (Belmont County).

By 1813, enough Friends (Quakers) had migrated to western Pennsylvania, Ohio, and Indiana to warrant establishing the Ohio Yearly Meeting. A painful schism in yearly meetings in the eastern United States in 1827 affected Ohio Friends as well, and in 1828 the Barnesville Friends separated into Hicksite and Orthodox groups. In 1854 another separation divided the Stillwater Friends into Wilburites, or Conservative Friends, and the more emotional Gurneyites, who became the largest group of Friends west of the Alleghenies. Lizzie Stanton's family allied themselves with the Conservative Friends.

Although this stress on the Stillwater Friends officially occurred in 1854, its effects lingered, as disputes over ownership of property continued for twenty years. Lizzie Stanton was only eight when this separation began, and it affected her family deeply.

Lizzie's quilt, in an Ohio Star pattern, is signed by her family and friends in Barnesville. All names on it are of Conservative Friends; the quilt affirms Lizzie's ties to that church group, while at the same time affirming her family ties through her arrangement of quilt blocks. Each pieced block preserves the names of individuals or couples. Like Sarah Mahan and the church society in Rome (see illustration 14 on page 18), Lizzie arranged her signed blocks in family groups. The only inscribed plain block was signed by Lizzie herself. The notation, "Lizzie/Stanton/Barnesville/Ohio/1865," is surrounded by four blocks bearing the names of her immediate family: her parents, a sister and her husband, and two brothers and their wives (see illustration 174). On the quilt, as in her life, Lizzie was surrounded by family.

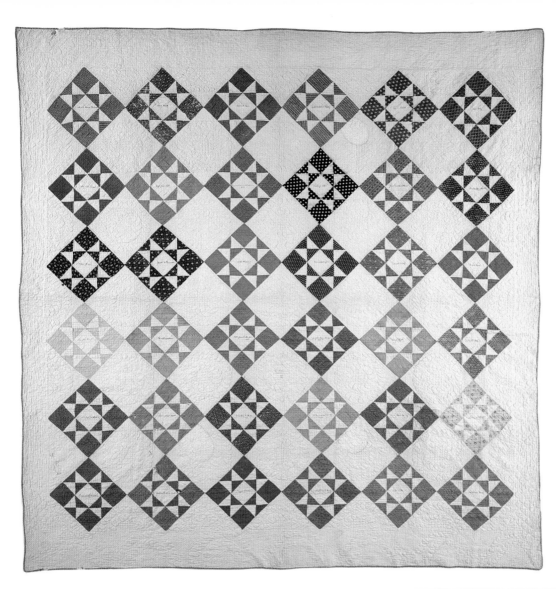

[174] Elizabeth Stanton

[173] *Ohio Star.* Elizabeth Stanton (1846–1936), Barnesville (Belmont County), 1859–1865. 86″ x 83″ (218 cm x 211 cm). Pieced. Cotton. From a family collection.

Lizzie Stanton made this quilt shortly after an unfortunate separation in her Quaker community when a large group withdrew from Stillwater Friends Meeting to reorganize as Gurneyites, forerunner of today's Evangelical Friends church. Lizzie and her family remained with the other group, known as Conservative Friends, and the quilt affirms her ties to them. Lizzie had her relatives and friends, all of them Conservative Friends, sign the pieced blocks.

[175] Lizzie signed the only inscribed plain block "Lizzie Stanton/Barnesville/Ohio/1865" and surrounded herself with her immediate family. Names in the pieced blocks are of her parents and siblings. The names of both husband and wife appear on each signed block, which is characteristic of Quaker signature quilts, but rare outside the Friends' community.

CHURCH SEWING SOCIETIES

While family quilts were typically made by individual women or collaborating family members, a second large category of quilts we found was designed and sewn by groups of women working together for a common cause. The earliest of these were drawn from another "community" important to women: the church and its sewing society.

Sometimes the common cause was simply human need, as in the case of the Dorcas Society, which organized in Cincinnati in 1816 to make quilts for the "worthy poor," i.e., those who were "poor and pious" or "poor but industrious." In other instances, there was an evangelical or even polemic thrust to their efforts. Those women in the Ladies' Benevolent Sewing Society of Strongsville cited earlier (see illustration 130 on page 118), made quilts for victims of social injustices such as slavery, alcoholism, physical abuse, and poverty, as well as for "heathens" not yet "won to Christ" by the society's favorite missionaries. The society's members, although all Protestants, were not concerned with denominational loyalty; women from at least two of Strongsville's churches worked together to make quilts and clothing for the needy.

FROM LADIES' Benevolent Sewing Society, Pierpont

one bed quilt, valued at	$4.50
one pr. sheets	1.00
7 pillow cases	1.00
one woman's sack	1.25
5 children's sacks	4.00
one sun bonnet	.25
two night caps	.18
20 shirts averaging 62¢ each	12.40
	$24.68

From Ladies' Benevolent Sewing Society, Williamsfield and Wayne

19 white shirts at 50¢ each	$9.50
8 striped shirts at 62½ cts	5.00
3 loos dresses, one 1.00 2 75 cts each	2.50
6 small dresses, 3 50 cts each, 3 37½ cts each.	2.62½
2 pr men's pants 50 cts each, 2 boys 31 cts each	2.62½
1 small shirt 37 cts	.37
1 dress 1.50	1.50
15 lbs of dried apples	.50
	$23.61

Report of boxes collected from Ashtabula County for American Missionary Association
November, 1852

This attitude of ecumenical benevolence is characteristic of Ohio church women who made quilts during the mid nineteenth century and reflects the nature of the evangelical Protestant church in Ohio during that period, when it was the prevailing religion there, as elsewhere in America. Because most church sewing groups gave away the quilts they made, usually to distant recipients, few such quilts remain in Ohio. We learn about them mainly from the written records of church sewing societies like those in Cincinnati and Strongsville.

MARCH 28, 1849
Society met at Mrs. A. Pope's. Over 20 were present and spent the time in quilting. It was proposed to have a Daguerreotype of the scene taken and send with the Bedquilt to the Home in N. York—Meet tomorrow forenoon for the purpose—Prayer by Mrs. Moore—Adjourned to meet in one week at Mrs. Whitney's.
Record Book, Ladies Benevolent Sewing Society
Strongsville (Cuyahoga County)
1849

Quiltmakers' involvement in the church community not only motivated their efforts, it often affected the design of the quilts themselves. Once again, Sarah Mahan's quilt serves as a good example. Inscribed by forty-five friends, of whom twenty-three were members of her own church and eight of other Protestant churches, Sarah's quilt reflects a Christian community intimately familiar with the Bible and relying on it as authoritative. Thirty-one of the inscriptions on Sarah's quilt are biblical references or quotations, and, of those, twenty-one are messages of comfort, including specific references to the death of a child. Many of these citations are probably unfamiliar to today's church members, but not so for the biblically literate signers of this quilt, members of at least four churches in three states.

Other mid-century Ohio quilts reflect a culture of quiltmaking women remarkably well-versed in the Bible (see illustration 192 on page 144). One is filled with biblical references to pain and suffering, suggesting that it was made for a friend who was terminally ill. Several others, made for women about to leave their communities, are inscribed "Mizpah," followed by the relevant biblical citation from Genesis 31:49 ["The Lord watch between me and thee, when we are absent one from another" (KJV)]. Erroneously interpreted as early as 1846 as a benediction rather than an uneasy truce, this Bible verse still serves in many Protestant churches in rituals of separation.

That Bible verse is one of many that decorate a later quilt made by a group in the Free Will Baptist Church in Auburn Corners (Geauga County). On April 29, 1883, twelve ladies from the church met to organize "a society for the up-building and advancement of the cause of

[176] *Parson's Quilt*. Ladies of the Free Will Baptist Church, Auburn Corners (Geauga County), 1886. 79″ x 66″ (199 cm x 168 cm). Pieced. Cotton. Collection of the Geauga County Historical Society.

This quilt apparently had multiple functions. Some inscriptions suggest it was made as a gift to a new minister. According to a Geauga County history, it was also a fund-raiser. The unusual drawings accompanying inked Bible verses and hymn texts reflect the biblical literalism of the denomination.

[177] Detail of illustration 176

[178] Detail of illustration 176

SISTERS, SAINTS, AND SEWING SOCIETIES: QUILTMAKERS' COMMUNITIES • 135

Christ." Three years later, they decided to make a quilt inscribed with Bible verses and religious sentiments (see illustration 176). The verses were selected by anyone wanting to have his or her name signed on the quilt and who was willing to pay ten cents for the privilege. The quilt is decorated with inked pictures literally illustrating each Bible verse (see illustrations 177 and 178). Although there is no record of how the ladies used the three dollars raised by their project, two inscriptions suggest that the quilt might have been a gift welcoming a new minister to their congregation.

The Free Will Baptist Church, a New England-based denomination, organized its Auburn Corners congregation in 1839. Established in reaction against a dour, rigid, New England Calvinism, the Free Will Baptists had at various times in their brief history also opposed creeds, an educated and paid clergy, the advance preparation of sermons, and the collection of church statistics. The church in Auburn Corners was suspicious of science as well. In 1845, when Samuel Morse was invited to speak there about his recently invented electric telegraph, the church members refused permission to lend their church building for the occasion, believing a scientific lecture to be sacrilegious. In response, Morse's host, Dr. O. W. Ludlow, composed a poem, which he tacked to the door of the church:

The Goddess, Ignorance, o'er this Temple reigns,
Her 'special care the Rev. Mr. Ames,
Him they both feed, and also clothe
And frequently for him a begging goes.

Nice quilt patch-work, she for him prepares;
And striped vestments war [sic], from her loom he wears.
And then this little upstart, beardless youth,
Becomes an expounder of Divine Truth.

She spurns all Science from within her walls,
And music from her consecrated halls.
There Ignoramuses in numbers meet,
Each other with Salvation to greet.

Ye Heavens that do God's glory declare,
Let your veteran of this Temple beware:
Let not the optic glass be raised on high
To unfold the wonders of the midnight sky.

Ye cursed sons of Ham's degenerate Race,
Your magic art keep from this Holy Place.
Your chemical Laws would only disgrace
The child out of God's peculiar Grace.

The electric spark from the Voltanic pile
This sanctum Sanctorium would greatly defile,
And Morse's extended Telegraphic line
Would outrage all things heavenly and Divine.

Ye sinners all, with one accord,
Ne'er more enter this House of the Lord
But seek a more congenial spot to dwell
And bid this Sacred Place a lasting Farewell.

Let Ignorance triumph with Hindoo zeal,
And sing, and shout, and bawl and squeal,
'Til Gabriel's trumpet shall sound the Knell,
And send them bawling down to Hell.

CHURCH FUND-RAISING QUILTS

Although Ohio's earliest church-made quilts tended to reflect the Bible-oriented ideology of their makers, by 1885 and continuing until 1920 many church groups made quilts for the primary purpose of raising funds. The biblical inscriptions found on mid-century quilts were now replaced by long lists of names; and rather than being made to commemorate personal ties, these later quilts were made solely to raise money for local projects. Quiltmakers began by charging church members a certain amount of money for the privilege of having their names signed or embroidered on the quilt. Occasionally, the completed quilt was raffled, thus increasing the revenue, although some churches considered the raffle a form of gambling and thus unacceptable.

In terms of design, fund-raising quilts were remarkably diverse. Some, made early in this period, include the names of donors and the amounts of their gifts printed on the quilt back. Other churches were less discreet about concealing their donors' generosity and broadcast their names and contributions on the front of the quilt (see illustrations 179 and 180).

Makers of these quilts were primarily drawn from Protestant (most frequently Methodist) churches. Characteristic is the quilt made by the ladies in the Amboy Methodist Episcopal Church (Ashtabula County) in 1891 (see illustration 181). Its blocks are embroidered with names of present and past ministers, boards of deacons and trustees, teachers and assistant teachers in the Sabbath school, students and contributors (along with amounts contributed), as well as embroidered images of the church, and tombstones memorializing deceased members. The quiltmakers even solicited advertisements from local businesses, which they embroidered in prominent locations (see illustration 182).

This change in the nature of church-made quilts parallels a changing attitude in American society in the

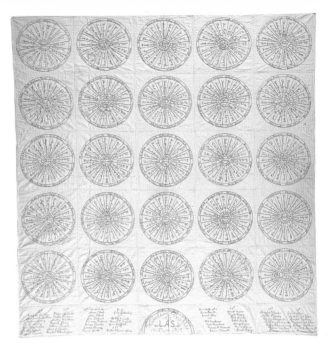

[179] *Fund-raising Quilt.* Ladies' Aid Society, Episcopal Church of Windsor Mills (Ashtabula County), 1917–1919. 90″ x 83″ (229 cm x 211 cm). Embroidered. Cotton. Collection of the Windsor Historical Society.

This church fund-raiser is in a style popular in the early twentieth century, with embroidered names forming spokes of a wheel.

[180] Detail of illustration 179. Amounts contributed by donors were emblazoned on the front of this quilt and included the donation of cloth worth $1.60 by the Devoe Brothers Company.

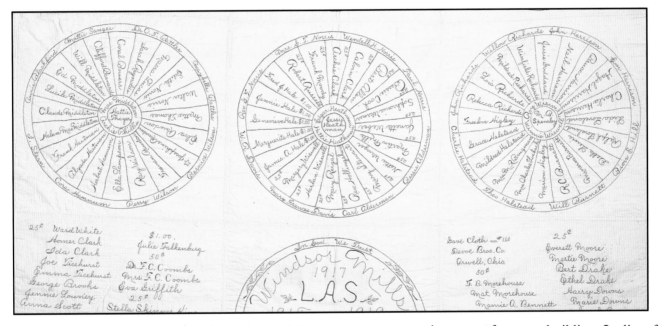

late nineteenth century, as science, mathematics, and the gathering of statistics came to the fore as a dominant interest of America's middle class. In many Protestant churches, "attendance came to count for more than genuine adherence," as Ann Douglas notes in *The Feminization of American Culture* (New York: Alfred A. Knopf, 1977). Ushers counted heads during worship services and posted attendance statistics on boards confronting the congregation: "Attendance last Sunday 103/Attendance Today 89."

Almost all such quilts were made by ladies' aid societies, which emerged from earlier sewing societies like the ones in Cincinnati and Strongsville, but whose responsibility was usually the maintenance of a local church building or parsonage. Consequently, the money raised through these quilts (as well as from bazaars and church suppers) went for specific, local "bricks and mortar" projects: to purchase carpeting, a pulpit Bible or organ, or to raise money for a new building. Ladies of the Park Congregational Church in Cleveland underscored their specific fund-raising project by stitching to their 1910 revenue quilt an actual blueprint of the proposed church building that the quilt would help finance.

■

THE OLD CHURCH bell had long been cracked;
Its call was like a groan.
It seemed to sound a funeral knell
With every broken tone.
"We need a bell," the brethren said,
"But taxes must be paid.
We have no money we can spare . . .
Let's ask the Ladies' Aid."
　　Dorothy Bailey
　　East Ohio Conference, United Methodist Church
　　"The Ladies' Aid," 1983

■

[181] *Fund-raising Quilt.* Ladies of the Methodist Episcopal Church, Amboy (Ashtabula County), 1891. 98″ x 80″ (249 cm x 201 cm). Embroidered. Cotton. Collection of Mrs. Robert Bossley.

This fund-raising quilt, characteristic of many made 1880–1920, reflects a change in the nature of the Protestant church over the nineteenth century. These quiltmakers were concerned with lists and statistics, rather than with Bible verses as their mid-century quiltmaking sisters had been.

The sewing and quilting activities of the Old Mennonites, a conservative branch of the Mennonite church, are particularly well documented by Mennonite historian Melvin Gingerich in "The Mennonite Woman's Missionary Society," *Mennonite Quarterly Review* (37:2, 3, 1963). The Sewing Circle of the Oak Grove Mennonite Church in Smithville (Wayne County), organized in 1905, is an impressive example. This group sewed for the poor of the Canton (Stark County) Mission, as well as for needy local families and for residents of a nearby Mennonite home for the aged. In a typical sewing day, from twenty to fifty women worked together to make thirty to forty items of clothing. They also made quilts, comforters, and "several hundred yards of carpet." At a "sewing" on March 6, 1906, fifty members of this circle made "seven bonnets, ten caps, eight petticoats, one dress, one apron, three pair of pants, also quilted a quilt and knotted a comforter, all of which was sent to the Canton Mission." They contributed $8.17 to the mission as well.

[182] Detail of illustration 181. The church building, lists of ministers and class leaders, and money contributed are centrally located on the Amboy church quilt. An advertisement solicited from "H. Whitman & Son's [*sic*], Builders" reflects the growing secularization of American society.

At the same time, however, church women continued to make quilts either to send directly to the needy or to sell to raise money for community needs. As is true of such quilts made by church sewing societies, few have been preserved, and we know of their existence primarily through written records or rare visual images (see illustration 183).

This tradition continues in many Ohio churches. The Sewing Circle of the United Bethel Mennonite Church in Plain City, for instance, meets once a month to make quilts for benevolence. Since 1982 these women have made approximately thirty quilts each year to be auctioned at an annual fund-raising event to benefit the Shekinah Christian School, as well as others to support other programs for the needy.

The amount of time they spend on each quilt depends on its intended use. The circle makes approximately three quilts each month to send to the Mennonite Central Committee, the denomination's national distribution center for worldwide relief projects. These quilts, which one circle member describes as "scrap quilts," will be sent to recipients selected by the Mennonite Central Committee. In addition, the Sewing Circle makes better quality quilts that they keep in reserve for local families victimized by fire, the greatest threat in any agricultural community. The Sewing Circle also makes one quilt each year to be auctioned at the Ohio Mennonite Relief Sale in Kidron (Wayne County) to benefit the Mennonite Central Committee. This quilt is the finest the women can make.

The Ohio Mennonite Relief Sale, held the first Saturday in August each year, is Ohio's major annual fund-raising event for the Mennonite Central Committee (see illustration 184). It attracts thousands, Mennonites and non-Mennonites alike. Many locally made craft items are

[183] Quilting at the Ebenezer Mennonite Church, Bluffton (Allen County), c. 1900. Note four fully opened quilting frames in the back of the sanctuary. Women in the foreground are sewing clothing. Quilts and garments made by these Swiss Mennonite women were sent to American Indians on reservations in the West. *Photo courtesy of the Swiss Community Historical Society.*

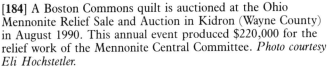

[184] A Boston Commons quilt is auctioned at the Ohio Mennonite Relief Sale and Auction in Kidron (Wayne County) in August 1990. This annual event produced $220,000 for the relief work of the Mennonite Central Committee. *Photo courtesy Eli Hochstetler.*

[185] Posters and brochures publicizing a variety of benefit auctions held in Ohio's Amish and Mennonite communities in 1990. *Photo by Terry A. Jonasson, Photo Imagery.*

sold or auctioned; however, the most popular aspect of the sale is the quilt auction. Sewing circles from Amish, Mennonite, Brethren, and other Germanic sectarian churches throughout Ohio and western Pennsylvania contribute at least one quilt, usually made the previous winter, to be auctioned. In 1990, the twenty-fifth anniversary of the Ohio Mennonite Relief Sale, 190 quilts, comforters, and quilted wall hangings were auctioned, netting almost half the amount raised by the entire relief sale.

While the annual Kidron quilt auction and a similar one benefiting the Sunshine Children's Home in Maumee (Lucas County) are widely known in Ohio, they are not the only such events. The benefit auction is an important event in Ohio's Amish and Mennonite communities and a popular form of fundraising for a variety of causes, from supporting the Adriel School for troubled children in West Liberty (Logan County) to raising money to cover medical costs for uninsured Amish children (see illustration 185).

With a strong tradition of aid, Ohio's Amish, Mennonite, and Brethren churches may be the largest source of quilts made to benefit the needy (see illustration 186). However, such benevolent impulses are not limited to Germanic quiltmakers.

In 1885 Martha Ann Lupton, a Quaker woman in Colerain (Harrison County), lost her home in a fire. Immediately, her fellow members of Harrisville Friends Meeting began a quilt for her (see illustration 187). Each woman in Meeting made a block and signed her name in ink, then completed the quilt top and gave it to Martha unfinished. After Martha's death in 1900, her sister-in-law, Ellen Lupton, found the quilt top while going through Martha's possessions and gave it to Martha's close friend, Ida Binns, as a memento. It was seventeen years before Ida decided to complete the quilt. In the fall of 1917 she invited all the women still living whose names were on the blocks to come to her home and finish Martha's quilt. Among these few was Rachel Taber. After the women completed the quilt begun in 1885, Rachel composed a poem about it, "Lines on an Album Quilt." Her poem indicates that the quilt begun so many years ago to offer solace to a friend now held added meaning for Rachel, as it evoked so many memories of her friends and family.

■

Lines on an Album Quilt

Mementos of our loving ones
  Whose lives were closely knit with ours;
To memory how oft they bring
  The joy of long past social hours.

'Twas as friendship's recorded page;
  Though not in script or print are read,
Events whereon our musing dwell,
  That with the passing seasons sped.

The winter blasts are wild and high;
  They stir the fire to keep back cold;
From heated prod the sparks arise,
  And soon that home the flames unfold.

Though naught such loss could all repair,
  Eliza then this quilt outlined;
And called on friend to take a share,
  Thus show their sympathy entwined.

Each took a willing hand therein:
  But one for whom this token made,
Placed it away and in the chest
  The long unfinished treasure laid.

Whilst yet in prime of womanhood,
  From 'mong the living she passed on;
Devoted, cared for Father frail,
  Who mourned an only daughter gone.

Her brother's spouse to girlhood friend,
  The uncompleted token gave;
Assured 'twould be where duly prized,
  For sake of Martha in her grave.

One year and three decades had passed,
  Since album pieces all were done;
When Ida bids, both near and far,
  The quilters who, responsive, come.

The needles flash, there's hum of tongues;
  While each her task plies swift and well,
They talk of this event as one
  Which ne'er hath had a parallel.

Some pieced by Mothers of that band;
  They count the names and find a score
Whose faithful hands are folded now,
  Whose earthy pilgrimage is o'er.

Among the shade and colors seen,
  One is more dear than any other;
To which my heart most closely clings,
  Enrobed the form of precious Mother.

Her adminition still controls,
  Upon my heart stamped indelible;
Therefore desist where once I strove;
  "Don't wrangle with the inevitable."

And this that's of a silver gray,
  A matron wore with placid brow;
Her kindly deeds, her words of cheer,
  "Rise up and call her blessed" now.

With her consort who sat at head,
  To our devotions added grace;
A charm the silent hour all through,
  The sweet adoring on each face.

When thus assembled, no words spoke,
  The potency of silence theirs;
And yet it seemed we almost heard
  The fervency of spirit prayers.

Young feet were drawn toward surest path;
  "The beauty of holiness behold"
In humble followers of right,
  From whence their living sermons unfold.

There, too, my sire in vision see;
  And oft 'mid stress where's left no choice,
I'm soothed by tones from out the years,
  The melody of Father's voice.

With cadence as of far off song,
  The soul that's sorely tried and riven,
Entices gently on its way
  To deeper faith and hope in heaven;

Which calms the aching throb of thought,
  And sets its unstrung chords in tune;
To chafing spirit brings a balm,
  Sweet as the springtime rose perfume.

Then as in waves melodious,
  Seems bathed this helpless form of mine,
Which, from the present, drifts away
  To maidenhood's sweet singbird clime.

The whilst my step was quick and light,
  Ere I could tread the floor no more;
In wheel chair, moving slowly round,
  In dreamland, walking as of yore.

These currents of emotions past,
  Again within my being flow,
From founts of joy and grief unsealed
  By remnants, thus, of long ago.

One who with care these names inscribed,
  On journey, far, hath gone to stay;
With misty eye and tendered heart,
  We slowly fold this quilt away.
    Rachel Taber Hirst
    Tacoma, Ohio
    1920

■

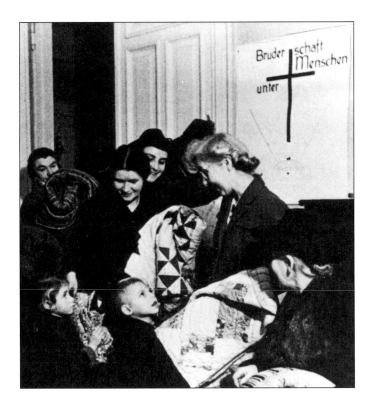

[186] Brethren Service Commission worker Cecile Burke, b. Fayette (Fulton County), distributing quilts to war victims in Bremen, Germany, c. 1947. *Photo courtesy Brethren Historical Library and Archives.*

[187] *Album Block.* Women of Harrisville Friends Meeting, Harrisville (Harrison County), pieced 1885, quilted 1917. 82″ x 73″ (208 cm x 185 cm). Pieced. Cotton. Collection of Virginia Smith.

The top of this quilt was made for Martha Lupton by her fellow church members after her home burned in 1885 and completed by some of the same women in 1917. Rachel Taber, one of the group, wrote a poem recounting the story of the quilt and its meaning to the women who worked on it.

For other quiltmakers, the "family" was national. Rhoda Warner's quilt, made in Painesville (Lake County) in 1855 when the maker was seventy-one, celebrates American history. In this quilt Rhoda chronicles received memories, rather than personal experiences. In addition, her quilt became a personal family record for the Painesville family in which it has descended (see illustration 189).

Rhoda's "revolutionary quilt" (her term) is an impassioned statement of patriotism in words and images, as well as an elaborate and skillful exhibition of technique.

The appliquéd quilt is decorated with stuffed fruit and ruched (gathered) flowers. The center area is a large circle filled with thirteen smaller circles, each enclosing a thirteen-pointed star with two progressively smaller thirteen-pointed stars within it. A fabric label in each of these circles is embroidered with the name of one of the original colonies. The large circle also encloses an American eagle holding in its mouth a banner proclaiming, "O Washington Live Forever." A label below the eagle reads, "The British King Lost States Thirteen." Further inscriptions are embroidered above two roses, each identified as "The Rose of Mt. Libanus": "Our Fathers Fought Bled and Died for Our Liberty. How Dear How Sweet" and "May Our Political Horizons Glow with Truth and the Nation Learn Righteousness." This central area is encircled with fifty-five small muslin labels, each embroidered with the name of a signer of the Declaration of Independence, grouped by state and arranged, clockwise in geographic order from north (New Hampshire) to south (Georgia). Rhoda Warner was an informed patriot. Above this, a curved label declares: "A Star Lighted Visitants to Bethlehem. By the Same Power These Noblemen Stood in 1776 on the 4th of July & Became the Glory of the New World. May Their Names Never Be Forgotten, No Never." A smaller label above this proclaims the theme, perhaps intended as a title of the quilt: "Heroes of the Revolution."

[188] Detail of illustration 189. Rhoda Warner recorded on a label stitched to the quilt details that other quiltmakers must certainly have appreciated. A similar label apparently accompanied a quilt she exhibited two years earlier.

A label attached to the quilt back records construction details (see illustration 188). Both the handwriting style and the content indicate that the inscription was written by Rhoda Warner herself as it recounts statistics only a needlewoman could appreciate: "This revolutionary Quilt Containes [sic] 2404 Pieces,/57 names, 80 words, 1063 letters of needlework./By Mrs. Rhoda Warner Aged 71 Years of Painesville Ohio/Sept. 1. 1855/This Quilt for Sale."

A particularly intriguing detail of Rhoda Warner's quilt is a small fabric hand pinned to the quilt, its index finger pointing toward the names "J. Witherspoon" and "R. Stockton" in the circle of signers (see illustration 190). Newspapers of the time (including the *Painesville Telegraph*) used similar hands as a convention intended to draw the readers' attention to items of particular interest (see illustration 190).

In 1856 Dr. Charles Lewis Stockton of Painesville, a descendent of Richard Stockton, a signer of the Declaration of Independence, purchased the quilt. His son Charles, also a physician, who practiced in Buffalo, New York, inherited it and eventually donated it to the Buffalo and Erie County Historical Society. Dr. Stockton, Sr., may have seen the quilt at the Lake County Fair, held in Painesville on Oc-

■

Class L—Domestic Manufactures and Farm Tools.

IN THIS CLASS there were 110 entries, in all of which we found much to admire; and while we would not have any think us *partial*, we must notice two or three articles in brief, and conclude by giving the names of the exhibitors; merely adding that the articles they exhibited were calculated to win the praise and admiration of all who saw them. A quilt, worked by Mrs. R. Warner, aged 70 years, was admired by all as the most accomplished piece of ladies' work on exhibition. It contained 2,200 pieces, 44 names and 32 words, and was very handsomely embroidered throughout.

THE COUNTY FAIR
Painesville Telegraph (Lake County)
November 1, 1854

■

tober 13, 1856. Rhoda Warner, who exhibited two bed quilts at that fair, was one of only two prize winners; she received a diploma as second prize for one of her quilts. In the same year she entered two quilts in the Ohio State Fair in nearby Cleveland and won three dollars and a diploma for the "best worked quilt" (see illustration 191).

Another quilt exhibited in the 1856 Lake County Fair and intriguingly similar to the "Heroes of the Revolution" apparently stole the show. According to a reporter for the *Painesville Telegraph*, "A Worked Quilt representing the Garden of Eden, in which were Adam and Eve, the tree of forbidden fruit, &, &, . . . attracted much attention." It was very likely the Garden of Eden quilt now attributed to Olive Batchelor Wells of Painesville (see illustration 192).

[189] *Heroes of the Revolution.* Mrs. Rhoda Warner, Painesville (Lake County), 1855. 83″ x 82″ (211 cm x 208 cm). Appliquéd, pieced, stuffed, gathered, embroidered. Cotton, possibly silk. Collection Buffalo and Erie County Historical Society (#57.280).

Rhoda Warner commemorated America's past in her magnificent "Heroes of the Revolution" quilt. She embroidered on it the names of all the signers of the Declaration of Independence, as well as impassioned patriotic and religious sentiments. Although she was too young to have been directly involved in the Revolution (she was born in 1784), her parents lived through it and undoubtedly shared their memories with her.

Understandably, Rhoda was acclaimed as an outstanding quiltmaker at the time she made this quilt. In 1854 she exhibited at the Lake County Fair a quilt that the local newspaper deemed "the most accomplished piece of ladies' work on exhibition." In 1856 her quilts were awarded a second prize at the Lake County Fair and first prize at the Ohio State Fair.

OUR COUNTY FAIR

IN DOMESTIC Manufactures the show was good. The list of entries will show what was on exhibition. The list, however, gives no idea of the character or quality of the various articles named. . . . There was among numerous other beautiful ones, a Worked Quilt representing the Garden of Eden, in which were Adam and Eve, the tree of forbidden fruit, &, &, which attracted much attention.
Painesville Telegraph (Lake County)
October 8, 1856

[190] Detail of illustration 189. An appliquéd hand, similar to those printed in newspapers of the time to draw the readers' attention to items of particular interest, points toward the names of Declaration of Independence signers J. Witherspoon and R. Stockton. In 1856 Dr. Charles Stockton of Painesville, a descendent of signer Richard Stockton, purchased Rhoda's quilt.

[191] View of the Ohio State Fair Grounds, 1856

[192] *The Garden of Eden*. Olive Batchelor Wells (1822–1873), Painesville (Lake County), c. 1856. 86″ x 76″ (218 cm x 193 cm). Appliquéd, pieced, stuffed, gathered, embroidered. Cotton, wool, silk. Collection of the Spencer Museum of Art, University of Kansas. Gift of C. Wells Haren.

This extraordinary quilt was also made in Painesville and was probably the "Garden of Eden" quilt exhibited at the Lake County Fair in 1856. It is remarkably similar to Rhoda Warner's quilt in techniques, quality, and details.

[193] Detail of illustration 192. Like Rhoda Warner's quilt, this one includes red and blue stars and an appliquéd hand pointing to text embroidered on a fabric strip that was then appliquéd to the quilt. This "fiery, flying serpent" (Is. 14:29; 30:6) seems far more threatening than the traditional slithery snake.

This quilt commemorates the well-known biblical Creation story against a background of flower-filled trelliswork, an arrangement probably inspired by similarly designed printed fabrics popular at the same time. The quilt was the work of a biblically literate quiltmaker. Although the incident depicted is recorded only in the Book of Genesis, she drew on many books of the Bible, as well as on Milton's *Paradise Lost,* and the popular hymn "Brightest and Best of the Sons of the Morning" to tell her story. The quiltmaker identifies two trees on her quilt as "The Tree of Knowledge" (Gen. 2:17) and "The Tree of Life/the Leaves of the Tree were for the healing of the nations" (Rev. 22:2). Appropriately, the Tree of Life bears several kinds of fruit, as recorded in Revelation. These images are drawn not only from the Old and New Testaments, but also from the first and last books of the Bible. A flower in the center of the quilt, labeled "Plant of Renown," alludes to Ezekiel 34:29.

The conversation between Adam and Eve draws on the Books of Job and Genesis, as well as on Milton's masterpiece: "The morning stars sung together and all the sons of god shouted for joy (Job 38:7). But now, Adam, paradise is lost" (Milton, *Paradise Lost*). "No, Eve, the promised seed shall bruise the serpent's head" (Genesis 3:15). "River Tigris," as she identifies the river, was a name used by Milton, but not by the writer of the Genesis account.

Most dramatic is the quiltmaker's "fiery flying serpent," which emerges from the "morning stars," heads toward the "Star of the East" (mentioned in the hymn text and appropriately located in the eastern sky), and settles in the Tree of Knowledge (see illustration 193). The quiltmaker's source for this repulsive creature is the Book of Isaiah (14:29; 30:6).

■ **. . . OUT OF THE SERPENT'S ROOT** shall come forth a cockatrice, and his fruit shall be a fiery flying serpent.
Isaiah 14:29 ■

The similarities between Rhoda Warner's "Heroes of the Revolution" and the "Garden of Eden" quilt are remarkable. Both quilts, made in Painesville at approximately the same time, are thematic and bear titles. Both depict realistic fruit and flowers, worked in the three-dimensional techniques of stuffing (grapes and strawberries) and ruching (flowers), with similar grape leaves in both quilts. In each quilt at least one flower (the Rose of Mount Libanus and the Plant of Renown) is symbolically significant to the maker. Each quilt incorporates red, yellow, and blue stars. On both quilts, the lettering is embroidered on cotton strips, which are then appliquéd to the quilts. Furthermore, the "type-face" of the embroidered labels is identical on the two quilts. Finally, both quilts have identical appliquéd hands pointing to significant labels.

The "Garden of Eden" quilt is attributed by the family in which it descended to Olive Batchelor Wells of Painesville, whose husband, Leonidas Knight Wells, was a bootmaker and merchant. Leonidas Wells is listed in the 1840 and 1850 censuses for Painesville. He married Olive Batchelor in 1843; and they lived in Painesville until 1859, when they moved to Monmouth, Illinois. In 1860, according to the Painesville census, Rhoda Warner lived with a relative of Leonidas Wells, Ophelia Wells Slocum, and her husband, Doty Slocum. Mrs. Slocum was probably Leonidas Wells's sister; according to the Wells's family Bible, they were born two years apart.

One hundred years after the event whose heroes Rhoda Warner commemorated on her quilt, Maria Whetstone Hallett made a quilt to celebrate the birthday of the nation they established (see illustration 194). "This Is the Centennial Year 1876," she proclaimed along the lower border and on other borders, "From Washington to Grant, One Hundred Years" and her name, "Mrs. Maria Whetstone Hallett." An American eagle and the dates 1776 and 1876 form the center of this eight-pointed star quilt made to celebrate America's centennial year.

Maria Hallett lived in Washington County near Marietta, Ohio's first settlement. She exhibited her quilt in the Washington County Fair in 1876; her descendents, to whom the quilt was passed, exhibited it in 1989 at the Ohio State Fair where it took third place.

This is only one example of the many quilts inspired by America's one hundredth birthday and made in celebration of that glorious event. The nation's bicentennial year in 1976 elicited still more quilts from the needles of skilled, patriotic American women.

[194] *Centennial Quilt.* Maria Whetstone Hallet, Washington County, 1876. 78″ x 78″ (198 cm x 198 cm). Pieced, appliquéd. Cotton. From a private collection.

Maria Hallet was one of many quiltmakers who celebrated America's centennial year with their needles. She designed her quilt with stars and an American eagle and notes the succession of presidents over the preceding one hundred years.

CIVIL WAR QUILTS

Not all quilts that marked national events were celebratory. In times of national emergency, Ohio quiltmakers mobilized to make quilts for relief. During the Civil War they transformed their church sewing circles into Soldiers' Aid societies to collect and make clothing, quilts, and bandages for Union soldiers. These groups, affiliates of regional branches of the United States Sanitary Commission (forerunner of the American Red Cross and an organization of northern women who contributed needed articles of food and clothing to the Union troops), were admirably effective. They organized immediately and efficiently, since their goals and structure as charitable sewing societies had existed for years. The Strongsville society, for instance, simply changed a few words in its constitution, retained its membership, and instantly became a Soldiers' Aid Society, fifty-eight members strong.

WHEREAS, OBSERVATION and experience teach that more efficient aid is rendered in any cause, and greater good accomplished by combined than by single individual effort, and believing that patriotism and humanity no less than christian [sic] duty urgently call us to more vigorous effort in behalf of our sick and suffering soldiers, therefore we, the Subscribers, form ourselves into a Society, to continue our organisation so long as may be deemed necessary to be governed by the following Constitution. . . .

Soldiers' Aid Society
Strongsville (Cuyahoga County)
June 1862

The need for bedcoverings in military camps and hospitals was so great that Soldiers' Aid societies began by collecting existing quilts from their communities. A week after the war began and two months before the Soldiers' Aid societies officially organized, Cleveland women collected 729 quilts, comforters, and blankets in a single day to answer an emergency need at nearby Camp Taylor. In the first fifteen months of its existence the Cleveland Soldiers' Aid Society, to which Strongsville and other nearby communities sent their work for disbursal, received 6,830 "Comfortables and Blankets," the category that included quilts. In her article "Quilts for Union Soldiers in the Civil War" (*Uncoverings* 6 [1985]: 95–121), Virginia Gunn estimates that northern women contributed more than 250,000 quilts to the Union cause. The figures for Cleveland and Cincinnati alone total 27,369. As is true of other quilts contributed directly for benevolent causes, we found none of those thousands given by Ohio women to the Sanitary Commission and know about them only through written records.

I PARTICULARLY noticed a large invoice of quilts from your society, received here just when fly-blown blankets could not be endured another day, and one of the most timely of all of your favors.

Surgeon A. G. Hart to U.S. Sanitary Commission,
Cleveland Branch (Cuyahoga County)
1862

We did, however, find a few quilts made by Ohio women during the Civil War and kept within their families (see illustrations 131 on page 117 and 132 on page 118). One of the most notable was made in 1862 by Love Davis Campbell of Valley Township (Guernsey County), when she was thirty-one (see illustration 195). It was her community's involvement in the Civil War that enabled Love to make her quilt.

A week after the fall of Fort Sumter, Guernsey County was ordered to raise eleven companies of militia, each made up of one hundred men or fewer, between the ages of eighteen and forty-five. Each company member was required to live in the township in which the company was organized. One such company was the Valley Guards. These volunteers from Valley Township asked Love Davis Campbell, who evidently had a well-deserved reputation as a seamstress, to make their silk company banner. In return for her favor, they purchased enough red and white cotton for her to make this masterpiece quilt. It is in a traditional Evening Star pattern, with elaborate stuffed quilted designs in the plain blocks. Love's designs for her stuffed work are varied and include flower-filled vases, plant forms, and a fish (see illustration 196).

This quilt has much in common with the quilt made by Mary Kelly for her daughter's wedding (see illustration 164 on page 131). Both are red and white pieced quilts with saw-tooth borders. Both include elaborate stuffed work of original design. The two quilts were made in adjacent counties four years apart. Love Campbell may have made this quilt, as Mary Kelly did, for her daughter; the initials "V. C." in stuffed work may refer to Love's daughter, Veroqua, who was five years old when the quilt was made.

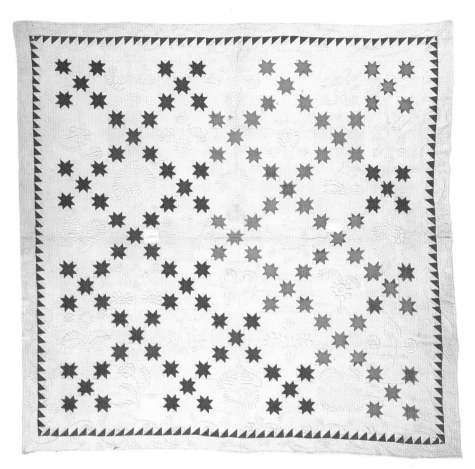

[195] *Evening Star.* Love Davis Campbell (1831–1899), Valley Township (Guernsey County), 1862. 79″ x 77″ (201 cm x 196 cm). Pieced, stuffed. Cotton. Collection of the Campbell family.

Love Davis Campbell, a superb seamstress, made the company banner for the Valley Guards, a Civil War company from Valley Township. In return, the men bought Love enough red and white cotton to allow her to make this quilt.

[196] Detail of illustration 195

WORLD WAR I QUILTS

The end of the Civil War did not obviate quiltmakers' patriotic and social concerns. The United States Sanitary Commission was succeeded during World War I by the American Red Cross, whose members sewed, knitted, and rolled bandages for the American troops. In 1917 the ladies' magazine *Modern Priscilla* published detailed instructions for a Red Cross "quilt campaign," whereby one thousand dollars (the cost of an ambulance, bedding for 129 beds, or 280 pounds of yarn to knit socks) could be raised by making a quilt embroidered with the names of contributors.

Strongsville, with its long history of benevolent quiltmakers, responded to the plan and made a Red Cross quilt (see illustration 197). By selling names at ten cents, the ladies raised thirty-eight dollars. Lila Bedford Burnham wrote the names on the quilt; and the Red Cross members, working together in the Strongsville town hall, embroidered them. They added blue stars after the names of each of Strongsville's seventeen servicemen and later added gold stars to honor the city's two servicemen killed in the war.

Two days before the armistice was signed in 1918, the ladies auctioned the quilt. William Roy was the successful bidder at twelve dollars. His name and several others from his family are embroidered in the center blocks.

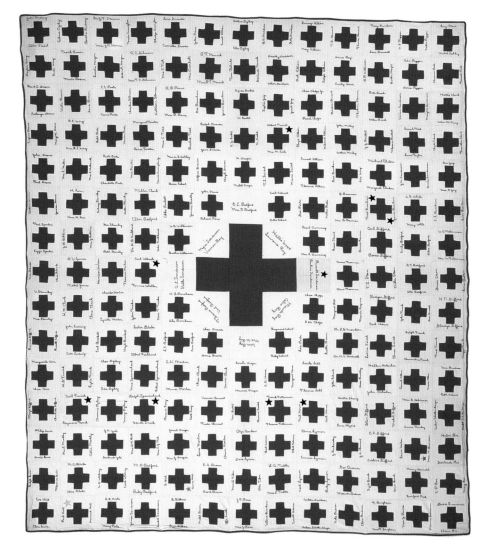

[197] *Red Cross Quilt.* Strongsville Red Cross, Strongsville (Cuyahoga County), 1917. 99″ x 86″ (251 cm x 218 cm). Pieced, embroidered. Cotton. Collection of Maude Roy Hirt.

This quilt was one of countless identical ones used to raise money for the Red Cross during World War I. Instructions for a Red Cross "quilt campaign" were published in *Modern Priscilla* in 1917, the year this quilt was made. The ladies raised thirty-eight dollars through the project.

SOCIAL REFORM

These quilts illustrate clearly the responsiveness of individual women and groups of women, often church-oriented, to social and human needs. The third and final category of quilts that we found in abundance in Ohio are those that were designed or used to emphasize the need for social reform and to address specific social ills. To be sure, the beginnings of this category can be found in the early church quilts; but, increasingly, these quilts came out of groups motivated by a stronger desire to change society than merely respond to its needs.

The quilt in the 1849 daguerreotype of the Ladies' Benevolent Sewing Society, for instance, was destined for the Home for the Friendless in New York City, an institution established a few months earlier by the American Female Reform and Guardian Society to meet the needs of abused, neglected, and "vagrant" children. This was only one of many organizations dealing with social ills threatening family life to which women responded. The women considered their support a natural part of their duties as Christian wives and mothers. Meetings of the Ladies' Benevolent Sewing Society and hundreds of others like it included hymn-singing, prayer, and discussion of issues important to Christian women. One woman in this daguerreotype (see illustration 130 on page 114) is reading aloud to the quilters, probably from a religious newspaper, a regular occurrence at such meetings. Thus the women were informed about the problems of the day and responded to them with their needles.

The earliest instance known to us in which Ohio women made quilts to provide humanitarian aid is the Dorcas Society of Cincinnati (1817), cited above, although Adrienne Saint-Pierre, who researched it, cites an earlier sewing association, the Dayton Female Charitable and Bible Society, which organized in 1815 to make shirts for General Harrison's "brave defenders" during the War of 1812 ("Clothing and Clothing Textiles in Ohio, Circa 1788 to 1835: A Study Based on Manuscript and Artifact Evidence" [Master's thesis, Wright State University, 1988], 111–112). Ohio women worked for a wide variety of social reforms, and excepting only one—the mid-nineteenth-century suffrage movement—they used quilts to express their concern. Ohio women were such active and effective reformers that the 1888 Ohio Centennial Exposition included a display entitled "Women in Reforms."

The Work of Women

OHIO WOMEN have been among the foremost in all reforms of the hundred years behind us. No history of Ohio would be complete if it did not show what part our women have borne in correcting social and political evils, and in raising the standards of social life and morals.
Norwalk Chronicle (Huron County)
January 19, 1888

OHIO CRUSADE QUILT

One of the most remarkable quilts made to raise money for social reform bridges the gap between church-related and secular reform societies. It is the Ohio Crusade Quilt, made in 1876 by Ohio members of the Woman's Christian Temperance Union (WCTU), an organization that combined religion and social reform (see illustration 198).

Alcohol abuse had been a problem in America from its earliest days. In the early nineteenth century, Americans drank three times as much alcohol as they do today. Temperance societies had existed since 1826; but the leaders were almost always men, even though women and children were alcoholism's most susceptible victims. The situation in Ohio in 1873, when the temperance crusade began there, was critical. The availability of liquor and beer in Ohio had increased enormously between 1860 and 1870 and was most evident in Ohio's small towns,

especially its county seats. The statistics are astonishing. One historian estimates that in its heyday, Cheyenne, Wyoming (in the hard-drinking "Wild West"), had one saloon per one hundred drinkers. During the crusade years, Ohio's well-populated regions had three times as many: one saloon per thirty drinkers.

Although drinking was a predominantly male activity, its primary victims were wives, sisters, and mothers: women who suffered physical abuse, humiliation, and economic loss. Ohio had both state and local laws designed to control the use of liquor, yet they were inadequately enforced. And women, who suffered the greatest consequences, were denied the vote and were therefore legally powerless to change the situation.

On December 22, 1873, however, reformer and lecturer Diocletian ("Dio") Lewis of Massachusetts lectured

[198] *Ohio Crusade Quilt.* Woman's Christian Temperance Union of Ohio, statewide, 1876. 97″ x 81″ (246 cm x 206 cm). Pieced, appliquéd, embroidered. Silk, linen, cotton. Collection of the National Woman's Christian Temperance Union.

Ohio temperance women (and children) contributed blocks to this quilt made to raise funds for the temperance cause. The back of each block and border is inscribed with religious sentiments and the names of three thousand crusaders and their supporters. Hanging tabs sewn to the top of the quilt at the time it was made underscore the quilt's function as a political document, rather than a bedcover. Numbers pinned to the fronts of the blocks suggest it was displayed shortly after it was made, along with a corresponding key to the groups that made each block, since the signed back would not have been visible.

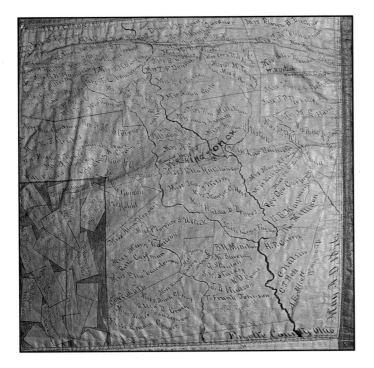

[199] Detail of illustration 198. Women in and around Washington Court House, where crusaders succeeded in closing eleven saloons in eight days, designed the back of their block as a map of Fayette County. Crusaders and supportive husbands signed their names in the townships where they lived. The red-backed area at the lower left bears the names of Fayette County officials who espoused the ladies' cause.

in Hillsboro, seat of Highland County, on "The Duty of Christian Women in Temperance Work." He described his mother's temperance campaign in Fredonia, New York, forty years earlier in which she and other women had knelt on the floors of saloons praying and singing hymns until the saloon keepers agreed to close their establishments. Although Mrs. Lewis's efforts had only limited success, her approach appealed to Hillsboro's women, who organized the following day under the leadership of "Mother" Eliza Trimble Thompson (daughter of a governor and mother of an alcoholic) to march on liquor-selling drugstores and saloons. The "praying band" succeeded the first day in securing pledges from three of the town's four druggists to cease selling liquor. Following an identical lecture by Dio Lewis in nearby Washington Court House, seat of Fayette County, on Christmas day, forty-two of that community's women marched on their town's liquor establishments. Within eight days the crusaders in Washington Court House succeeded in closing all eleven saloons and securing no-sale pledges from all three druggists (see illustration 199).

Ohio women's involvement in the crusade can hardly be exaggerated. Even Oberlin (Lorain County), a town that had been "dry" since it was settled in 1833, had a woman's temperance organization that at one point met *daily* for more than two weeks. The temperance crusade spread like wildfire throughout Ohio and thirty other states. It was strongest and most successful in Ohio, particularly in its small towns, and led directly to the organization in 1874 of the WCTU, which became the largest and most effective women's organization in American history.

From its beginnings, the WCTU needed funds to promote its work. In 1875 the state president, Harriet McCabe of Delaware (Delaware County), wrote to local temperance groups proposing a way to accomplish this. As Mother Thompson records in her reminiscences (*Hillsboro Crusade Sketches and Family Records* [Cincinnati: Jennings and Graham, 1906]), "Each local Union was requested to send to [Mrs. McCabe], at Delaware, a square of silk of given dimensions, patchwork, quilted or embroidered, but lined with linen, the usual gray color, and on that linen lining the names of all members who would send a dime or more must be written legibly, and if possible, in fadeless ink." The idea was popular and the response greater than Mrs. McCabe had hoped. In Hillsboro the ladies made a block representing their union and contributed ten dollars in dimes as well. They also worked with young members of Hillsboro's Children's Temperance Band to make a square that was contributed, along with five dollars in dimes, "each child giving five cents with the name."

NOBLE WOMEN often have watched them on the coldest days of winter when denied the privilege of admittance to saloons, to ask those who sold the accursed stuff to sell no more, knelt on the cold pavement in front of these places to ask God to change the hearts of these wicked men, whose drinking cursed their homes. . . .
  L[ouisa] Detwiler, "Prophecy"
    sewn to Ohio crusade quilt in 1876, to
    be "opened in the year, 1976."

CRUSADE MEMORIAL QUILT.

BUCYRUS,

CRAWFORD COUNTY, OHIO.

"Let us not be weary in well doing; for, in due season, we shall reap, if we faint not."

1 Mrs. LYDIA OFLYNG	28 Mrs. RACHEL HOWENSTEIN	55 Mrs. E. P. PENFIELD
2 Miss ELIZABETH JENKINS	29 Mrs. ADA SHECKLER	56 Mrs. HENRIETTA FISHER
3 Mrs. MARTHA BARCLAY	30 Mrs. JAMES B. GORMLY	57 Mrs. ICY BOWERS
4 Mrs. DR. NELSON	31 Mrs. REV. J. CROUSE	58 Mrs. M. A. BOWERS
5 Miss LULIE MONNETT	32 Mrs. REBECCA MAXWELL	59 Mrs. KATE McHIBBEN
6 Mrs. ZERUIAH CAISON	33 Mrs. EVA CAMPBELL	60 Mrs. AMY YOST
7 Mrs. E. P. BOYER	34 Mrs. J. P. MONNETT	61 Mrs. SUSAN KEARSLEY
8 Mrs. E. M. BOYER	35 Mrs. BARBARA YOST	62 Mrs. C. K. WARD
9 Mrs. MARY NEWELL	36 Miss JANE DOBBINS	63 Mrs. GEORGE G. GORMLY
10 Mrs. JUDGE SCOTT	37 Mrs. W. McBOURE	64 Mrs. MARTHA ECCLESTON
11 Mrs. RACHEL BOYER	38 Miss NETTIE SHECKLER	65 Mrs. H. M. FISHER
12 Mrs. ANNA KELLER	39 Mrs. MARY L. SERGENT	66 Mrs. ELLEN BARDLEY
13 Mrs. D. PICKING	40 Mrs. MARY JONES	67 Mrs. J. A. SERVISS
14 Mrs. REV. BALAZLY	41 Mrs. ANNA OSMAN	68 Mrs. M. I. BASOHE
15 Mrs. HARRIET WADE	42 Mrs. LIZZIE EABLEY	69 Mrs. PARK
16 Mrs. ANNA DOUGHERTY	43 Mrs. LIZZIE BEARD	70 Mrs. C. C. SHECKLER
17 Mrs. J. HOPLEY	44 Mrs. E. L. WISE	71 Mrs. IDA BUHL
18 Mrs. SARAH AUKERS	45 Miss HATTIE LIGHTNER	72 Mrs. MARTHA JOHNSTON
19 Mrs. MARTHA J. AUKERS	46 Miss SALLY LIGHTNER	73 Mrs. S. B. HARRIS
20 Mrs. WM. TRIMBLE	47 Mrs. E. HERSHNER	74 Mrs. DANE M. HAMAN
21 Mrs. S. ROBINSON	48 Mrs. MARTIN DEAL	75 Miss GEORGIANNA LEONARD
22 Mrs. MARY C. THRUSH	49 Mrs. KATE ROWLAND	76 Mrs. E. WENNER
23 Mrs. REV. J. H. SHEPPARD	50 Mrs. SUSAN MODERWELL	77 Mrs. CATHARINE SHULL
24 Mrs. ELIZABETH YOST	51 Mrs. EMILY REID	78 Mrs. ELIZABETH JONES
25 Mrs. WM. ROWSE	52 Mrs. LORENA FISHER	79 Mrs. ELLEN DENTON
26 Miss PLACIDA SHAW	53 Mrs. LAURA LAUCK	80 Miss HATTIE LEONARD
27 Mrs. ROBERT McCRORY	54 Mrs. C. C. MUNSON	81 Mrs. EMMA POGUE

[200] Detail of illustration 198. Bucyrus crusaders had the linen backing of their block commercially printed.

[201] Crusaders praying outside neighboring saloons in Bucyrus (Crawford County). This photo conveys something of the courage it must have taken for women to kneel and pray in the mud before crowds of saloon patrons. *Photo courtesy the Ohio Historical Society.*

Eventually, eighty quilt blocks documented the Ohio temperance crusade (see illustration 200). Over three thousand names of Ohio's temperance women and men are written or printed on this textile record of one of the most significant and successful reform projects undertaken by women anywhere (see illustration 201).

Temperance historians rightly identify Dio Lewis as the catalyst who made possible this extraordinarily successful movement. Zanesville's temperance quilters credited him as well with proposing the idea, but were even more impressed with "the example of his widowed, by worse than death—widowed mother." In much the same way that Sarah Mahan saw her quilt as a way to complete her stepdaughter's unfinished work, Zanesville's women viewed the temperance crusade as the culmination of the unfinished life work of a woman they admired and with whom they identified. On one of their four blocks forming the center of the quilt they wrote: "The Crusade—1873/harvest of the prayers/of the mother of Dr. Dio Lewis many years before" (see illustration 202).

At the 1877 national meeting of the WCTU, the Ohio members presented the Ohio Crusade Quilt to Mother Thompson. Frances Willard, who would become the brilliant second president of the organization, reported on the event in her memoirs, *Glimpses of Fifty Years: The Autobiography of an American Woman* (Chicago: 1889). She considered it "beautiful evidence of woman's skill and taste in needle handicraft, and, as it hung in graceful folds from the gallery . . . a banner of which no body of men or women need have been ashamed." Willard, a woman keenly sensitive to the power of symbols, reported:

[I]t must, indeed, be a women's convention that would make so curious a testimonial as a quilt. . . . Within its folds are hidden all our hearts. The day will come when, beside the death-sentence of a woman who was burned as a witch in Massachusetts, beside the block from which a woman was sold as a slave in South Carolina, and besides [sic] the liquor license that was issued by the State of Illinois to ruin its young men, there will hang this beautiful quilt, to which young men and women will point with pride, and say, "There is the name of my great-grandmother, who took part in Ohio's great crusade."

Another speaker considered the quilt "evidence of woman's patience in matters of detail—a quality that had been valuable in temperance reform." For Mother Thompson, it now became a symbol of the enormous organization that resulted from her Christmas-week activities four years earlier. She responded to the gathering that "when the quilt was made by the women of Ohio, from the ten-cent contributions of over 3,000 mothers and daughters, she had no idea it would ever become hers as a testimonial of the National W.C.T.U."

The crusade curiously affected Ohio's textile economy. A reporter for the *Cincinnati Commercial* wrote on

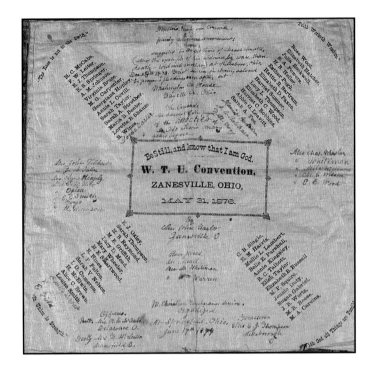

[202] In addition to the names of Zanesville crusaders, this block of illustration 198 is imprinted with the names of other well-known leaders such as Eliza Jane Thompson, Matilda Gilruth Carpenter, and Harriet McCabe, who proposed that Ohio temperance women make this quilt.

March 30, 1874, that in Cincinnati, Marysville, Delaware, and Cardington, dealers in dry goods and "fancy articles" were making no sales whatever. "Hundreds of women engaged in this Crusade talk freely of 'consecrating to God and humanity' what they would have expended on the spring goods," he wrote, "and even those not so heroic have abundant reasons for not purchasing now. Old clothes will do very well to visit saloons in, particularly where they are barred out and have to conduct their devotions on the dirty pavement."

Twelve years after they made the Crusade Quilt, another Ohio woman attempted to solve the interrelated problems of poverty and old age. In 1887 Eliza Jennings, a wealthy Cleveland woman, learned through her minister the sad story of Miss Mary Love, a fellow church member who had cared all her life for an invalid sister. Miss Love herself was now ill and elderly, but as she had no family to help she had been taken to the city infirmary. Much moved by Mary Love's plight, Eliza Jennings immediately contributed land and money to the Women's Christian Association for the "erection of a home or hospital for invalid and incurable women" who "had known the better things in life . . . and had no peaceful place in

[203] *Morning Glory.* Residents and trustees of the Eliza
Jennings Home, Cleveland (Cuyahoga County), 1925–1931. 87″
x 87″ (221 cm x 221 cm). Appliquéd. Cotton. Collection of the
Western Reserve Historical Society.

Residents and trustees of this home for "invalid and incurable
women" raised funds by making quilts and selling them
annually on Rose Day. This practice ended in 1931 when the
wealthy Van Sweringen brothers of Cleveland purchased this
quilt and a companion one for four hundred dollars each. The
Marie Webster design is characteristic of the Colonial Revival
quilt kits popular at the time.

which to end their days in comfort and with proper care." Mary Love was one of the first residents of the Eliza Jennings Home, still in existence more than one hundred years later and recently expanded.

From the day of its opening, the Eliza Jennings Home established a fundraising tradition. On one day each year, designated "Rose Day," the home sold roses and quilts made by the residents and trustees of the home. Proceeds contributed to the support of the residents. The tradition continued until 1931, when the home sold the last of the "Eliza" quilts, an appliquéd Morning Glory (see illustration 203). The wealthy Van Sweringen brothers of Cleveland, who had developed the community of Shaker Heights and built Cleveland's Terminal Tower, purchased the quilt for four hundred dollars. It was apparently never used, and in 1955 it was donated to the Western Reserve Historical Society.

A less-successful attempt to solve the problems of the aging was conceived during the Great Depression by Dr. Francis E. Townsend of Long Beach, California, in the days before Social Security was enacted. Townsend proposed that the federal government give all Americans over age sixty a pension of two hundred dollars a month, provided they spend the money in that month and thus pump money into a depressed economy. The plan was entirely unrealistic during the Depression when the federal government could ill afford to implement it, but it was nonetheless popular with many economically desperate Americans.

Supporters established "Townsend clubs," whose quiltmaking members attempted to raise money by making and raffling quilts (see illustration 204). Bertha Abbott made a pieced Schoolhouse quilt as a fundraiser for the Townsend clubs of Lima (Allen County) in 1935 (see illustration 205). Lula Abbott embroidered the names of contributors, and the completed quilt raised $111.60 through raffle tickets, sold by Sarah Voltz (see illustration 206).

Quilts made by women hoping to reform society did not end with the Depression. A group of students at Oberlin College made an Ecology Quilt in 1974 to express their environmental concerns. In 1990 their suc-

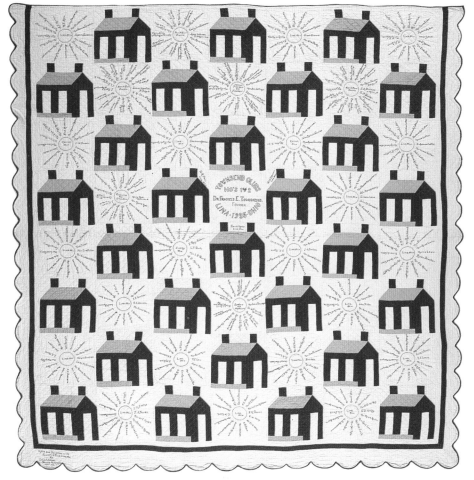

[204] *Schoolhouse.* Bertha Abbott and Lula Abbott, Lima (Allen County), 1935. 85″ x 83″ (216 cm x 211 cm). Pieced, embroidered. Cotton. Collection of the Allen County Historical Society.

The Abbott sisters made this quilt to raise funds for the Townsend clubs of Lima, supporters of an unrealistic and doomed old-age pension plan proposed by Dr. Francis E. Townsend before the enactment of Social Security. Using the same fund-raising techniques as Ladies' Aid societies, the women succeeded in raising $111.60 for their cause.

[205] Detail of illustration 204

[206] Makers of the Townsend Club quilt. *Left to right:* Bertha Abbott, Lula Abbott, and Sarah Voltz, who sold raffle tickets for the quilt.

cessors made a quilt to celebrate the twentieth anniversary of Earth Day, similarly dedicated to increasing awareness of environmental matters.

In 1985 women all over Ohio and the other forty-nine states made segments of a "peace ribbon" illustrating "what I can't bear to think of as being lost forever in a nuclear war." These yard-long segments joined together to create a peace ribbon eighteen and one-half miles long, which its makers wrapped around the Pentagon to publicize their concerns. Since then, quiltmakers all over the nation have joined together in the Names Project to memorialize victims of AIDS and create awareness of this new catastrophe and in the related ABC (AIDS Babies Crib Quilts) project to make quilts for babies suffering from AIDS.

A recent quilted political protest from Ohio by the Southwestern Ohio chapter of MADD (Mothers Against Drunk Driving) was completed in 1988 (see illustration 216 on page 162). When the parents of Judy Scheyer, the victim of a drunk driver, filed a civil suit against the man responsible for Judy's death, her mother introduced the MADD Memorial Quilt as part of her court testimony, explaining its symbolism and testifying to the quilt's significance to her.

As these recent quilts indicate, quilting traditions established early in Ohio's history continue. Throughout the nineteenth and twentieth centuries, Ohio quiltmakers have made quilts to affirm family bonds, worked in church quilting groups to meet human needs and raise funds to support their religious and social concerns, and created quilts to protest social problems. As in the cases of the Ohio Crusade Quilt, the Ecology Quilt, peace ribbon, AIDS quilts, and MADD quilt are contemporary quiltmakers' reactions to social problems so vast as to be overwhelming. Individuals feel unable to solve them alone, but by participating in communities of the concerned, Ohio's quiltmaking descendents of the Ladies' Benevolent Sewing Society give voice to their social concerns, dramatically publicize the problems, and confront their frustrations. In much the same way, grieving Ohio mothers made quilts as links between themselves, their deceased children, and their progeny, so many of whom came forward with the quilts illustrated here and almost seven thousand more during the Ohio Quilt Research Project.

CONTINUING TRADITIONS

D espite the social, economic, and technological changes in Ohio over its two-hundred-year history, and in the quilts that reflect those changes, some quiltmaking traditions persist and inspire today's quiltmakers to uphold or respond to those traditions.

[209] *Carolina Lily.* Martha Hostetler (b. 1940), Bluffton (Allen County), 1987. 98″ x 82″ (249 cm x 209 cm). Pieced, cotton. Collection of Mary A. Stahlman.

Martha Hostetler made this quilt from Laura Ashley prints and hand-dyed cottons as a gift to her sister and a memento of her trip to Europe. It is in the tradition of Germanic sectarian quilts: pieced blocks alternating with plain blocks, surrounded with multiple plain borders and contrasting binding. The quiltmaker and her sister come from a Swiss Mennonite family in Bluffton; Martha Hostetler is active in her church's quilting guild.

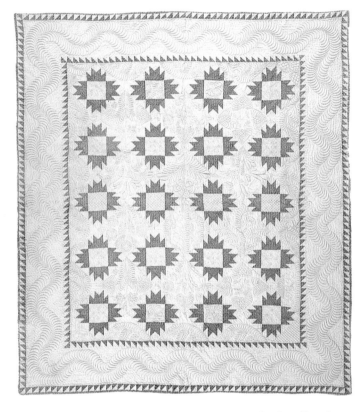

[207] *King's Crown.* Pauline Bryant, Columbia Station (Lorain County), 1959. 85″ x 74″ (216 cm x 188 cm). Pieced, stuffed. Cotton. Collection of Pauline C. Bryant.

After seeing this quilt published in an issue of *Woman's Day Magazine* in the 1950s, Pauline Bryant traveled to Washington to study the original in the Smithsonian Institution. When she returned to Ohio, Pauline replicated it exactly, even to the elaborate stuffed work. She quilted her own initials, PCB, near the inner border and the date, 1959, near the center.

[208] Pauline C. Bryant

[210] *Twelve Good Reasons for Grandmother to Stop Flower Gardening.* Ellen B. Hess (b. 1946), and friends, Amlin (Franklin County), 1987. 62″ x 50″ (157 cm x 127 cm). Pieced, appliquéd, embroidered. Cotton and cotton blends. Collection of Ellen B. Hess.

Familiar with the traditional *Grandmother's Flower Garden* pattern of the 1930s and recent humorous quilted reactions to another favorite pattern of the time, Sunbonnet Sue, Ellen B. Hess conceived this quilt as a joke and an enjoyable group project for the FROG (Final Rendition of Grandmother's Flower Garden) Society. Block titles and makers are, *left to right:* "The Cow Got Loose I" (Ellen Hess); "Giant Slugs" (Nancy Halpern); "Granny Paved It and Put Up a Parking Lot" (Linda Scholten); "Runaway Lawnmower" (Carol Cleaves); "Stomped On: Grandfather's Revenge" (Ami Simms); "Acid Rain" (Jeannette Muir); "Strangled by a Weed" (Barbara Caron); "Annexed for a Landfill" (Poppy Sanks); "Grandmother's Cash Crop" (Lisa Smith); "The Drunk in the Garden" (Katy Christopherson); "Rabbits Rampant" (Pat Morris); and "The Cow Got Loose II" (Ellen Hess).

[211] *Fourth of July—Opus 25.* Alice Hegy (1870–1955), and Arnold Hegy Savage (b. 1926), Rose Township (Carroll County) and Avon (Lorain County), 1876 and 1976. 81″ x 83″ (206 cm x 211 cm). Pieced. Cotton. Collection of Arnold Hegy Savage.

In the tradition of commemorating national celebrations with quilts, Alice Hegy began this as a centennial quilt in 1876 but never completed it. In 1976 her grandnephew, Arnold Hegy Savage, who had inherited her blocks and fabrics, completed the quilt to celebrate America's bicentennial year. Arnold added the outer row of blocks, which include some made by Alice (the Ohio Star and Jacob's Ladder blocks) and others designed and made by Arnold from Alice Hegy's fabrics (Ohio and American flags). It is truly a centennial/bicentennial family quilt.

[212] Mary Alice Hegy   [213] Arnold Hegy Savage

[214] *Greg's Mourning Glory Quilt*. Lois K. Ide, Bucyrus (Crawford County), 1981. 87″ x 84″ (221 cm x 213 cm). Appliquéd. Cotton and cotton blends. Collection of Lois K. Ide.

Lois Ide began this quilt five days after the unexpected death of her son, Greg, in 1981. She based its design on one of the many condolence cards the family received, unaware at the time that in nineteenth-century mourning art the morning glory symbolized death in childhood. "I literally drowned my grief in the making of this quilt," Lois reports. "It is my therapeutic quilt. It did indeed allow me to keep my sanity."

[215] Lois K. Ide

[216] *MADD Memorial Quilt*. Members of Mothers Against Drunk Driving, Southwestern Ohio chapter, Ross (Butler County), 1988–1989. 98″ x 82″ (249 cm x 207 cm). Appliqué, embroidery, paint. Cotton, cotton blends. Collection of MADD, Southwestern Ohio chapter; victims of drunk driving crashes.

In the traditions of nineteenth-century mourning quilts and those created for social reform (especially the Ohio Crusade Quilt), relatives of victims of drunk driving crashes made this quilt as a memorial to their loved ones and as a teaching tool to publicize their goals. MADD members June Taylor of Ross and Andrea Rehkamp of Oxford conceived the idea; Ariel Biggs and Taylor put the quilt together from the completed blocks. This quilt has inspired similar projects in MADD chapters across the country.

[217] *Underground Railroad Quilt*. Oberlin Senior Citizens, Oberlin (Lorain County), 1982. 103″ x 70″ (262 cm x 178 cm). Appliquéd, embroidered. Cotton blends, synthetics. Collection of Oberlin Seniors, Inc. Photography by Nicholas Whitman, courtesy Williams College Museum of Art.

In this quilt, Oberlin's senior citizens commemorated their town's active involvement in the Underground Railroad one hundred years earlier. Quiltmakers studied Oberlin's history, then designed and made the blocks. This arrangement of pictorial blocks in a horizontal set was popular with quiltmakers throughout Ohio beginning in 1976, when so many of them made quilts to celebrate America's bicentennial year.

[218] Thirteen of the twenty-five makers of the Underground Railroad Quilt gather for their picture. Some of these women descend from blacks who came to Oberlin during the Civil War to escape slavery. The group also includes descendents of Oberlin citizens active in the Underground Railroad. *Photo by Myron Miller, Lady's Circle Patchwork Quilts.*

[219] *Pride of Ohio.* Mary Borkowski, Dayton (Montgomery County), 1962. 94" x 75" (239 cm x 191 cm). Appliquéd, stuffed, embroidered. Cotton, cotton blends. Collection of the Ohio Historical Society.

Like Rhoda Warner, Mary Borkowski celebrates national events in a masterful and highly symbolic quilt. Pride of Ohio was completed the year Ohio's John Glenn became the first American astronaut to circle the earth. The Ohio map includes its eighty-eight counties, with a star identifying Muskingum County, Glenn's home. Below the map seven scarlet carnations (Ohio's state flower) honor the seven astronauts; the three carnations above the map represent Glenn as the third American in space and the Ohioan who orbited the globe three times. Eight seals of the state of Ohio represent the eight United States presidents from Ohio. Each seal is surrounded by seventeen stars, the number on Ohio's state flag. Eight cardinals (Ohio's state bird) and several buckeyes (Ohio's state tree) are depicted. The side edges of the quilt are decorated with fifty blue stars, one for each state in the Union; the upper and lower edges with the letter *O* for Ohio. Diagonal quilting represents Ohio's (frequent) rainfall.

[220] Mary Borkowski, an Ohio native who "loves every stick and stone and every hill and valley in Ohio."

CONCLUSION

Over the past six years as we traveled throughout Ohio documenting quilts, we often recalled George Knepper's telling image: early Ohio was more like a salad bowl than a melting pot. In some respects, it still is. I leave my New England-based, English-speaking community, driving my car past an orderly town square still flanked by its cultural icons, the church and the school, then travel through miles of farmland boasting substantial, red brick farmhouses and comparatively small barns. In season, the hay will be harvested and bound mechanically into a few enormous rolls that will border the fields. A wide variety of flowers graces gardens variously located in front, back, or side yards, on rail fences, or trellises climbing the house walls. Telephone poles and the wires they support create a mesmerizing pattern along the highway.

I cross the West Branch of the Black River and, a short time later, a tributary of another river—this time, a "fork." I enter Holmes County. Here the landscape is steep and the farms lush, each anchored by two white clapboard and yellow brick houses in close proximity, and massive bank barns. After the corn is harvested, the stalks will be arranged by hand in small, orderly shocks that will dot the fields at regular intervals. In front of each house is an immaculate, rectangular flower garden filled with blazing orange and red coxcomb and framed with a low, frilly border of green and purple kale. The coxcomb might have been taken directly from quilts. No power lines edge the roads I travel. I enter the town center, here running along both sides of the main street. The Amish people in Holmes County are trilingual; they will speak English to me, a German dialect to other members of their community, and High German in their worship services. They dress in solid-colored clothes of uniform style and travel by horse and buggy.

It seems incredible that almost two hundred years after Easterners began migrating to the area that would become Ohio, I can still leave one sectional settlement and an hour and a half later enter another whose language and material culture are notably different. Because of where I live, the contrast is dramatic. Yet similar experiences were shared by so many project members as they traveled from southern and western Ohio to quilt documentation days in other parts of the state that none of us was surprised to find regional differences in quilt styles,

just as we did in architecture and agriculture. And in spite of the urbanization and industrialization of much of Ohio, in some rural areas—especially those that have remained stable over several generations—we discovered instances of quilt designs that were favored by so many quiltmakers that they constitute regional styles. Many examples illustrate George Knepper's chapter, "Early Migrants to Ohio."

We did not expect to discover that two particular quilt styles, which we have called "floral appliqué" and "sectarian," are associated, not with a geographic region but with a particular, widely dispersed ethnic group, and within that group, with two religiously different communities. We consider this significant enough to warrant a separate chapter.

Studying the materials, construction, and design of Ohio's quilts, individually and in comparison with others, led us to identify many as characteristic of a specific regional, ethnic, or religious community. Further studying each quilt's history and functions and considering these properties in the context of state and national history enabled us to identify other communities significant to their makers and subsequent owners. These communities, we discovered, were family, church, and reform society. In one sense, they were sequential; nineteenth-century women's most significant social groups when they first came to Ohio were their immediate families, for whom they made quilts. As villages organized, women met under the aegis of the organized church, where they also made quilts, now as tangible bonds with other church women or as objects of direct benevolence. Late in the nineteenth century, most dramatically in the instance of the Ohio Crusade Quilt, women increasingly used quilts as instruments of social reform.

While these kinds of communities succeeded each other, they also overlapped. As early church-made signature quilts testify, the women who created them were both fellow church members and relatives. They were also concerned with social problems and used their quilts to address them. Members of the Ladies' Benevolent Sewing Society in Strongsville, sisters and fellow Christians, for instance, made the quilt in the 1849 daguerreotype to support the efforts of the American Female Moral Reform Society to rescue "fallen women" and the children of "dissipated and vicious parents." The name of the organization that made the Crusade Quilt—

Woman's Christian Temperance Union—reflects the gender-based and religious bonds of the quiltmaking women who united to reform an alcoholic society.

Our basic premise is that quilts are historical documents. If this is valid, we should expect Ohio's quilts to reflect changes over time. In fact, this is what we found. As Ellice Ronsheim has noted ("From Bolt to Bed: Quilts in Context"), each quilt is "part of a flowing continuum, each a product of its time and environment." In terms of materials, most Ohio quilts were made of cotton, until some women began making quilts of silk during a period appropriately called the Gilded Age. During the Depression of 1929 and following, inexpensive feed sacks supplemented the cotton scraps many women used. As textile technologists increasingly developed myriad synthetic fabrics, Ohio quiltmakers incorporated most of these, including knitted polyesters, into quilts.

Another technological achievement, the development of the sewing machine, is also mirrored in Ohio's quilts. The finest handwork brought to our attention was in quilts made in the decade before the Civil War, after the end of Ohio's frontier period and just before the successful marketing of the sewing machine in the 1860s. In the 1850s most of Ohio's families lived in settled communities and had more leisure time than earlier; however, women still made their family's garments and household linens by hand. With years of practice behind them, many had developed their hand sewing skills to a remarkable degree and lavished them on quilts. With the advent of the sewing machine, however, quiltmakers' hand sewing skills declined as they turned to this new technological marvel. We documented one quilt whose owner was so impressed with her recently invented sewing machine, she embellished her masterpiece with machine stitching.

Some quilts we saw reflect specific events. Ohio's quiltmakers made quilts to mark personal occasions, like rites of passage, and to commemorate major historical victories, such as America's birth and its centennial and bicentennial anniversaries. In times of war they dispersed quilts to needy soldiers and refugees or made them to raise funds for the war effort. They also quilted metaphoric communities at times when their most significant social groups were disrupted. Most of the quilts made and signed by families and friends date to the period of westward expansion or to times when major separations occurred within religious communities.

More gradual trends are also reflected in quilts as we compare many over a period of time. Ronsheim notes the changes in the nature of the quilting frolic throughout the nineteenth century, citing the comments of those involved. We also saw changing religious concerns during this century as we studied quilts made by Ohio's church women. Mid-nineteenth-century Ohio women were biblically literate to an admirable degree. During the Progressive Era in the late nineteenth century, they joined the rest of America in an obsession with statistics, ecclesiastical though they might be. At the same time we saw the increasing secularization of American society echoed in church-made quilts, some of which include embroidered advertisements for local businesses. Quilts intended as instruments of social reform were first made in churches or religiously based groups. Increasingly, reform societies became totally secular organizations. This is reflected in the fact that the largest number of quilts made by secular social agencies were made in the last decade.

In addition to these changes in some quiltmaking traditions, we discovered continuity in others. Traditions that persist are effective responses to experiences that are both universal and, often, intensely personal. Human needs and human nature are constants. In their quilts included here, Pauline Bryant and Ellen Hess respond to quilts of the past, albeit in different ways. Pauline revives the lost art of skillful handwork she so admires in quilts from the 1850s; Ellen makes a humorous comment on a favorite pattern from an earlier day. For Martha Hostetler, a quilt she made as a gift for her sister affirms their family bonds, as do the quilts made by Phebe Cook, Sadie Wells, and so many other nineteenth-century Ohio women. Because Martha made her quilt in the Germanic sectarian style, it also ties her to earlier Mennonite quiltmakers such as Rebecca Ramseyer and Barbara Welty.

Like Sarah Mahan and Rachel Fisher, Lois Ide found that making a quilt as a deliberate and tangible link to her deceased child was therapeutic. Arnold Savage joined his great-aunt in designing and completing her unfinished quilt one hundred years later to celebrate anniversaries of the same event that Rhoda Warner and Maria Hallett commemorated in their quilts. Mary Borkowski and the Oberlin Senior Citizens worked in this same tradition. Makers of the MADD Memorial Quilt carry on two nineteenth-century quiltmaking traditions: mourning quilts and the use of quilts as political propaganda. They are grieving women and social reformers, as were the makers of the Ohio Crusade Quilt over one hundred years earlier.

Our study of Ohio's quilts, quiltmakers, and quiltmaking traditions would not be complete if we failed to ask what quilts mean to us today. What accounts for the current quilt revival? There are probably as many answers as there are lovers of quilts. Revivals often occur during times of social stress, when people find comfort in a selectively remembered past. The 1980s might well be considered such a stressful period. It may not be coincidental that so many of our respondents value quilts as symbols of family bonds at a time when the breakdown of the traditional family is epidemic.

The strong, positive response to our quilt documentation days indicates that many Ohio residents have kept their family quilts, that they cherish them and are willing to share them with project members, even though they have never met us before. Their comments on inherited quilts taught us that for these people, quilts signify loving relationships to their quiltmaking mothers and grandmothers. They want to share these relationships with their descendents as so many tell us their treasured family quilts will be passed on to daughters. That quilt owners value family history is further supported by the volumes of genealogical material they bring to share with us. It certainly makes our job easier; but, more importantly, it underscores the significance of family to so many descendents of quiltmakers.

The willingness of hundreds of Ohio women and men to volunteer their time and efforts to document Ohio's quilts further substantiates this widespread interest in quilts. Many of these volunteers are themselves quiltmakers or owners; all love quilts and are eager to study them as intensely as we must in quilt days. As Ronsheim has noted, the volunteers respond to different aspects of each quilt. Some admire skillful handwork; others, strong graphic design; and still others, quilt-related family stories.

Today's quilt revival is the most extensive in American history. The proliferation of quilters, quilt guilds, classes, and quilt-related publications testifies to this. These aspects of a quilt revival are not new. However, the widespread involvement in quilt historical research undertaken by the Ohio Quilt Research Project and similar ventures in more than thirty other states is unprecedented. The existence of these state-wide organizations and the national American Quilt Study Group, five hundred members strong, indicates that for many Americans studying quilts as historical documents is a matter of passionate importance. This raises another question: Why is involvement in historical research a major aspect of the current quilt revival when it played such a minor role in the revival of the 1920s?

The answer probably lies in changing attitudes toward the study of history. In the last twenty years, three new and relevant academic disciplines have emerged: women's history, material culture, and the "new" social history. All seek to learn about the past by studying "ordinary" people, and sources for study include the ob-

jects they created and used. The approaches of investigators in these new disciplines converge in the study of quilts and their makers. Quilts are material objects made primarily by women, most of them ordinary people with whom we can readily identify. We saw no quilts made by kings, queens, popes, or presidents, the leading characters in traditional history textbooks. Furthermore, unlike the architecture of seventeenth-century St. Mary's City in Maryland or the prehistoric petroglyphs of Clear Creek, Arizona, quilts and their makers can be found everywhere in the United States, made by women of all economic levels and accessible as subjects for study by all who are interested. And thousands are interested. Quilt documentation at the grass-roots level is, in the words of historian Larry Tise, an example of "the democratization of American history."

It's exciting to be on the cutting edge. All our research is original. Most of the seven thousand quilts we have documented have never before been studied. We have read published and unpublished diaries, newspaper advertisements, county fair records, and letters to editors who died a century ago. A diary entry as vague as "worked on my quilt today" leaps from the page and thrills us; at the same time we find it frustrating, since it raises more questions than it answers.

Enough regional quilt documentation projects have now published their findings that we can begin to make comparisons. We see common threads among quilts in different states and are beginning to see distinctions. In North Carolina, for instance, one researcher worked full time documenting the many high-style chintz appliqué quilts found there; in Ohio we saw only two. Tennessee quiltmakers frame their quilt blocks with sashes and contrasting corner blocks; we found very few examples of sashwork in Ohio. Researchers in some eastern states discovered regional styles apparently dictated by the state's geography; in the "salad bowl" of Ohio, we attribute regionalism to Ohio's settlement patterns. Each quilt documentation project's public presentations will be unique and should communicate a sense of place. As researchers, we have certainly experienced this in Ohio. We hope we have successfully shared it with our readers.

Ricky Clark, Editor

EXPLANATORY NOTES

All quilts discussed here came to our attention through our five years of research. Although every quilt we documented is recorded in the Ohio Quilt Research Project archives (to be deposited at the Ohio Historical Society), we had specific criteria for those selected for inclusion here: they were made in Ohio, they best illustrate the points made by the contributors, and they are accompanied by strong family history. In cases where quilts meeting these criteria exist in both family and institutional collections, we have selected those that are privately owned.

Quilt pattern names are those used by the quiltmakers, when known; otherwise, by the quilt owners. When no pattern names were reported to us, we have used for identical and closely related designs names found in the sources listed in the "Pattern Identification" section of Suggested Readings (page 166) or names descriptive of the quilts' primary function, for instance, Fundraising Quilt.

Measurements are rounded to the nearest inch and centimeter. Length precedes width.

Several Amish quiltmakers asked that their names not be used. In those cases, we have identified the makers as "Amish quiltmaker."

SUGGESTED READINGS

HISTORICAL BACKGROUND

Ahlstrom, Sydney E. *A Religious History of the American People.* New Haven: Yale University Press, 1973.

Auditor [State of Ohio]. *A Short History [of] Ohio Land Grants.* Columbus: various dates.

Banta, R.E. *The Ohio.* New York: Rinehart, 1949.

Barnhart, John D. *Valley of Democracy: The Frontier Versus the Plantation in the Ohio Valley, 1775–1818.* Bloomington: Indiana University Press, 1953.

Blocker, Jack S., Jr. *"Give to the Winds Thy Fears": The Women's Temperance Crusade, 1873–1874.* Westport, Connecticut: Greenwood Press, 1985.

Bond, Beverly W., Jr. *The Foundations of Ohio.* Columbus: Ohio State Archaeological and Historical Society, 1941.

Buley, R. Carlyle. *The Old Northwest: Pioneer Period 1815–1840.* 2 vols. Indianapolis: Indiana Historical Society, 1950.

Cayton, Andrew R.L. *The Frontier Republic: Ideology and Politics in the Ohio Country, 1780–1825.* Kent, Ohio: Kent State University Press, 1986.

Durnbaugh, Donald E, ed. *The Brethren Encyclopedia.* Philadelphia: Brethren Encyclopedia, Inc., 1983–1984.

——————. *Meet the Brethren.* Elgin, IL: The Brethren Press, 1984.

Elliot, Errol T. *Quakers on the American Frontier: A History of the Westward Migrations, Settlements, and Developments of Friends on the American Continent.* Richmond, Indiana: The Friends United Press, 1969.

Hatcher, Harlan. *The Western Reserve: The Story of New Connecticut in Ohio.* Indianapolis: Bobbs-Merrill, 1949.

Hildreth, S.P. *Pioneer History of the Ohio Valley.* 2 vols. Cincinnati: H.W. Derby & Co., 1848.

Holbrook, Stewart H. *The Yankee Exodus: An Account of Migration from New England.* New York: Macmillan, 1950.

Hostetler, John A. *Amish Society.* Baltimore: Johns Hopkins University Press, 1980.

——————. *Annotated Bibliography on the Amish; An Annotated Bibliography of Source Materials Pertaining to the Old Order Amish Mennonites.* Scottdale, Pennsylvania: Mennonite Publishing House, 1951.

Howe, Henry. *Historical Collections of Ohio.* Various editions.

Huntington, Abbie Gertrude Enders. "Dove at the Window: A Study of an Old Order Amish Community in Ohio." Ph.D. diss., Yale University, 1956.

Jakle, John. *Images of the Ohio Valley: A Historical Geography of Travel.* New York: Oxford University Press, 1977.

Knepper, George W. "Early Migration to the Western Reserve." *Western Reserve Magazine* (September 1977).

——————. *Ohio and Its People.* Kent, Ohio: Kent State University Press, 1989.

McFarland, Gerald W. *A Scattered People: An American Family Moves West.* New York: Pantheon Books, 1985.

The Mennonite Encyclopedia: A Comprehensive Reference Work on the Anabaptists. Hillsboro, Kansas: Mennonite Brethren Publishing House, 1955–1959.

Miller, Levi. *Our People: The Amish and Mennonites of Ohio.* Scottdale, Pennsylvania: Herald Press, 1983.

Parker, William N. "From Northwest to Mid-West: Social Bases of a Regional History." In David Klingaman and Richard Vedder, eds., *Essays in Nineteenth Century Economic History: The Old Northwest.* Athens, Ohio: Ohio University Press, 1975.

Rohrbaugh, Malcolm J. *The Trans-Appalachian Frontier: People, Societies and Institutions, 1775–1850.* New York: Oxford University Press, 1978.

Roseboom, Eugene. *The Civil War Era, 1850–1873.* Columbus: Ohio State Archaeological and Historical Society, 1944.

Ruether, Rosemary Radford, and Rosemary Skinner Keller, eds. *Women and Religion in America: The Nineteenth Century.* San Francisco: Harper & Row, 1982.

Schlabach, Theron F. *Peace, Faith, Nation: Mennonites and Amish in Nineteenth-Century America.* The Mennonite Experience in America, vol. 2. Scottdale, Pennsylvania: Herald Press, 1988.

Schreiber, William I. *Our Amish Neighbors.* Chicago: University of Chicago Press, 1962.

Smith, H.E. "The Quakers, Their Migration to the Upper Ohio, Their Customs and Discipline." *Ohio State Archeological and Historical Quarterly* (January 1928).

Stoltzfus, Grant M. *Mennonites of the Ohio and Eastern Conference: From the Colonial Period in Pennsylvania to 1968.* Scottdale, Pennsylvania: Herald Press, 1968.

Thompson, Mrs. Eliza Jane Trimble, et al. *Hillsboro Crusade Sketches and Family Records.* Cincinnati: Jennings and Graham, 1906.

Utter, William. *The Frontier State, 1803–1825.* Columbus: Ohio State Archaeological and Historical Society, 1941.

Weisenburger, Francis P. *The Passing of the Frontier, 1825–1850.* Columbus: Ohio State Archaeological and Historical Society, 1941.

Wilhelm, Hubert G.H. *The Origin and Distribution of Settlement Groups: Ohio, 1850.* Athens, Ohio, 1982.

Wittenmyer, Mrs. Annie. *History of the Woman's Temperance Crusade.* Philadelphia: Office of the Christian Woman, 1878.

QUILTS AND QUILT HISTORY

Bishop, Robert, and Elizabeth Safanda. *A Gallery of Amish Quilts: Design Diversity from a Plain People.* New York: E.P. Dutton, 1976.

Bishop, Robert. *New Discoveries in American Quilts.* New York: E.P. Dutton, 1975.

Cooper, Patricia, and Norma Bradley Buferd. *The Quilters: Women and Domestic Art.* Garden City, New York: Doubleday, 1978.

Ferrero, Pat, Elaine Hedges, and Julie Silber. *Hearts and Hands: The Influence of Women & Quilts on American Society.* San Francisco: The Quilt Digest Press, 1987.

Garoutte, Sally. "Marseilles Quilts and Their Woven Offspring." *Uncoverings* 3 (1982).

Granick, Eve Wheatcroft. *The Amish Quilt.* Intercourse, Pennsylvania: Good Books, 1989.

Gunn, Virginia. "Quilts at Nineteenth Century State and County Fairs: An Ohio Study." *Uncoverings* 9 (1988).

——————. "Quilts for Union Soldiers in the Civil War." *Uncoverings* 6 (1986).

——————. "Yo-Yo or Bed-of-Roses Quilts: Nineteenth-Century Origins." *Uncoverings* 8 (1987).

Holstein, Jonathan. *The Pieced Quilt: An American Design Tradition.* Boston: New York Graphic Society, 1973.

Horton, Laurel, and Lynn Robertson Myers. *Social Fabric: South Carolina's Traditional Quilts.* Columbia, South Carolina: McKissick Museum, n.d.

Kansas History 13:1 (Spring 1990) [special issue on the Kansas Quilt Project].

Kentucky Quilts 1800–1900. Louisville: The Kentucky Quilt Project, 1982.

Kile, Michael, ed. *The Quilt Digest.* San Francisco: The Quilt Digest Press, 1983.

Lasansky, Jeannette. *In the Heart of Pennsylvania: 19th and 20th Century Quiltmaking Traditions.* Lewisburg, Pennsylvania: Oral Traditions Project, 1985.

—————. *Pieced by Mother: Over 100 Years of Quiltmaking Traditions.* Lewisburg, Pennsylvania: Oral Traditions Project, 1987.

Lasansky, Jeannette, ed. *In the Heart of Pennsylvania Symposium Papers.* Lewisburg, PA: Oral Traditions Project, 1986.

—————. *Pieced by Mother: Symposium Papers.* Lewisburg, PA: Oral Traditions Project, 1988.

Laury, Jean Ray and California Heritage Quilt Project. *Ho for California!* New York: E.P. Dutton, 1990.

MacDowell, Marsha, and Ruth D. Fitzgerald, eds. *Michigan Quilts: 150 Years of a Textile Tradition.* East Lansing, Michigan: Michigan State University Museum, 1987.

McMorris, Penny. *Crazy Quilts.* New York: E.P. Dutton, 1984.

Pellman, Rachel, and Kenneth Pellman. *The World of Amish Quilts.* Intercourse, Pennsylvania: Good Books, 1984.

Philbin, Marianne, ed. *The Ribbon: A Celebration of Life.* Asheville, North Carolina: Lark Books, 1983.

Ramsey, Bets, and Merikay Waldvogel. *The Quilts of Tennessee.* Nashville: Rutledge Hill Press, 1986.

Roberson, Ruth Haislip, ed. *North Carolina Quilts.* Chapel Hill: The University of North Carolina Press, 1988.

Ruskin, Cindy. *The Quilt: Stories from the NAMES Project.* New York: Pocket Books, 1988.

Safford, Carleton, and Robert Bishop. *America's Quilts and Coverlets.* New York: E.P. Dutton, 1980.

Tomlonson, Judy Schroeder. *Mennonite Quilts and Pieces.* Intercourse, Pennsylvania: Good Books, 1985.

Uncoverings. Sally Garoutte, ed. 1980–1986; Laurel Horton, ed. 1987–. Mill Valley, California: American Quilt Study Group.

Waldvogel, Merikay. *Soft Covers for Hard Times: Quiltmaking and the Great Depression.* Nashville: Rutledge Hill Press, 1990.

Woodard, Thomas K., and Blanche Greenstein. *Twentieth Century Quilts 1900–1950.* New York: E.P. Dutton, 1988.

MATERIALS

Affleck, Diane L. Fagan. *Just New from the Mills.* North Andover: Museum of American Textile History, 1987.

Beer, Alice Baldwin. *Trade Goods: A Study of Indian Chintz in the Collection of the Cooper-Hewitt Museum of Decorative Arts and Design, Smithsonian Institution.* Washington, DC: Smithsonian Institution Press, 1970.

Brackman, Barbara. *Clues in the Calico. A Guide to Identifying and Dating Antique Quilts.* EPM Publications, Inc., 1989.

—————. "Quilts from Feed Sacks." *Quilter's Newsletter Magazine* 16:9 (October 1985).

Liles, James M. "Dyes in American Quilts Made Before 1930." *Uncoverings* 5 (1984).

Montgomery, Florence. *Printed Textiles: English and American Cottons and Linens 1700–1850.* London: Thames and Hudson, 1970.

—————. *Textiles in America 1650–1870.* New York: W.W. Norton & Co., 1984.

Nickols, Pat L. "The Use of Cotton Sacks in Quiltmaking." *Uncoverings* 9 (1988).

Pettit, Florence H. *America's Printed & Painted Fabrics.* Toronto, Saunders, Ltd., 1970.

Schoeser, Mary, and Celia Rufey. *English and American Textiles: from 1790 to the Present.* London: Thames and Hudson, 1989.

Scott, Stephen. *Why Do They Dress That Way?* Intercourse, Pennsylvania: Good Books, 1986.

CARE AND CONSERVATION

Division of Textiles, Smithsonian Institution. *The Care and Cleaning of Antique Cotton and Linen Quilts.* Washington, DC: The National Museum of History and Technology, n.d.

—————. *Care of Victorian Silk Quilts and Slumberthrows.* Washington, DC: The National Museum of American History, n.d.

Gunn, Virginia. "The Care and Conservation of Quilts." *Technical Guide #3.* San Francisco: American Quilt Study Group, 1988.

Mailand, Harold F. *Considerations for the Care of Textiles and Costumes: A Handbook for the Non-Specialist.* Indianapolis: Indianapolis Museum of Art, 1980.

Ordonez, Margaret and Zoe Slinkman. *Quilt Conservation.* Manhattan, Kansas: Cooperative Extension Service, Kansas State University Kansas 1981. (Extension Bulletin C-632)

PATTERN IDENTIFICATION

Brackman, Barbara. *An Encyclopedia of Pieced Quilt Patterns.* 8 vols. Lawrence, Kansas: Prairie Flower Publishing, 1984.

Hall, Carrie A., and Rose Kretsinger. *The Romance of the Patchwork Quilt in America.* New York: Bonanza, 1935.

Rehmel, Judy. *Key to 1000 Appliqué Quilt Patterns.* Self published, 1984.

—————. *Key to 1000 Quilt Patterns.* Self published, 1978.

QUILT DOCUMENTATION

Brackman, Barbara. "Dating Antique Quilts: Two Hundred Years of Style, Pattern and Technique." *Technical Guide #4.* San Francisco: American Quilt Study Group, 1990.

Clark, Ricky. "Quilt Documentation: A Case Study." *Making the American Home: Middle-Class Women and Domestic Material Culture 1840–1940,* edited by Marilyn Ferris Motz and Pat Browne. Bowling Green, Ohio: BGSU Popular Press, 1988.

Fitzgerald, Ruth D., Marsha MacDowell, and C. Kurt Dewhurst. "The Michigan Quilt Project." *Michigan Quilts: 150 Years of Textile Tradition.* East Lansing: MSU Museum, 1987.

Fleming, E. McClung. "Artifact Study: A Proposed Model." *Winterthur Portfolio 9* (June 1974).

Holstein, Jonathan. "Collecting Quilt Data: History from Statistics." *The Quilt Digest* (1983).

Horton, Laurel. "Format for a Quilt Research Project." *Lady's Circle Patchwork Quilts* (Fall 1984).

—————. "The Oral Interview in Quilt Research." *Technical Guide #2.* San Francisco: American Quilt Study Group, 1988.

Lasansky, Jeannette. "Quilt Documentation: A Step-by-Step Guide." *Pieced by Mother: Over 100 Years of Quiltmaking Traditions.* Lewisburg, Pennsylvania: Oral Traditions Project, 1987.

Melvin, Patricia Mooney. "Tracing the Quiltmaker." *Technical Guide #1.* San Francisco: American Quilt Study Group, 1987.

Prown, Jules David, "Mind in Matter: An Introduction to Material Culture Theory and Method." *Winterthur Portfolio 17:1* (Spring 1982).

Richards, Elizabeth, Sherri Martin Scott, and Kerry Maguire. "Quilts as Material History: Identifying Research Models." *Uncoverings 11* (1990).

"Towards a Material History Methodology." *Material History Bulletin 22* (Fall, 1985).

EXHIBITION CATALOGS—OHIO
(Some may be out of print)

Albacete, M.J., Sharon D'Atri and Jane Reeves. *Ohio Quilts: A Living Tradition.* Canton, Ohio: The Canton Art Institute, 1981.

Clark, Ricky, ed. *Quilts and Carousels: Folk Art in the Firelands.* Oberlin, Ohio: Firelands Association for the Visual Arts, 1983.

Gunn, Virginia, Stephanie N. Tan and Ricky Clark. *Treasures from Trunks: Early Quilts from Wayne and Holmes Counties.* Wooster, Ohio: The College of Wooster Art Museum, 1987.

Melvin, Patricia Mooney. *Ohio Quilts and Quilters 1800–1981.* Wooster, Ohio: The College of Wooster Art Museum, 1981.

Quilts from Cincinnati Collections. Cincinnati: Cincinnati Art Museum, 1985.

Walsh, Susan. *The Elmer R. Webster and Robert A. Tisch Collection of American Quilts and Coverlets.* Dayton: The Dayton Art Institute, 1988.

ACKNOWLEDGMENTS

The Ohio Quilt Research Project would not have been possible without the thousands of Ohio quiltmakers and quilt owners who shared with us their quilts, quilt related items, and family stories. We also thank the hundreds of members, volunteers, and Quilt Discovery Day hosts who enabled us to document Ohio's quilts, quiltmakers, and quiltmaking traditions. We are indebted to them and trust that they enjoyed the exhilarating and often exhausting experience as much as we did.

The following consultants have offered invaluable suggestions and encouragement throughout the project: Katy Christopherson, Virginia Gunn, George Knepper, Jeannette Lasansky, Penny McMorris, and Bari Oyler Stith.

Special acknowledgment must go to Price Waterhouse, Columbus, Ohio; Tom Reed, photographer, The Photographic Illustrators, Inc.; and Jules Sanks, attorney. Our thanks also go to numerous archivists, librarians, and historians throughout the country, and especially to staff members of the Dayton Art Institute and the Ohio Historical Society.

Research, planning, and manuscript preparation could not have occurred without the generous financial support of the following agencies: for research, the Grants-In-Aid-Program for Research in State and Local History (supported by the National Endowment for the Humanities through the American Association for State and Local History, with matching funds from the Ohio Historical Society), the Ohio Arts Council, and The Stocker Foundation; for manuscript preparation, the Helping Hand Quilting Craft Foundation and the Stocker Foundation.

Finally, we are indebted to the many organizations and individuals whose donations supported our research and photography:

The Antiquists Study Guild
Bob Evans Farm, Inc., Rio Grande, Ohio
Canal Quilters
Cellar Sewers
Chagrin Valley Quilt Guild
Palmer Clement
Colonial Dames
Columbus Metropolitan Quilters
Common Threads Quilting Club
Conneaut Quilt Club
Country Crossroads Quilters
Country Piecemakers
Country Quilters
Crazy Quilters; Columbus Metropolitan Quilters
Creative Quilters Guild
Darke County Cooperative Extension Service
Firelands Historical Society
Foundry Guild
Friends Around the Block; Columbus Metropolitan Quilters
Gathering of Quilters Guild
Geauga County Historical Society
German Culture Museum, Stanley A. Kaufman, Director
Glass City Quilt Commission
Huron Public Library
Knox County Quilters
Legendary Quilters
Marilyn Lemmon
Logan Piecemakers
Miami Valley Quilters Guild
Milan Historical Museum
Mohican Quilters

Northcoast Needlers Quilt Guild
Ohio State Quilters
Ohio Valley Quilters Guild
Oxford Piecemakers
Patchwork Partners; Columbus Metropolitan Quilters
Piecemakers; Columbus Metropolitan Quilters
Pioneer Historical Society
Pioneer Quilters
Portage Patchers Quilt Guild
Quilt Guild of Metro Detroit
Quintessential Quilters
Satellites; Columbus Metropolitan Quilters
Sheauga Quilters Guild
Sherman's March; Columbus Metropolitan Quilters
Townsquare Quilt Lovers Guild
Towne Squares Quilt Club
Barbara Wamelink
West Central Ohio Quilters Guild
Western Reserve Quilt Guild

Quilt Discovery Days were held in the following locations, listed by county:

Adams (Peebles)
Allen (Bluffton, Lima [2])
Ashland (Loudonville)
Ashtabula (Austinburg)
Belmont (Barnesville)
Brown (Ripley)
Butler (Oxford)
Champaign (Urbana)
Clinton (Clarksville)
Crawford (Bucyrus)
Cuyahoga (Cleveland [2], Parma)
Darke (Greenville)
Erie (Huron)
Fairfield (Lancaster)
Franklin (Columbus [2], New Albany)
Fulton (Archbold [2])
Gallia (Rio Grande)
Geauga (Burton [2])
Hamilton (Cincinnati [2], College Hill, Montgomery [2])
Hardin (Ada)
Harrison (Cadiz)
Holmes (Berlin)
Lake (Mentor)
Lawrence (Ironton)
Logan (Bellefontaine)
Lorain (Lorain, Oberlin)
Lucas (Toledo [2])
Madison (Plain City)
Montgomery (Dayton)
Muskingum (Zanesville)
Paulding (Paulding)
Portage (Brimfield)
Putnam (Continental)
Stark (Canton, North Canton)
Trumbull (Cortland)
Tuscarawas (Zoar)
Wayne (Smithville)

THE OHIO QUILT RESEARCH PROJECT

Chairman: Edith Richmond
Vice Chairman: Ellen Hess
Secretary: Madelyn Horvath
Treasurer: Carol Cleaves

EDITOR: Ricky Clark

CONTRIBUTORS:
Ricky Clark
George W. Knepper
Ellice Ronsheim

PHOTOGRAPHER:
The Photographic Illustrators, Inc., Tom Reed, Photographer

INDEXERS:
Ellen Hess
Patricia Williamsen

Captions are by Ellice Ronsheim for her article and by Ricky Clark for all other articles.

RICKY CLARK, an affiliate scholar at Oberlin College, is a quilt researcher particularly interested in quilts as cultural documents. A graduate of Oberlin College, she has published numerous articles on quilt history. She has served on the Traditional and Ethnic Arts panel of the Ohio Arts Council and is currently on the board of directors of the American Quilt Study Group, as well as a founding member of the Ohio Quilt Research Project.

GEORGE W. KNEPPER, Distinguished Professor of History at the University of Akron, is recognized as an outstanding Ohio scholar and teacher. After earning his doctorate at the University of Michigan, he was a Fulbright scholar at the University of London. He has served both as academic dean and vice president at the University of Akron and won an award for teaching excellence in 1978. His many articles, books, and public addresses on Ohio subjects include a recent major work on Ohio history, *Ohio and Its People*, published in 1989. Dr. Knepper has served as president of the Ohio Historical Association, the Ohio Academy of History, and the Summit County Historical Society, and as member of the editorial boards of *Ohio History* and *The Old Northwest*.

ELLICE RONSHEIM is collections manager and textile curator at the Ohio Historical Society. She is a graduate of Antioch College, where she majored in art history and minored in American history. Since 1986 she has served as a member of the Ohio Quilt Research Project, curator of the project's exhibition at the Ohio Historical Society, and co-curator of the exhibition at the Dayton Art Institute.

[221] Locations of where Quilt Discovery Days were held, county by county.

INDEX

Boldface words indicate a quilt illustrated in the book.
Boldface numbers refer to illustration numbers, not page numbers.